HANDEHOOL

H.C. Robbins Lan
In 1949 he founded the Haydn Society, which began to issue the Collected Edition of Haydn's music and also made a number of gramophone records. Later he was a Special Correspondent of *The Times* for which he wrote mostly from Eastern Europe. He has published books on Haydn, Mozart and other composers of the eighteenth century, and was also responsible for the first editions of many of his other works. In addition, he has shared in the editing of the new Collected Edition of Mozart's works. He has received honorary doctoral degrees from Boston University, Queen's College, Belfast, and Bristol University. He is at present Honorary Professorial Fellow of University College, Cardiff. H. C. Robbins Landon lives near Toulouse with his wife Else Radant, an Austrian historian and writer. Another of his books, *1791: Mozart's Last Year*, is also available in Flamingo paperback.

Handel and His World

H.C. ROBBINS LANDON

Flamingo
An Imprint of HarperCollins*Publishers*

Flamingo
An Imprint of HarperCollins*Publishers*,
77–85 Fulham Palace Road,
Hammersmith, London W6 8JB

Published by Flamingo 1992
9 8 7 6 5 4 3 2 1

First Edition published in Great Britain by
Weidenfeld & Nicolson 1984

ISBN 0 00 654460 6

Set in New Caledonia

Printed in Great Britain by HarperCollins Manufacturing, Glasgow

For Lavinia and David Hankinson,
with much affection

Preface to the Flamingo Edition (1992)

In the intervening period between 1984, when this book was first published, and 1992, when it appears for the first time in paperback, there has been a revolution in our ability to listen to Handel: the emergence of compact discs. For other composers, like Haydn, this technical development has been also fundamental – three complete new recordings of all the symphonies planned, two on period instruments. The same, perhaps to an even greater extent, applies to Handel. With the full Summer of CD upon us, there are now major new recordings of almost all the oratorios, including some (like *Susanna*) hardly known except to connoisseurs beforehand. But the particularly gratifying change in our attitude towards Handel has been the ever increasing availability of the operas, on CD and often in spectacularly good performances, but also in the opera house. Seeing a Handel opera at Covent Garden is no longer a rarity, as Marc Minkowsky's recent revival of *Riccardo Primo* – a distinct rarity even to avid Handelians – graphically shows.

It cannot, however, be said that this remarkable upswing of attention to Handel's vocal music on CD and in concert or opera house has produced a fundamental difference in his overall popularity in Mediterranean countries such as Spain, France or Italy, though France is rapidly becoming the centre of a large Handel cult (as was the case with Mozart's music here in the 1930s), at least in such centres as Paris and Lyon. Handel is still not really one of the genuinely popular composers except in Anglo-Saxon countries. Perhaps this situation will change: there are signs of it happening in Germany, where there was always a flourishing audience for the more esoteric Handel (e.g. the famous Göttingen operatic revivals in the 1920s and 1930s).

A great deal of this increase in popularity is, in Handel's case, bound up with the revival of period instruments. An *Israel in Egypt* conducted by Gardiner, or Hogwood's epochal recording of *La Resurrezione* (1981) before there was even a proper published score, will illustrate the matter in a vivid fashion: and nowadays there are no less than three period performances on CD of the latter work. I am personally pleased to see the *Roman Vespers* so cultivated on CD. Since publication of the original edition of this book, the principal source for the *Vespers* – authentic performance material of most of the principal sections – was sold by auction at Sotheby's (November 1985) and is now in private possession in New York City.

In the present circumstances, it was hardly possible to provide any extensive update in the Handel literature, but one exception must be made: the National Portrait Gallery's magnificent Handel exhibition catalogue (*Handel: A Celebration of His Life & Times 1685–1759*) for the bicentenary (London 1985), with many new discoveries and many facts clarified and reassessed.

I should be pleased and gratified if this very modest contribution to the Handelian literature can win new friends for this great and noble musician, a composer who painted with such large and generous strokes.

H.C.R.L.

Château de Foncoussières
July 1991

Contents

Author's Preface

In the mind of the average concert-goer, music's hero is usually Ludwig van Beethoven: the man who (in the title of one 1929 biography) 'freed music'; the man who, battling incomprehension, adversity and deafness, conquered all to write the *Missa Solemnis*, the Ninth Symphony and the late quartets. No one would want to dethrone Beethoven; but it seems to me that Handel is an almost equally valid candidate for one of the grand heroes of music history. At the outset we have a young German, trained in Italy, who imported his successful Italian operatic style into England where, after a series of initial triumphs, the genre fell into a kind of generic disrepute and failed. Handel for season after season attempted to persuade the British public that they were wrong, and he flatly refused to give up opera (partly, no doubt, because of his famous Saxon stubbornness but also because of his profound conviction of the validity of the form as well as his contribution to it); on its failure followed the saga of the composer's physical and mental breakdown, his near-miraculous cure at Aix (Aachen) and his return to battle with opera but also with two of the greatest oratorios of all time – *Saul* and *Israel in Egypt*. Soon thereafter came the total failure of *Israel* (a sublime masterpiece) but also his gradual conversion, *faute de mieux*, to English oratorio. Then in rapid succession occur his near bankruptcy and his retreat to Ireland, where *Messiah* was a triumph; but when it was introduced in London, *Messiah* was a failure, although that failure was in the course of a few years totally reversed and the work became a household name within the composer's lifetime. Meanwhile Handel was enjoying a phenomenal success as a composer of instrumental music – the *Water Musick* and *Fireworks Musick* and the Grand Concertos Opus 6 –

and of anthems for the church, such as the Coronation music, public music of a nobility and depth that was (and is) unique. The remainder of Handel's career is, in the oratorio, equally mixed: some works were instant successes (like *Judas Maccabaeus*), others, far greater (*Jephtha*), were coolly received. Handel could have enjoyed an even and tranquil career writing organ concertos, orchestral music, trio sonatas and English anthems, but his life was primarily dedicated to music for the voice. And even when blindness struck him, he found a way to dictate his thoughts to J. C. Smith, Jr. His contemporaries' hearts melted when the boys led him out to play the organ, his fat fingers finding the keys which his eyes could no longer see. Is not all this the stuff of heroes?

It is quite clear that Handel has always had a very special place in the hearts of the British: if you go to Rome, to seek out the scenes of Handel's triumphs in the aula of the Palazzo della Cancelleria in Rome, where Cardinal Ottoboni pitted Handel against Domenico Scarlatti; or to the Palazzo Bonelli where *La Resurrezione* was staged, hardly any Italian knows that the events even took place. And in the gaunt town of Vignanello, where the Ruspoli castle looms over the sloping vineyards, no one has even heard of Handel, who conducted there for several summers (giving, amongst others, his austerely lovely *Salve Regina* in the summer of 1707). In Britain and Ireland, most of the places where Handel lived and worked have disappeared: not the composer's house in Brook Street; but the old Covent Garden, the old Haymarket Theatre, the Dublin hall where *Messiah* saw the light – all exist no longer. Yet although Handel's Italian triumphs took place in extant halls, Handel as a composer is a negligible force in Italian life nowadays, and the same applies, perhaps less drastically, to musical life in Leningrad, Prague, Budapest or Vienna. Apart from the usual few war-horses, Handel is largely an unknown quantity in those places.

Not so in England. And how did this curious state of affairs come to pass? Charles Burney, the great British music scholar who in his youth knew Handel, has this to say:

> Handel spent the greatest part of his life in the service of its inhabitants: improving our taste, delighting us in the church, the theatre, and the chamber; and introducing among us so many

> species of musical excellence, that, during more than half a century, while sentiment, not fashion, guided our applause, we neither wanted nor wished for any other standard. He arrived among us at a barbarous period for almost every kind of music, except that of the church. But, besides his oratorio choruses, which are so well intitled to immortality, his organ-pieces, and manner of playing, are still such models of perfection as no master in Europe has surpassed; and his operas were composed in a style so new and excellent, that no Music has since, with all its refinements of melody and symmetry of air, in performance, had such effects on the audience. Indeed his works were so long the models of perfection in this country, that they may be said to have formed our national taste. The English, a manly, military race, were instantly captivated by the grave, bold, and nervous style of Handel, which is congenial with their manners and sentiments. [Burney 1785, pp. iii–iv]

This modest new biographical study of Handel might best be subtitled 'a documentary survey'. For ever since the publications of Otto Erich Deutsch's great documentary biographies of Schubert, Handel and Mozart, the death-knell of the usual kind of narrative biography of great musicians has sounded. Naturally, not every contemporary document about Handel is true, perfect or even necessarily valuable. But *in toto* contemporary documents give a truer picture of the man, and reveal an authentic flavour of an age, which not even the most astute modern biographer can supplant. Hence, this is primarily a documentary biography, although necessarily on a small scale. The massive documentary tribute to Handel by O. E. Deutsch (*Handel: A Documentary Biography*, London, A. & C. Black, 1954) is, astonishingly, out of print and the publishers inform us that there are no plans to reprint it. Naturally, I have used this indispensable book as the basis of my new study. Many new documents, particularly about Handel's Italian years, have since come to light, expanding and altering Deutsch's picture; but the work is still of unique value.

In 1760, the first book-length biography of a musician appeared in London, anonymously: it was John Mainwaring's study of Handel, using in large part oral testimony from the composer's amanuensis, John Christopher Smith Jr. There was a time when the evidence of this valuable and near-contemporary biography was considered of less importance than nowadays. Although Mainwaring frequently gets his dates wrong and the chronology mixed, recent evidence has often come to light that affirms a vague, even an improbable statement – such as Handel's supposed affair with the Italian *primadonna*, Vittoria Tarquini. For many periods in Handel's life, indeed, Mainwaring is the only evidence at all; and therefore, although he must be used with caution, we have allowed him to provide the backbone of our documentary study (we have, incidentally, not modernized his language, even though some of his spellings, such as 'Hamburgh', 'Hall', 'uncontroulable' and 'stedfastly' may strike modern readers as slightly odd). Similarly, the illustrations were not chosen in order to create a pretty 'coffee table' book but were regarded as necessary adjuncts to the contemporary documents: many of these illustrations appear for the first time in these pages, and many of the others will not be familiar to most readers.

In a book such as this one, there was hardly room to explore in any depth the vexed problem of authenticity in Handel's music, whether in the actual printed (manuscript) notes or the modern performances thereof. But if there be any necessity to chart the progress towards a genuinely authentic Handelian style, the reader need only compare (say) the recent (1979) recording of *Partenope* conducted by Sigiswald Kuijken using La Petite Bande and period instruments with the performance (now recorded) of *Hercules*, made at La Scala, Milan, in 1958 with Elizabeth Schwarzkopf, Franco Corelli, Fedora Barbien, Ettore Bastianini and Jerome Hines, and conducted by Lovro von Matacic, an excellent and celebrated Bruckner interpreter. This *Hercules* is stylistically a total disaster from beginning to end, whereas the Kuijken *Partenope* is a model of our current attempt to play Handel's music approximately as we believe he would have heard it. The differences between the two recordings are in many respects more instructive than many long articles on the subject.

As regards scholarly performing editions, Handel is, for some unaccountable reason, the most neglected of all the great composers: many of his works are still unpublished, including such a major Motet as 'Saeviat tellus' (part of the great Roman Vespereal cycle which is, however, now in the process of publication by the University Press,

Cardiff); and as this book goes to press, we learn that a large collection of authentic Handel sources from the Earl of Shaftesbury's library has just been discovered in one of the great stately homes of Britain, the details of which will soon be revealed by the scholars who are at present investigating these important manuscripts.

In the present biography, some attempt has been made to provide a new view of Handel's vast production: for example, the position of *Messiah*. Among sophisticated Handelians, it is currently the fashion to extol many of the lesser-known works – not quite at the expense of, but certainly (shall we say) despite the popularity of, the famous war-horses of the Handelian canon. I think this tendency, which is also happening to a certain extent with other composers such as Haydn, is possibly unproductive. *Messiah* is a phenomenon which cannot and should not be explained away. In a perceptive article recently published by Nicholas Temperley we read:

> The overwhelming power of *The Messiah*, as the Victorians called it, is attested by countless sources from all classes and all parts of the English-speaking world, not so speak of other countries. . . . Such stature was not the product of Handel's music alone. Handel certainly composed some of his finest music in *Messiah*. And he did begin the processes that led to its Victorian apotheosis. In the first place he knew that he was writing a deeply religious work. His own beliefs have little to do with it, since Baroque composers wrote for their patrons or public, not for themselves. Handel recognized the English public's deep wells of religious emotion, and in his oratorios, above all in *Messiah*, he eventually succeeded in tapping them. [*Early Music*, February 1984, pp. 19f.]

Similar reasons account for the overwhelming success of the (strongly Handelian) oratorio that Haydn wrote with a different public in mind at the end of the eighteenth century – *The Creation*. Both drew upon the public's profound need for an article of faith transcending just the word, or just wordless music.

The reader will perhaps pardon a personal note at the end of this brief introduction. When an editor of Weidenfeld & Nicolson came to Italy in 1972 to try to persuade me to write a Handel biography for that firm, I was in the middle of my five-volume Haydn biography and was totally unable to accept the commission; but when some ten years later Lord Weidenfeld again suggested the book, I agreed, and for several reasons. In the first place, my parents had always revered Handel – and not just *Messiah*, either: I grew up with the strains of an old recording by Sir Thomas Beecham containing extracts from *Israel in Egypt* in my ears. As the years went on, and I came to live in Austria and Italy, I was constantly astonished at the complete neglect and incomprehension with which Handel was greeted. When my old and much lamented friend, the late Vittorio Gui, conducted *Israel* in Vienna in the 1950s, the then leading music critic, Baron Mittag, met me in the interval: 'almost as boring as Corelli', he said. The idea of Handel as a poor man's Bach I found as insane as the then customary view of Haydn as a watered-down Mozart. This small contribution to the tercentenary celebration of Handel, which falls in the year 1985, is therefore a personal tribute (in documentary form, whenever possible) to a composer whose true stature and boundless greatness will one day, and perhaps very soon, be recognized by more than just the Anglo-Saxon community.

Saturnia, H.C.R.L.
Easter 1984.

List of Illustrations

I
The early years 1685–1706

HANDEL WAS BAPTIZED Georg Friedrich Händel at the Church 'Zu unser lieben Frauen' at Halle-on-Saal on 24 February 1685; his father was the 'noble, honourable, greatly respected and renowned Herr Georg Händel [1622–97], duly appointed Valet [*recte*: court surgeon] to the Elector of Brandenburg' – this is the father's description in his second marriage register – and his mother was Dorothea *née* Taust (1651–1730), the daughter of Pastor Georg Taust at the Church of St Bartholomew in Giebichenstein. Handel's father was by profession a barber-surgeon and this was his second marriage; he was nearly sixty-three years of age when George Frideric (as he later styled himself) was born, probably a day before the baptism, on 23 February; Dorothea, nearly thirty years younger than her husband, lived to survive him by more than thirty years. Handel's father had children by his first marriage and, by his second, Georg and two girls: Dorothea Sophia, born on 6 October 1687 and, after Handel's father had suffered an alarming illness in September 1689, there was another, younger sister, Johanna Christiana, born on 10 January 1690.[1]

What little we know about Handel's life from the time of his birth in Halle to his sojourn in Hamburg comes, principally, from Mainwaring, who (as we have seen in the preface) based this information on J.C. Smith Jr, Handel's confidant and principal copyist. One of the first facts that Mainwaring got wrong was the date of Handel's birth, which also appears on his tombstone in Westminster Abbey and, being a year too early (1684), resulted in the first of the great Handel Commemorations being performed in 1784 rather than the real centenary date, 1785. Mainwaring takes us from Halle to Hamburg (we shall attempt to correct the author's worst mistakes in chronology, as far as is possible from existing corroboratory evidence, see the footnotes and also the chronology on p. 23.):

GEORGE FREDERIC HANDEL was born at HALL, a city in the circle of Upper-Saxony, the 24th February 1684, by a second wife of his father, who was an eminent surgeon and physician of the same place, and above sixty when his son was born. He had also one daughter[2] by the same wife. HANDEL always retained the strongest affection for this sister, to whose only daughter, *i.e.* his niece now living, he bequeathed the greatest part of his ample fortune.

While he was yet under seven years of age, he went with his father to the Duke of Saxe-Weisenfels. His strong desire to pay a visit to his half-brother, a good deal older[3] than himself, (for we have before observed that he was the issue of a second marriage) and at that time valet de chambre to the Prince, was the occasion of his going. His father intended to have left him behind, and had actually set out without him. He thought one of his age a very improper companion when he was going to the court of a Prince, and to attend the duties of his profession. The boy finding all his solicitations ineffectual, had recourse to the only method which was left for the accomplishment of his wish. Having watched the time of his father's setting out, and concealed his intention from the rest of the family, he followed the chaise on foot. It was probably retarded by the roughness of the roads, or some other accident, for he overtook it before it had advanced to any considerable distance from the town. His father, greatly surprised at his courage, and somewhat displeased with his obstinacy, could hardly resolve what course to take. When he was asked, how he could think of the journey, after such a plain refusal had been given him; instead of answering the question, he renewed his intreaties in the most pressing manner, and pleaded in language too moving to be resisted. Being taken into the chaise, and carried to court, he discovered an unspeakable satisfaction at meeting with his brother above-mentioned, whom till then he had never seen.

This was not the first instance of the father's ill success, when he judged it expedient to oppose or over-rule his son's inclinations. This matter demands a more particular explication, before an account can properly be given of what afterwards passed at the court of Weisenfels.

From his very childhood HANDEL had discovered such a strong propensity to Music, that his father, who always intended him for the study of the Civil Law, had reason to be alarmed. Perceiving that this inclination still increased, he took every method to oppose it. He strictly forbad him to meddle with any musical instrument; nothing of that kind was suffered to remain in the house, nor was he ever permitted to go to any other, where such kind of furniture was in use. All this caution and art, instead of restraining, did but augment his passion. He had found means to get a little clavichord privately convey'd to a room at the top of the house. To this room he constantly stole when the family was asleep. He had made some progress before Music had been prohibited, and by his assiduous practice at the hours of rest, had made such farther advances, as, tho' not attended to at that time, were no slight prognostics of his future greatness.

And here it may not be unpleasing to the reader, just to remind him of the minute and surprising resemblance between these passages in the early periods of HANDEL's life, and some which are recorded in that of the celebrated monsieur Pascal, written by his sister. Nothing could equal the bias of the one to Mathematics, but the bias of the other to Music: both in their very childhood out-did the efforts of maturer age: they pursued their respective studies not only without any assistance, but against the consent of their parents, and in spite of all the opposition they contrived to give them.

We left our little traveller just on his arrival with his father at the Duke of Saxe-Weisenfels. In such a situation it was not easy to keep him from getting at harpsichords, and his father was too much engaged to watch him so closely there as he had done at home. He often mentioned to his friends, this uncontroulable humour of his son, which he told them he had taken great pains to subdue, but hitherto with little or no success. He said it was easy to foresee, that if it was not subdued very soon, it would preclude all improvements in the science for which he intended him, and wholly disconcert the plan that had been formed and agreed on for his education.

The reasonableness of such apprehensions every one admitted, in case it was determined to adhere to the scheme above-mentioned. But the prudence of adhering to it was doubted by many. It was observed with reason, that where Nature seemed to declare herself in so strong a manner, resistance was often not only fruitless, but pernicious. Some said, that, from all the accounts, the case appeared so desperate, that nothing but the cutting off his fingers could prevent his playing; and others affirmed, that it was a pity any thing *should* prevent it. Such were the sentiments and declarations of the Doctor's friends in regard to his son. It is not likely they would have had any great effect, but for the following incident, which gave their advice all the weight and authority it seems to have deserved.

It happened one morning, that while he was playing on the organ after the service was over, the Duke was in the church. Something there was in the manner of playing, which drew his attention so strongly, that his Highness, as soon as he returned, asked his valet de chambre who it was that he had heard at the organ, when the service was over. The valet replied, that it was his brother. The Duke demanded to see him.

After he had seen him, and made all the inquiries which it was natural for a man of taste and discernment to make on such an occasion, he told his physician, that every father must judge for himself in what manner to dispose of his children; but that, for his own part, he could not but consider it as a sort of crime against the public and posterity, to rob the world of such a rising Genius!

The old Doctor still retained his prepossessions in favour of the Civil Law. Though he was convinced it was almost become an act of necessity to yield to his son's inclinations (as it seemed an act of duty to yield to the Prince's advice and authority) yet it was not without the utmost reluctance that he brought himself to this resolution. He was sensible of the Prince's goodness in taking such notice of his son, and giving his opinion concerning the best method of education. But he begged leave humbly to represent to his Highness, that though Music was an elegant art, and a fine amusement, yet if considered as an occupation, it had little dignity, as having for its object nothing better than mere pleasure and entertainment: that whatever degree of eminence his son might arrive at in such a profession, he thought that a much less degree in many others would be far preferable.

The Prince could not agree with him in his notions of Music as a profession, which he said were much too low and disparaging, as great excellence of any kind entitled men to great honour. And as to profit, he observed how much more likely he would be to succeed, if suffered to pursue the path that Nature and Providence seemed to have marked out for him; than if he was forced into another track to which he had no such bias; nay, to which he had a direct aversion. He concluded with saying, that he was far from recommending the study of Music in exclusion of the Languages, or of the Civil Law, provided it was possible to reconcile them together: what he wished was, that all of them might have fair play; that no violence might be used, but the boy be left at liberty to follow the natural bent of his faculties, whatever that might be.

All this while he had kept his eyes stedfastly fixed on his powerful advocate; and his ears were as watchful and attentive to the impressions which the Prince's discourse made upon his father.

The issue of their debate was this: not only a toleration was obtained for Music, but consent for a master to be employed, who should forward and assist him in his advances on his return to Hall. At his departure from Weisenfels, the Prince fill'd his pockets with money, and told him, with a smile, that if he minded his studies, no encouragements should be wanting.

The great civilities which he had received at the court of Weisenfels, the prosperous issue of the debate just mentioned, but especially the friendly and generous dismission which the Prince had given him, were often the subject of his thoughts. These fortunate incidents served to foment that native emulation, and to inflame that inbred ambition, which, even at this early period it was easy to discover in him.

The first thing which his father did at his return to Hall, was to place him under one ZACKAW,[4] who was organist to the cathedral church. This person had great abilities in his profession, and was not more qualified than inclined to do justice to any pupil of a hopeful disposition. HANDEL pleased him so much, that he never thought he could do enough for him. The first object of his attention was to ground him thoroughly in the principles of harmony. His next care was to cultivate his imagination, and form his taste. He had a large collection of Italian as well as German music: he shewed him the different styles of different nations; the excellences and defects of each particular author; and, that he might equally advance in the practical part, he frequently gave him subjects to work, and made him copy, and play, and compose in his head. Thus he had more exercise, and more experience than usually falls to the share of any learner at his years.

ZACKAW was proud of a pupil, who already began to attract the attention of all persons who lived near Hall, or resorted thither from distant quarters. And he was glad of an assistant, who, by his uncommon talents, was capable of supplying his place, whenever he had an inclination to be absent, as he often was, from his love of company, and a chearful glass. It may seem strange to talk of an assistant at seven years of age,[5] for he could not be more, if indeed he was quite so much, when first he was committed to the care of this person. But it will appear much stranger, that by the time he was nine he began to compose the church service for voices and instruments, and from that time actually did compose a service every week for three years successively. However, it must not be forgot, that he had made some progress at home, before his father began to be alarmed, and, in consequence thereof, had forbid him to touch any musical instrument: that, after this severe prohibition, he had made further advances at stolen intervals by his practice on the clavichord; and after that had made the most of his moderate stay at the court of Weisenfels, where he found many instruments, and more admirers.

We have already hinted at some striking coincidences of life and character, which are found in him, and the famous Pascal. In this place we may just observe, that the latter, at the age of twelve compos'd a treatise on the propagation of sounds, and at sixteen another upon conic sections.

From the few facts just related it is easy to guess, that from the time of HANDEL's having a master in form, the Civil Law could have had no great share of his attention. The bent of his mind to Music was now so evident, and so prevailing, that the

Prince's advice was punctually followed. No further endeavours were used to alter or correct it. The consequence of this full liberty was soon perceived, the pupil surpassed the master, the master himself confessed his superiority. HALL was not a place for so aspiring a youth to be long confined to. During this interval of three or four years, he had made all the improvements that were any way consistent with the opportunities it afforded; but he was impatient for another situation, which would afford him better, and such a one at length presented itself. After some consultation, BERLIN was the place agreed on. He had a friend and relation at that court, on whose care and kindness his parents could rely. It was in the year 1698[6] that he went to Berlin. The Opera there was in a flourishing condition, under the direction of the King of Prussia (grandfather of the present) who, by the encouragement which he gave to singers and composers, drew thither some of the most eminent from Italy, and other parts. Among these were BUONONCINI[7] and ATTILIO,[8] the same who afterwards came to England while HANDEL was here, and of whom the former was at the head of a formidable opposition against him. This person was in high request for his compositions, probably the best which that court had known. But from his natural temper, he was easily elated with success, and apt to be intoxicated with admiration and applause. Though HANDEL was talk'd of as a most extraordinary player on the harpsichord for one so young, yet on account of his years he had always considered him as a mere child. But as people still persisted in their encomiums, it was his fancy to try the truth of them. For this end he composed a Cantata in the chromatic style, difficult in every respect, and such as even a master, he thought, would be puzzled to play, or accompany without some previous practice. When he found that he, whom he had regarded as a mere child, treated this formidable composition as a mere trifle, not only executing it at sight, but with a degree of accuracy, truth, and expression hardly to be expected even from repeated practice; – then indeed he began to see him in another light, and to talk of him in another tone.

ATTILIO, somewhat his inferior as a composer, was a better performer on the harpsichord, and, from the sweetness of his temper, and modesty of his character, was much more beloved as a man. His fondness for HANDEL commenced at his first coming to Berlin, and continued to the time of his leaving it. He would often take him on his knee, and make him play on his harpsichord for an hour together, equally pleased and surprized with the extraordinary proficiency of so young a person; for at this time he could not exceed thirteen, as may easily be seen by comparing dates. The kindness of ATTILIO was not thrown away; as he was always welcome, he never lost any opportunity of being with him, or of learning from him all that a person of his age and experience was capable of shewing him. It would be injustice to BUONONCINI not to mention his civilities to HANDEL, but they were accompanied with that kind of distance and reserve, which always lessen the value of an obligation, by the very endeavour to enhance it. The age of the person to be obliged seems to remove all suspicion of rivalship or jealousy. One so young could hardly be the object of either; and yet from what afterwards happened, such a notion may appear to some persons not altogether destitute of probability. Those who are fond of explaining former passages by subsequent events, would be apt to say, that the seeds of enmity were sown at Berlin; and that though they did not appear 'till the scene was changed, they waited only for time and occasion to produce them.

This much is certain, that the little stranger had not been long at court before his abilities became known to the King, who frequently sent for him, and made him large presents. Indeed his Majesty, convinc'd of his singular endowments, and unwilling to lose the opportunity of patronizing so rare a genius, had conceived a design of cultivating it at his own expence. His intention was to send him to Italy, where he might be formed under the best masters, and have opportunities of hearing and seeing all that was excellent in the kind. As soon as it was intimated to HANDEL's friends (for he was yet too young to determine for himself) they deliberated what answer it would be proper to return, in case this scheme should be proposed in form. It was the opinion of many that his fortune was already made, and that his relations would certainly embrace such an offer with the utmost alacrity. Others, who better understood the temper and spirit of the court at Berlin, thought this a matter of nice speculation, and cautious debate. For they well knew, that if he once engag'd in the King's service, he must remain in it, whether he liked it, or not; that if he continued to please, it would be a reason for not parting with him; and that if he happened to displease, his ruin would be the certain consequence. To accept an offer of this nature, was the same thing as to enter into a formal engagement, but how to refuse it was still the difficulty. At length it was resolved that some excuse must be found. It was not long before the King caused his intentions to be signified, and the answer was, that the Doctor would always retain the profoundest sense of the honour done to him by the notice which his Majesty had been graciously pleased to take of his son; but as he himself was now grown old, and could not expect to have him long with him, he humbly hoped the King would forgive his desire to decline the offer which had been made him by order of his Majesty.

I am not able to inform the reader how this answer was relished by the King, whom we may suppose not much accustomed to refusals, especially of this sort. Such an incident made it improper for HANDEL to stay much longer at the court of Berlin, where the more his abilities should be known and commended, the more some persons would be apt to sift and scrutinize the motives of his father's conduct.

Many and great were the compliments and civilities which he received on his leaving Berlin. As yet he had been but twice from home, and both times had received such marks of honour and distinction, as are seldom, if ever, paid to one of his age and condition. On his return to Hall, he began to feel himself more, to be conscious of his own superiority, to discover that spirit of emulation, and passion for fame, which urged him strongly to go out into the world, and try what success he should have in it. His acquaintance with the eminent masters at Berlin had opened his mind to new ideas of excellence, and shewn him in a more extended view the perfections of his art. After his friends had refused such offers as the King had made him, he never could endure the thought of staying long at home, either as a pupil or substitute to his old master ZACKAW. He had heard so high a character of the singers and composers of Italy, that his thoughts ran much on a journey into that country. But this project required a longer purse than he was as yet provided with, and was therefore suspended till such time as it could be compassed without hazard or inconvenience. In the mean while, as his fortune was to depend on his skill in his profession, it was necessary to consider of some place less distant, where he might employ his time to advantage, and be still improving in knowledge and experience. Next to the Opera of Berlin, that of HAMBURGH was in the highest request. It was resolved to send him thither on his own bottom, and chiefly with a view to improvement. It was a wise resolution not to engage him too early with a view to profit. How many parents have murdered the fine talents of their children by weakly sacrificing that liberty and independency, which are essential to their exertion! This consideration had ever been attended to by his friends while he was under their direction. And it is very remarkable that HANDEL, when he came to act for himself, constantly pursued the same salutary maxim. In the sequel of his life he refused the highest offers from persons of the greatest distinction; nay, the highest favours from the fairest of the sex, only because he would not be cramped or confined by particular attachments.

His father's death[9] happened not long after his return from Berlin. This event produced a considerable change for the worse in the income of his mother. That he might not add to her expences, the first thing which he did on his arrival at Hamburgh, was to procure scholars, and obtain some employment in the orchestra. Such was his industry and success in setting out, that the first remittance which his mother sent him he generously returned her, accompanied with a small present of his own. On this occasion it is but justice to observe, that the same generous regard for those with whom he had any natural or accidental connection, appeared in the later, as well as in the earlier periods of his life. But a very few years before his death, being informed that the widow of ZACKAW was left ill provided for, he sent her money more than once. He would have done the same by her son, for whose welfare he appeared to be equally anxious; but the assurances he received, that all such services would only furnish him with opportunities of increasing those sottish habits he had contracted, with-held his hand. [Mainwaring, pp. 1–30]

Before we continue with Handel's stay in Hamburg, it might be convenient to take stock of the composer's life in chronological sequence, as far as evidence other than Mainwaring can provide:

1685, 24 February: Handel baptized. His parents lived in the house 'Zum gelben Hirsch' in the Kleine Klausstrasse, now Nicolaistrasse, in Halle.

1696, 2 May: Elector grants Handel's father a fee of fifty Reichsthaler for having successfully operated on a man who had swallowed a knife.

1697, 11 February: Handel's father dies.

1697, 18 February: Funeral sermon for Handel's father given at Halle and later printed; among the mourning poems included is one by George Frideric.

1698: Under Zachau's tutelage Handel compiles a manuscript music book (see above).

1702, 10 February: Handel matriculates at the University of Halle (without entering a special faculty). The composer G.P. Telemann (1681–1767) visits Handel, 'who was *already famous*', at Halle. '. . . HANDEL and I were continually exercising our fancy, and reciprocally communicating our thoughts, both by letter and conversation, in the frequent visits we made to each other' (Mattheson's *Ehren-Pforte*, p. 354, trans. by Burney 1785, pp. 5f.).

1702, 13 March: Handel appointed organist to the Calvinist Cathedral 'in place of the recently departed Johann Christoph Leporin', whose assistant Handel may have been. Handel was a Lutheran. The appointment was 'for the probationary year' at a salary of 'fifty thalers' to be paid in quarterly instalments 'beginning next Trinity Sunday'. Contract: Deutsch, p. 9.

1703, 5 April: Handel takes part in the Communion Service at Halle.

1703, 9 July: Handel meets Johann Mattheson in the organ loft of the Church of St Mary Magdalene in Hamburg.

At this juncture a personal friend of Handel's now enters the scene: the composer and singer Johann Mattheson (1681–1764). Mattheson later wanted Handel to write his autobiography for a publication of Mattheson's, but alas Handel never found the time to do so. In 1740, however, Mattheson published the following note in his *Grundlage einer Ehren-Pforte* (Hamburg). After noting that it was a pity that 'no detailed and well planned essay by *Keiser* and *Händel*, etc., from their own hand, can be imparted, as it can in the case of the praiseworthy *Telemann*,' Matheson then continues (Deutsch, pp. 501–5):

> In the summer of 1703 he [Handel] came to Hamburg, rich in capability and goodwill. He made almost his first acquaintance with me, by means of which he had access to the organs and choirs of the town, to operas and concerts; especially, however, he was led to a certain house, where everything was ardently devoted to music. At first he played second violin in the Opera orchestra, and behaved as though he did not know how many beans made five, for he was inclined by nature to dry jokes.[10] When, however, on one occasion, a harpsichord player was missing, he let himself be persuaded to stand in his stead, and did it manfully; without anyone having suspected it possible, except me.
>
> He composed at that time long, long arias, and almost endless cantatas, which still had not yet the right skill or the right taste, albeit a perfect harmony; he was, however, soon fashioned in quite another form by the high school of the opera.
>
> He was a skilful organist: more skilful than *Kuhnau* in fugue and counterpoint, particularly *ex tempore*; but he knew very little about melodic writing before he got to the Hamburg Opera . . .
>
> Most of the time in those days my late father provided him with free board, and he repaid that by imparting to me several choice touches of counterpoint. However, I did no small service for him with regard to dramatic style, and one good turn deserved another.
>
> We journeyed together on 17th Aug. of that same year, 1703, to Lübeck, and in the coach constructed many double fugues, *da mente, non da penna*. The President of the Privy Council, *Magnus von Wedderkopp*, had invited me there: in order to find for the admirable organist *Dieterich Buxtehude* a future successor. I took *Händel* with me. We played there almost every organ and harpsichord, and by reason of our playing made a particular decision, of which I have made mention elsewhere: namely, that he should play only the organ, and I the harpsichord. Besides, we listened to the above-mentioned artist, in his Marienkirche,

with merited attention. Since, however, a marriage contract [with Buxtehude's daughter who was no longer in her first youth] was proposed in connection with the affair, for which neither one of us showed the slightest desire, we left the place, after receiving many tokens of respect and enjoying entertainments. *Johann Christian Schieferdecker* thenceforth devoted himself more closely to his aim, and after the death of the father, *Buxtehude*, gained the lady and the fair employment, which today is laudably filled by *Johann Paul Kuntzen*.

In the year 1704, when I was in Holland, intending to go to England,[11] I received on 21st March, in Amsterdam, such an obliging and emphatic letter from *Händel* in Hamburg, that it moved me, principally, to take the journey back home again. The said letter is dated 18th March 1704 and contains amongst other things these expressions . . . 'I wish very much to have the pleasure of seeing you and talking with you, and this is likely to be achieved soon, for the time is coming when nothing can be done at the Opera in your absence. I beg you respectfully to let me know when you leave, so that with Mlle Sbülens I may perform the pleasurable duty of meeting you . . .'

On 5th December of the above-mentioned year, when my third opera, *Cleopatra*, was performed, and *Händel* sat at the harpsichord, a misunderstanding arose: such a thing is nothing new with young people, who strive after honour with all their power and little consideration. I, as composer, conducted, and at the same time personated *Antonius*, who, about half-an-hour before the end of the play, commits suicide. Now until that occasion I had been accustomed, after this action, to go into the orchestra and accompany the rest myself: which unquestionably the author can do better than anyone else; this time, however, it was denied to me. Instigated by several people, we thereupon, at the exit of the Opera House, on the public market place and with a multitude of onlookers, fought a duel, which might have passed off very unfortunately for both of us, had God's guidance not graciously ordained that my blade, thrusting against the broad, metallic coat-button of my opponent, should be shattered. No especial harm therefore came of the affair, and through the intervention of one of the most eminent councillors in Hamburg, as well as of the then lessees of the Opera House, we were soon reconciled again; and I had the honour, on the same day, namely, 30th December, of entertaining *Händel*, whereupon we were both present in the evening at the rehearsal of his *Almira*, and became better friends than before. The words of Ecclesiasticus, ch. 22, fit the case here: *Though thou drawest a sword at thy friend, yet despair not: for there may be a returning to favour. If thou openest thy mouth against thy friend, fear not; for there may be a reconciliation: except for upbraiding, or pride, or disclosing of secrets, or a treacherous wound: for, for these things, every friend will depart.*[12] I relate this event according to the true circumstances of it, because it is not yet so long since, that crooked people have wished to construe it crookedly.

Händel successfully performed his aforesaid opera, *Almira*, on 8th January 1705.[13] *Nero* followed on 25th Febr. In the last two beautiful operas I played the chief parts amid general applause, and after that I took a pleasant farewell of the theatre. [Deutsch pp. 501–6]

At this point, when Mainwaring takes us to Hamburg, we have valuable and in part very annoyed comments by Mattheson, who of course not only translated the Mainwaring biography into German but also added notes, some of them extensive. We shall therefore quote the Mainwaring text verbatim from the first edition of 1760, adding the commentary provided by Mattheson:

Before we advance any farther in his history, it is necessary some accounts should be given of the Opera at Hamburgh, as well as some character of the composer and singers.

The principal singers were CONRATINI and MATHYSON. The latter was secretary to Sir Cyril Wych, who was resident for the English court, had HANDEL for his music-master, and was himself a fine player on the harpsichord. MATHYSON was no great singer, for which reason he sung only occasionally; but he was a good actor, a good composer of lessons, and a good player on the harpsichord. He wrote and translated several treaties. One that he wrote was on Composition. He had thoughts of writing the life of HANDEL many years before his death. Had he pursued this design, he would have had advantages beyond what we can pretend to, *i.e.* ampler and fresher materials; at least, for so much of the life as had then elapsed. All that is here intended, is to give a plain, artless account of such particulars as we have been able to learn, and such only as we have reason to believe authentic. To return to our narration . . . [pp. 31f.]

[Mattheson's commentary (abridged):] . . . Mad. Conradin (not Conratini) was possessed of an almost perfect personal beauty, and moreover had a most extraordinary voice that extended from A below middle c to d''' all in the same intensity. That made her a fine singer. Mattheson (not Mathyson) coached her year after year, that is, he sang every day for her until she was able to memorize the part. In those days no singers were considered great unless they were castrati . . . To say that [Mattheson] 'sung only occasionally' is ridiculous of someone who remained in the theatre for fifteen years and almost always had the principal roles . . . On 20 October [1703] Mattheson presented his fifth or sixth opera entitled *Kleopatra*; he conducted and Handel played the harpsichord. That same year on 7 November he [Mattheson] was engaged by Mr Johann Wich, British Resident for Lower Saxony . . . Mattheson was first engaged as governor and *Hofmeister* of Cyrill Wich, the nine-year-old son, soon thereafter [Mattheson] was promoted to be the well-remunerated Secretary at a salary of 300 Reichsthaler with 200 ditto emoluments per annum. There was annoyance at this since he had said good-bye to the theatre . . . The young Master Wich had enjoyed a few very superficial lessons from Handel, but they didn't amount to much and one turned forthwith to the *Hofmeister*, under whose tutelage the young man in time gained great proficiency. In 1727 he succeeded his father upon the latter's death . . .

[Mainwaring's text continues:] CONRATINI excelled greatly both as an actress and a singer. KEYSAR [Keiser] did the same as a composer, but being a man of gaiety and expence, involved himself in debts, which forced him to abscond. His Operas, for some time, continued to be performed during his absence. On his disappearing, the person who before had played the second harpsichord, demanded the first. This occasioned a dispute between him and HANDEL, the particulars of which, partly for the sake of their singularity, and partly on account of their importance, may deserve to be mentioned.

On what reasons HANDEL grounded his claim to the first harpsichord I do not understand: he had played a violin in the orchestra, he had a good command on this instrument, and was known to have a better on the other. But the older candidate was not unfit for the office, and insisted on the right of succession. HANDEL seemed to have no plea but that of natural superiority, of which he was conscious, and from which he would not recede. This dispute occasioned parties in the Opera-house. On the one side it was said, with great appearance of reason, that to set such a boy as HANDEL over a person so much his senior, was both unjust and unprecedented. On the other, it was urged with some plausibility, that the Opera was not to be ruined for punctilios; that it was easy to foresee, from the difficulties KEYSAR was under, that a Composer would soon be wanted, but not so easy to find a person capable of succeeding him, unless it were HANDEL. In short, matters (they said) were now at that pass, that the question, if fairly stated, was not who should conduct the Opera, but whether there should be any Opera at all.

These arguments prevailed; and he, to whom the first place seemed of course to be due, was constrained to yield it to his stripling-competitor. But how much he felt the indignity, may be guessed from the nature and degree of his resentment; more suited to the glowing temper of an Italian, than to the phlegmatic constitution of a German: For, determined to make HANDEL pay dear for his priority, he stifled his rage for the present, only to wait an opportunity of giving it full vent. As they were coming out of the orchestra, he made a push at him with a sword, which being aimed full at his heart, would for ever have removed him from the office he had usurped, but for the friendly *Score*, which he accidentally carried in his bosom; and through which to have forced it, would have demanded all the might of Ajax himself.

Had this happened in the early ages, not a mortal but would have been persuaded that APOLLO himself had interposed to preserve him, in the form of a music-book.

From the circumstances which are related of this affair, it has more the appearance of an assassination, than of a rencounter: if the latter, one of HANDEL's years might well be wanting in the courage, or the skill to defend himself: if the former, supposing him capable of making a defence, he could not be prepared for it.

How many great men, in the very dawning of their glory, have been planted, like him, on the very verge of destruction! as if Fortune, jealous of Nature, made a show of sacrificing her noblest productions, only to remind her of that supremacy to which she aspires! [pp. 32–6]

[Mattheson's commentary (abridged):] . . . In the Hamburg Opera Orchestra, there has never been, for as long as one can remember, two harpsichords but always just one . . . Since this is supposed to have been the bone of contention, the whole story thereby collapses . . . Handel played at the outset the ripieno second violin, of which there were in toto two players, and as might be guessed he did not play the instrument better than a ripieno player [Mattheson means that there were a total of two second violinists in the band, and Handel was the second] . . . The fisticuffs occurred on 5 December 1704. Since Handel, whom [Mainwaring] wishes to make younger as his tale proceeds, was nearly twenty-one years old [Mattheson is reckoning from the false birth date of 1784, hence in actuality Handel was nearly twenty] and was tall, strong, broad and equipped with muscles, hence man enough to defend himself, he could have made use of the sword at his side . . . [end Mattheson]

Whatever might be the merits of the quarrel at first, HANDEL seemed now to have purchased his title to precedence by the dangers he had incurred to support it. What he and his friends expected, soon happened. From conducting the performance, he became Composer to the Opera. KEYSAR, from his unhappy situation, could no longer supply the Manager, who therefore applied to HANDEL, and furnished him with a drama to set. The name of it was ALMERIA [*sic*], and this was the first Opera which he made. The success of it was so great, that it ran for thirty nights without interruption. He was at this time not much above fourteen: before he was quite fifteen, he made a second, entitled FLORINDA; and soon after, a third called NERONE, which were heard with the same applause. [p. 37]

[Mattheson's commentary (abridged):] . . . *Almira* [*recte*] was given for the first time on 8 January 1705. [Handel's age is thus corrected by Mattheson from about fourteen to nearly twenty-one, again using the wrong birth date, hence actually nearly twenty.] . . . *Nero* was not the third but the second Handel opera and was first given on 25 February 1705. There were 48 days between the two operas, or at the most seven weeks. In these seven weeks were seven Sundays, seven Saturdays, fourteen postal days (excepting holidays); where can those thirty performances of *Almira* have been squeezed in, one after the other? . . . The name is *Florindo*, a man, not *Florinda*, a woman, and it was not the second but the third and was given in 1708, three years after *Nero* . . . [In the event *Florindo* was thought too long and divided into two operas, *Florindo* and *Daphne*, both produced in January 1708 when Handel was already in Italy.]

It never was his intention to settle at Hamburg: he told the Manager, on his first application to him, that he came thither only as a traveller, and with a view to improvement: that till the Composer should be at liberty, or till some other successor or substitute could be found, he was willing to be employed, but was resolved to see more of the world before he entered into any engagements, which would confine him long to any particular place. The Manager left that matter for him and his friends to determine; but so long as he thought proper to be concerned in the Opera, he promised him advantages at least as great as any Composer that had gone before him. This indeed was no more than what interest would readily suggest to a person in his situation: for good houses will always afford good pay, to all who bear a part in the performance; and especially to that person, whose character and abilities can ensure its success.

At the time that ALMERIA and FLORINDA were performed, there were many persons of note at Hamburgh, among whom was the Prince[14] of Tuscany, brother to John Gaston de

Medicis, Grand Duke. The Prince was a great lover of the art for which his country is so renowned. HANDEL's proficiency in it, not only procured him access to his Highness, but occasioned a sort of intimacy betwixt them: they frequently discoursed together on the state of Music in general, Singers, and Performers in particular. The Prince would often lament that HANDEL was not acquainted with those of Italy; shewed him a large collection of Italian Music; and was very desirous he should return with him to Florence. HANDEL plainly confessed that he could see nothing in the Music which answered the high character his Highness had given it. On the contrary, he thought it so very indifferent, that the Singers, he said, must be angels to recommend it. The Prince smiled at the severity of his censure, and added, that there needed nothing but a journey to Italy to reconcile him to the style and taste which prevailed there. He assured him that there was no country in which a young proficient could spend his time to so much advantage; or in which every branch of his profession was cultivated with so much care. HANDEL replied, that if this were so, he was much at a loss to conceive how such great culture should be followed by so little fruit. However, what his Highness had told him, and what he had before heard of the fame of the Italians, would certainly induce him to undertake the journey he had been pleased to recommend, the moment it should be convenient. The Prince then intimated, that if he chose to return with him, no conveniences should be wanting. HANDEL, without intending to accept of the favour designed him, expressed his sense of the honour done him. For he resolved to go to Italy on his own bottom, as soon as he could make a purse for that occasion. This noble spirit of independency, which possessed him almost from his childhood, was never known to forsake him, not even in the most distressful seasons of his life.

During his continuance at Hamburgh, he made a considerable number of Sonatas. But what became of these pieces he never could learn, having been so imprudent as to let them go out of his hands.

Four or five years had elapsed from the time of his coming to Hamburgh, to that of his leaving it. It has already been observed, that instead of being chargeable to his mother, he began to be serviceable to her before he was well settled in his new situation. Tho' he had continued to send her remittances from time to time, yet, clear of his own expences, he had made up a purse of 200 ducats. On the strength of this fund he resolved to set out for Italy. [Mainwaring, pp. 37–42]

Detailed reports of what Handel actually composed during these important formative years are, except for the operas, strangely lacking. But although one must, in the interest of scholarly accuracy, dismiss many of the chronological attributions of music to these Halle-Hamburg years, we do have some works which undoubtedly belong to the period. We shall examine these one by one:

(1) Psalm 113 (112) 'Laudate pueri Dominum' ('Praise ye the Lord, Praise O ye servants of the Lord') for soprano solo, two violins and basso continuo in F major (Vol. 38 item 1 of Chrysander's *Händel-Gesellschaft*, the foreword dated Leipzig, 20 December 1872). The autograph, undated, is in the Royal Library (British Library), R. M. 20. h. 7., and is on very tall folio paper (33.0 × 21.1/2 cm.) from a German paper-mill (watermarks: a seven-pointed star, letters 'FD', a clover-leaf or fleur-de-lis, a column in an elaborate coat-of-arms with letters 'JG'), hence all speculation that it might have been written in Italy is superfluous. Chrysander dated it *c.* 1702 and wrote of it as follows: '[It] is the oldest extant in Handel's handwriting; it undoubtedly belongs to his residence in Halle, when he was from sixteen to eighteen years old. The original is written very hastily, and is moreover injured in the margin; so that the editor found his task by no means easy.' The handwriting is so different from even Handel's Roman autographs that at first one wonders if the 'Laudate pueri' is by Handel at all: but (a) it is undoubtedly an autograph, because there are certain compositional changes that suggest that it cannot be a copy; and also (b) it comes, significantly, from the Royal Library, *ex* Smith Jr. (the copyist), *ex* Handel himself; we must therefore deduce that it is indeed Handel's autograph, the earliest one known. Nowadays scholars date it slightly later than Chrysander. Anthony Hicks mentions Chrysander's date and then suggests: 'a slightly later date is more likely. An excerpt (the aria "Qui habitare facit") was played near the end of the paper so that the audience could place the piece stylistically in relation to the other

music played. The haphazard structure of the movements looks back to *Almira* while the exuberant voice and string writing indicates an affinity with the earliest Italian works. The piece may therefore have been written at Hamburg to take to Italy, or may be one of the first works composed on arrival (at Florence?).'[15] We have seen, however, that the autograph's watermarks seem to rule out the latter suggestion. This setting of the 'Laudate pueri', though not approaching the sophisticated treatment of the second 'Laudate pueri' in D major which will be considered in the forthcoming chapter, is nevertheless a work of remarkable genius. It contains that flair for the soprano voice which was soon to become a hallmark of Handel's style, and the music is bold, forthright and self-assured beyond (as it were) its years. The long-held notes in the soprano-writing show that Handel had already grasped the principle of the *messa di voce*, and the slow introduction 'Quis, quis?' that prefaces the 'Suscitans a terra inopem' is full of dramatic power. It is a rough diamond but it is a work that deserves special attention as being, perhaps, the first of a glorious line.

(2) Of the Hamburg operas for the Theatre in the Gänsemarkt, only *Almira* has survived in a nearly complete state. Like the other operas performed at the Hamburg theatre, the libretto has a German text but some arias in Italian: this was also a feature of Haydn's first opera, *Der (neue) krumme Teufel*, performed in Vienna half a century later. Critics have been rather hard on *Almira*, but it contains music of undoubted genius, even if the theatrical whole does not measure up even to Handel's Italian operas and oratorios. The ballet music is beautiful and one number, the sarabande, caught Handel's fancy and he used it several times in later works. Terence Best has used Handel's 'fingerprints' in *Almira* to back-date some keyboard music to the Hamburg period, especially the Harpsichord Suites in D minor and G minor (Nos 4 and 6 of the Second Collection, 1733), previously pirated in an Amsterdam edition of about 1719.[16] It seems to me that *Almira* would be an ideal candidate for the gramophone record, where one could enjoy its many striking beauties without worrying whether it is, or is not, stageworthy.

(3) One of Handel's admirers, and the author of several word-books for the composer (foremost of course *Messiah*), was Charles Jennens, whose highly important collection of Handeliana is now in the Manchester Public Library. There (press-mark MS 130 Hd 4

v. 312) is a copy of the trio sonatas known as Op. 2, and Jennens has written on the first page of Op. 2, No. 2: 'composed at the age of 14', information which Jennens must have had orally from the composer himself. As a piece of music, this trio sonata suffers from structural defects common to young, talented composers who have not yet learned, as it were, the tricks of the trade; but despite its weaknesses it shows talent and a 'musicianly' approach.

Among the works that used to be ascribed to this early period is the *St John Passion*, now regarded (and rightly) as very dubious, a viola da gamba sonata now attributed to M. Leffloth (1705–31), and a set of trio sonatas which, I think, require a re-examination. They are now in the Royal Library, (R. M. 18. g. 3) and have the following title: 'The first Compositions Mr Handel wrote in 3 Parts, when a School Boy, about Ten Years of Age, before he had any Instructions and ['then' added with caret] playd on the Hautboye, besides the Harpsichord . . .' The inner title is '6 / Sonata / compose par Mr Hendel / Sonata I[ma] Hautbois I[ma]' and the music is on tall folio paper with the following watermark: letters 'RIH' under a crown surmounted by a fleur-de-lis; and a coat-of-arms with the sign ⑨ at the bottom (probably indicating German paper). Nowadays, these sonatas are positively dismissed as being totally spurious (Hicks, op. cit., p. 85 n., '. . . the complete absence of thematic links with any authentic works by Handel is sufficient, in such substantial stretches of music, to rule out Handelian authorship . . .'); but I think this is wrong. In Burney 1785, we read the following note about these trio sonatas (p. 3):

> The late Mr Weideman was in possession of a set of Sonatas, in three parts, which HANDEL composed when he was only ten years old. The earl of Marchmont, in his travels through Germany, when Lord Polwarth, picked them up as great curiosities, and gave them to Mr Weideman, of whom he took lessons on the German flute. A friend, who favoured me with this anecdote, procured a copy of these juvenile productions, which are now in his Majesty's collection, and which Weideman shewed to HANDEL; who seemed to look at them with much pleasure, and laughing, said, 'I used to write like the D---l in those days, but chiefly for the hautbois, which was my favourite instrument.'

> This, and the having such an exquisite performer to write for, as San Martini, accounts for the frequent opportunities which HANDEL took of composing for that instrument, in the early part of his life.

It has been suggested that the pieces might be genuine but composed later than *c*. 1696, and that suggestion may be true; but it seems quite wrong to dismiss them entirely. This is bright, attractive music and some of its gaucheries vouch, it seems to me, for its authenticity *and* its very early position in Handel's *œuvre*. The music is easily viewed both in Chrysander's *Händel-Gesellschaft*, vol. 27 (pp. 58 ff.) and in the new Halle edition (iv/9, pp. 3ff.), and if they are really not by Handel, at least they are useful as early examples of woodwind trios of the period. But I think our knowledge of Handel's early music is so incomplete that to rule out their authenticity is unwise; how can we explain the sudden jump into full mastery that we see, blazingly, in such works as the 'Dixit Dominus' of April 1707 unless there existed a long hinterland behind it of music largely unidentified, unexplored, and certainly lost?[17]

But one must maintain a sense of perspective. Frankly, there is nothing in all the music hitherto mentioned that would prepare us even for the *Roman Vespers*, *La Resurrezione* or *Agrippina* (for all its borrowings; but that, too, is a mark of things to come), let alone for *Messiah* or *Israel in Egypt*. Handel's genius was to flower south of the Alps; and it is to that blessed part of Europe that we must now travel, in his brilliant company.[18]

NOTES

1 For further details about Handel's parents, his birth, baptism and his sisters' births, see Deutsch, pp. 1f.

2 As we have seen, he had two daughters. [H.C.R.L.]

3 Karl, thirty-six years older than George Frideric.

4 Friedrich Wilhelm Zachau (1663–1712), born at Leipzig.

5 Handel was, of course, considerably older than seven; if his copybook of 1698 (see below) may be taken to represent works studied under Zachau's tuition, then Handel was about thirteen at that date. He became the organist at Halle Cathedral in 1702.

6 In 1698 there was no king in Berlin. The Elector of Brandenburg, Frederick III, became King Frederick I in 1701 and reigned until his death in 1713, to be succeeded by his son, Frederick William I (reigned 1713–40), father of Frederick

the Great. Frederick I was married to Sophia Charlotte, who had studied music with Agostini Steffani (and he shall shortly enter Handel's life). 'Her favourite Diversion was Musick, in which she excell'd both in the Performance, on the Harpsicord [*sic*] and the Composition.' *The History Of the Reign of Queen Anne Digested into Annals, Year the Third*, London 1705, p. 177. The Queen died on 1 August 1714. Handel may or may not have made the journey in 1698, but that is the year when he assembled and dated a manuscript music book inscribed 'G.F.H,' and containing compositions by his master Zachau as well as other masters such as Johann Jakob Froberger and Johann Kaspar Kerl. The book was known until the end of the eighteenth century but has since disappeared; the book's existence seems to suggest that Handel was still studying with Zachau at that time.

7 Giovanni Battista Bononcini (1670–1747) the prolific composer whose name is often spelled with a 'u' as in Mainwaring. Handel cannot have met him in Berlin before 1702, which suggests that Mainwaring may have telescoped two or even more visits into one – as he was to do with the subsequent stay in Venice (see below p. 61).

8 Attilio Ariosti (1666–*c*. 1740), the celebrated opera composer, was not in Berlin before the death of Handel's father (i.e. 1697).

9 Handel's father, Georg, died on 11 February 1697.

10 I know for certain, should he read this, he will laugh inwardly, for outwardly he laughs little. Especially if he remembers the pigeon-dealer, who travelled with us at that time on the mail-coach to Lübeck, likewise the pastry-cook's son, who had to work the bellows for us while we played in the Mary-Magdalene Church there. That was on 30th July 1703, as we had been out on the water on the preceding 15th. And hundreds of similar incidents hover still in my thoughts. [original footnote]

11 My inclination was always to England: and behold! I gratified it in Hamburg, with more convenience. [original footnote]

12 The German quotation, from 'Syrach', is shorter. [Deutsch]

13 Not 1704 as erroneously stated in the *Musikalischer Patriot*, which please alter. [original footnote]

14 Mainwaring says 'Prince of Tuscany, brother to John Gaston de Medicis, Grand Duke'. In fact the protagonists of this Medici invitation may be listed as follows: Grand Duke was Cosimo III; his eldest son and heir was Ferdinando de' Medici, called *Gran Principe*. The second son, Prince Giovanni Gastone de' Medici, who was unhappily wedded to a Princess of Saxe-Lauenburg, later became a famous profligate and rampant homosexual. For an amusing account of his misdeeds, see *The Last of the Medici, done into English by Harold Acton with an Introduction by Norman Douglas*, Florence 1930. Although it is now thought, since Reinhard Strohm's 'Händel in Italia: nuovi contributi', *Rivista italiana di musicologia* IX (1974), pp. 154–6, that the Medici prince who came to Hamburg and invited Handel to Italy was Prince Ferdinando, the evidence is not at all clear and it might have been the dissolute Giovanni Gastone, who did not return to Florence until 11 June 1705 (*Last of the Medici*, p. 49). Although he was in Bohemia when *Almira* was first given at Hamburg, the last Medici ruler-to-be might have been in Hamburg another time. It is, however, clear that once in Italy, Handel's Florentine patron was Prince Ferdinando.

15 A. Hicks, 'Handel's Early Musical Development', *Proceedings of the Royal Musical Association*, ciii, (1976/7), p. 86.

16 See Best's brilliant and stimulating article in *Music in Eighteenth-Century England*, Essays in memory of Charles Cudworth, edited by Christopher Hogwood and Richard Luckett, Cambridge 1983, pp. 171–87.

17 Burney (1785, pp. 7f., note a) tells us of some of these lost works. 'I procured at Hamburgh, in 1773, a manuscript collection of cantatas, by the principal composers of the early part of the present century; among which are two by HANDEL, which I never saw elsewhere; and these, it is most probable, were produced in that city, during his residence there, previous to his arrival in England, or journey into Italy. One of these cantatas has a spirited accompaniment for a harpsichord, *obbligato*. At the end is a short air, which seems to contain the germ, or subject, of a favourite harpsichord lesson, printed in the second volume of his *Pièces de Clavecin*, p. 5, the identical movement with which he ended the last concerto which he ever played in public. This cantata is the more likely to have been composed early in his youth, as there are some little liberties and negligences in the composition, which have never appeared in his later productions.' Alas, Burney's MS volume has disappeared. Likewise, the printed word-books of Handel's German librettist, Senator B.H. Brockes, contain Handel cantatas which have not survived (Mr Albi Rosenthal, London & Oxford, owns these rare first editions of Brockes's works).

18 From Mattheson (*Grundlage einer Ebren-Pforte*, p. 95) we learn that '. . . the opportunity arose of embarking on a free journey to Italy with von *Binitz*', who has never been identified but was apparently a wealthy nobleman. It is possible that he shared lodgings with Handel in the Ruspoli Palace in Rome (see below, p. 69).

II
Handel in Italy 1706–1710

IT HAS ALWAYS been presumed that Florence was Handel's first goal, where he was expected by Prince Ferdinando de' Medici, heir presumptive to Grand Duke Cosimo III. But again, concerning this first Tuscan sojourn, our principal source is Mainwaring:

> We left him just on the point of his removal to Italy; where he is arrived soon after the Prince of Tuscany. FLORENCE, as it is natural to suppose, was his first destination; for he was too well known to his Highness to need any other recommendations at the court of the Grand Duke, to whose palace he had free access at all seasons, and whose kindness he experienced on all occasions. The fame of his abilities had raised the curiosity of the Duke and his court, and rendered them very impatient to have some performance of his composing. With less experience, and fewer years to mature his judgement, he had hitherto succeeded to the utmost extent of his wishes. But he was now to be brought to the trial in a strange country, where the style was as different from that of his own nation, as the manners and customs of the Italians are from those of the Germans. Sensible as he was of this disadvantage, his ambition would not suffer him to decline the trial to which he was invited. [pp.49f.]

On the other hand, Handel's arrival in Rome is documented by a note on an interesting manuscript: vocal duets by Agostino Steffani (1653–1728), the celebrated Italian composer who had been active in Germany and was soon to become Handel's friend; these duets were acquired by Handel and dated Rome, 1706 (British Library).[1] That year Handel was, presumably, a witness in Rome to the Christmas festivities, which included features new to a man from north of the Alps. First there were the players who came (and still come) from the Abruzzi hills, playing the *piffari*, a kind of rude oboe or bagpipe with an inflated sheepskin for reservoir. Called *pifferari*, they were garbed in the sheepskins of their native hills, and played tunes of the rocking *siciliano* kind (i.e., in such metres as 6/8 or 12/8) which soon became incorporated into 'art music' and were used as the final movements of 'Christmas' concertos, such as those by Corelli and others (manuscript copies of Corelli's Concerto, Opus 6 No. 12, published posthumously in January 1713, were in circulation many years before their publication; and the 'Christmas' Concerto is now thought to have been performed at the Vatican in the time of Pope Alexander VIII.) Years later, when he came to write *Messiah*, at one of the lowest points of his career (having recovered from his appalling stroke but with his operatic career more or less in ruins), Handel remembered the glowing dawn of his career in Rome and incorporated the 'pifa' of the Abruzzi shepherds into the famous 'Pastoral' Symphony. It was one of many extraordinary signposts of Handel's four years in Italy.

Handel's first public appearance in Rome is registered in a fascinating diary which was published in 1978 in a fine critical edition: Francesco Valesio's *Diario di Roma*.[2] In his entry for 14 January 1707 we read: 'È giunto in questa città un sassone eccellente sonatore di cembalo e compositore di musica, quale hoggi ha fatta pompa della sua virtù in sonare l'organo nella chiesa di S. Giovanni con stupore di tutti.' (There has arrived in this city a Saxon who is an excellent harpsichord player and composer of music who today exhibited his prowess by playing the organ at St John Lateran to the astonishment of everybody.') Of course, other 'Saxon' musicians came to Rome, such as Johann Heinichen who (the Italians being unable to spell German names) was referred to in the Ruspoli documents as 'Sig.r Giovanni Sassonese' in April 1711; and we shall see the problem at its most urgent when identifying Handel in the newly-discovered portrait by Ghezzi of 1720 where the sitter is merely described as 'Il Sassone . . . bravissimo Suona[tor]e di Cembalo.' But it seems almost certain that the Valesio Diary is really describing Handel's début in the Eternal City.[3]

How was it that Handel, a Protestant musician, could so swiftly acquire the enthusiastic patronage of three cardinals and an influential, wealthy marquis soon to be created prince? Did they all hope to convert the twenty-one-year-old composer? Various hints as to Handel's attraction to Roman Catholicism have been mooted, even as late as the 1950s. Percy Young notes, rightly (1954), that the *Salve Regina* of 1707 'is an unmistakable act of chivalrous devotion before the Queen of Heaven'.[4] Was Handel seriously contemplating a change of religion? Although it is still often considered to have been 'a near thing', it seems to have been unlikely.

> As he was familiar with so many of the Sacred Order, and of a persuasion so totally repugnant to theirs, it is natural to imagine that some of them would expostulate with him on that subject. For how could these good catholics be supposed to bear him any real regard, without endeavouring to lead him out of the road to damnation? Being pressed very closely on this article by one of these exalted Ecclesiastics, he replied, that he was neither qualified, nor disposed to enter into enquiries of this sort, but was resolved to die a member of that communion, whether true or false, in which he was born and bred. No hopes appearing of a real conversion, the next attempt was to win him over to outward conformity. But neither arguments, nor offers had any effect, unless it were that of confirming him still more in the principles of protestantism. These applications were made only by a few persons. The generality looked upon him as a man of honest, though mistaken principles, and therefore concluded that he would not easily be induced to change them. [Mainwaring, pp.64f.]

Even in the tolerant *settecento*, it was extraordinary that Handel was permitted to play the organ of one of the great churches of Mother Rome, and that he was soon at work on an extensive and astonishing series of Latin pieces in honour of the Blessed Virgin Mary. But before we enter into detailed discussion of this musical feast – the first evidence of Handel's genius on a stupendous scale – and its composer's association with the Roman Church, some background material about the city in Handel's time might be welcome.

The Pope was Clement XI (Giovanni Francesco Albani, born 1649, reigned 1700–21), a confirmed enemy of opera, which was strictly forbidden in Rome, who has gone down in history as having espoused the losing cause in the War of the Spanish Succession. Handel, apart from having to forgo composing opera in Rome, got into trouble together with Prince Ruspoli for using a soprano in *La Resurrezione* in 1708; and the Pope even informed Ruspoli, about to leave (with Handel and the musicians) for the Castello di Vignanello in February 1708 to celebrate Carnival away from papal watchfulness, that his Holiness did not approve of the 'improvised plays' which Ruspoli wanted to have staged at Vignanello. (By the autumn of 1710, Ruspoli was able to persuade the Pope to consecrate the new church of Monte Rosi, built by Ruspoli at Vignanello).

Our principal source for the daily life in Rome of Handel's time is the Valesio Diary, whose author, Francesco Valesio, was born at Rome on 14 April 1670. His father was a doctor from Bordeaux, his mother Roman, and Francesco was a censor of hagiographical publications who lived near the church of S. Carlo on The Corso. The Rome of Handel and Valesio was a labyrinth of narrow streets, houses of extreme antiquity, vast squares whose haphazard existence often derived from Roman times, with monasteries and nunneries which tended to squeeze into corners the houses of the people; but amidst this squalor and chaos there was, of course, the series of great churches, foremost St Peter's, the largest in Christendom, crowned by Michelangelo's cupola and framed by Bernini's majestic square. Roman temples and graves, overgrown with grass, abutted on the fabulous Baroque palaces of the nobility. The seven hills of Roman antiquity had proliferated into numerous suburbs or rather sections, ranging from Trastevere, with its church of St Cecilia (dear to musicians), to the Villa Medici, resting in a green paradise of pines and cypresses. Rome was not as large as Paris but had about 150,000 inhabitants, whose existence was mostly – the clerics and nobility apart – difficult. The colourful houses, crowding next to each other in appalling sanitary conditions, caught fire easily and helped to spread disease. The streets, paved with tiles, were full of pot-holes: hot and dusty in the summer, muddy and dank in rain and winter. The average Roman citizen suffered under the privileges of the nobility and high-ranking clergy, whose servants often behaved arrogantly and atrociously to the lower classes and were ensured protection from the prosecution that should have been their due. The Papal *sbirri* (constabulary) led an unsuccessful war against robbers who lurked behind every façade. But woe betide the man who fell into the clutches of the Papal courts; cruel punishments (often justified in the penal code of the times) were meted out to him unless he enjoyed high-ranking protection. Jews enjoyed no protection at all. Valesio tells of a Jew, whom the authorities discovered making salami with horsemeat, who was strapped to a donkey and paraded through the streets before being sent to the galleys (which was practically tantamount to a slow death under revolting circumstances). During Carnival of 1710, the Roman fishmongers were forbidden to have a 'baudy wagon' in the procession, so a 'Mask of the Jews' was hastily organized: 100 Jews on donkeys, awaiting the Messiah, among them a Rabbi with monster legs *al naturale*, then an old man with a white beard on a donkey, book of laws in hand, surrounded by devils who led him. In front of him a Rabbi sat on a horse backwards, held the horse's tail and pulled it high; in the other hand he held a sign in Hebrew. They all sang in imitation of Synagogue chants, much to the fury of the real Jews, who had crowded to the Corso to see the procession. Then, after the Jews had moved on, 'Il trionfo della Bellezza', with ten mounted trumpeters and six oboists, removed the bad taste of the Jews. Among the procession four white horses pulled a triumphal waggon, painted and gilded with musicians (flautists and oboists), and on the top Duchess Segni Cesarini as 'beauty' and Alessandro Sobieski as 'valour'. Despite icy winds, the procession halted in front of the Palazzo Chigi for a serenade.

Without the city walls life was even more difficult, for apart from the extended operation of bandits and robbers, malaria was rampant in the plains and towards the Mediterranean coast, where marauding corsairs were also a constant danger. A *settecento* variety of the Roman 'bread and circuses' was provided by the many church feast-days, some with gay processions, the cortèges of the nobility, ambassadors and the cardinals with their magnificent carriages, footmen, runners, torch-bearers and men-at-arms, and the wild festivities of Carnival (which if not so licentious as in Venice was sufficiently bawdy in Rome to cause papal displeasure, sometimes even to an actual banning of most events). The great palaces enjoyed the forbidden game of hazard, and if opera was not allowed, oratorio and large-scale religious music flourished, as did secular cantatas, duets, and all kinds of instrumental music. The new forms of sonata and concerto grosso had achieved a brilliant level in Rome which was now a world-famous centre of all kinds of music. Concerts with refreshments were regular features of the great palazzi.

Valesio and Handel witnessed the War of the Spanish Succession, a struggle between France and the Habsburgs into which Pope Clement XI was unwillingly dragged. Imperial troops crossed, to great local discomfort, papal territories and entered Rome itself. Spanish, French and Imperial troops fought in Italy, with the inevitable plundering and 'contributions' raised from unwilling cities. Taxes rose spectacularly, roads for the troops had to be constructed, ancient Roman bridges strengthened, and there was the ever-present need to supply and feed thousands of hungry troops. At one time the Roman nobility had to provide horses. We hear of all these things, some at first hand, some in the form of gossip or remote hearsay, in Valesio's Diary.

We learn of the wretched finances of the Papal State, the state of health not only of the Pope but of important cardinals, princes and ambassadors. We hear of nepotism, rampant in papal Rome, we take note of great concerts led by Arcangelo Corelli or Alessandro Scarlatti. We hear of a fruit-vendor who was packing pears into a straw bag and as he leaned over, a horse (grazing nearby) walked over, thrust his nose between the vendor's legs and, as Valesio puts it, bit off a sizeable chunk *'dell' instrumento'*, to yells of protest from the vendor and his wife and children.

Human life was not worth much in the Eternal City. All gentlemen wore swords, pistols, or daggers (but pistols were considered noisy and slightly vulgar). Robbers liked to use a knife. The thieves were bold despite grim punishments if they were caught: objects like iron chains in front of palace gates, wrought-iron window grates and the leather curtains in the salon of the Curia in Monte Citorio disappeared on wet winter nights. During Mass at the church of the Madonna del Popolo, frequented by many cardinals, two of their coachmen got into an argument in front of the church and drew their knives. When a Pope died, there were huge funeral ceremonies and processions, and when Innocent XII died (September 1700) some robbers made off with the alms boxes in St John Lateran.

There were two political parties in Rome: the one supported the French king who had placed his nephew Philip of Anjou on the Spanish throne, the other supported Emperor Joseph I, whose brother (Carlos III) wanted the Spanish succession for himself (hence the war's name). The conflict raged in Spain, on the Rhine and then in north Italy; papal lands in northern Italy were quickly drawn into the conflict. Imperial troops took up positions in the Papal States of Bologna and Ferrara and demanded high 'contributions', which Rome had to pay directly by increased taxation and indirectly by inflation. Moreover, the rival factions were constantly at daggers drawn in Rome itself. Shortly after Handel arrived, on New Year's Day 1707, a row exploded in the Catalan Church of the Madonna Santissima di Monserrato, where they read a Pater and Ave for King Philip V of Spain. Adherents of Carlos III at once required an Ave and Pater for their candidate, a fight broke out, and the papal troops had to patrol the church all night. The Pope, who was a genuinely pious man, decided to forbid the Carnival, and the *sbirri* confiscated the decorations, arrested masked revellers in the street and tried to find out which of the great palazzi were enjoying forbidden secret carnival parties (there was not much the Pope could do about those given by foreign embassies or the very highest nobility).

When Prince Eugène of Savoy won his great battle over the French at Mantua and drove them out of northern Italy, Cardinal Grimani (an Imperial follower) gave a great celebration with a *Te Deum*, and distributed bread and wine to the populace, who responded with '*vivat*' calls. The very next day, the Feast of St Joseph (19 March 1707) Grimani gave a huge *festa* to celebrate the Emperor's name-day. There was a solemn mass at the Church dell'Anima, with an enormous congregation and over a hundred musicians participating.

It was into this extraordinary atmosphere that Handel, just turned twenty-two years of age, was plunged. His biographer, Mainwaring, gives us a resumé which, although it mixes up chronology, is indispensable because (as we have seen) much of the information came directly from the composer, through his pupil John Christopher Smith, Jr. We shall quote from it fully as far as the Italian period is concerned, but before we begin Handel's own Roman Diary, we must single out three cardinals specially mentioned in the Mainwaring report: Pietro Ottoboni, Carlo Colonna, and Benedetto Pamphilj

(Panfili is the usual spelling today). Since we will be examining Handel's first series of religious works composed in Italy, we must also consider how they might have been commissioned, which brings us to the three cardinals in question.

The most important of the three, historically, was Pietro Ottoboni, nephew of the late Pope Alexander VIII (reigned 1689–91) who, as the Italians like to relate, was the reason that *nepotismo* entered the Italian language. Vastly favoured with sinecures and rents of all kinds, Pietro Ottoboni was made Papal Chancellor – a position of great power – by his uncle, immediately after the latter had been elected Pope. Pietro's preference was so flagrant that after Alexander's death the next pope, Innocent XII, issued in 1692 a bull forbidding any subsequent pope to bestow more than a modest benefice on his relatives and making it unlawful for a pope to raise more than one relative to the purple.

Pietro Ottoboni (1667–1740) came of an old and noble family of the Veneto, and with his position and wealth he became one of the great Maecenas of Handel's Rome, a littérateur (he wrote his own libretti), composer, great connoisseur of pictures and a patron of all the arts. Although he emerges as a highly sensitive and cultivated man, he could be ruthless (as when he suppressed the Freemasons in Florence). When he died he left astronomical debts, but also a collection of great pictures, including works by Raphael, Titian, Rubens, and Rembrandt; sculptures, furniture and several harpsichords, some with elaborately gilded *putti* as legs, and with their inside lids painted by great masters such as Poussin and Ottoboni's own painter, Trevisani (the latter instrument has survived). Arcangelo Corelli was his *maestro di concerto* and a valued friend; he lived in an Ottoboni apartment. Ottoboni's soirées were held at his Palazzo della Cancelleria on Mondays, and were famous as much for their artistic quality as for the excellence of the refreshments served. Ottoboni's great library is now in the Vatican, and his 'special' church was SS Lorenzo e Damaso, where he was buried. Valesio tells us of one such *festa* at the Cancelleria on 10 February 1706, where (according to papal wishes) there was music in the theatre without costumes, a '*nobile sinfonia*' and then a two-act satirical comedy by Ottoboni himself, followed by an evening *souper* of five courses, including partridges, hazel-hens and *galli di monte*. The day after, Cardinal

Pietro offered luncheon to the eleven men of the purple (himself included) who had been created cardinals by the Ottoboni Pope Alexander VIII, and at ten o'clock that evening a great procession along the Corso revealed Cardinal Pietro and four other cardinals in his newly-restored carriage with rich inlay, gold decorations and embroidered curtains. On 18 February the coffin with the body of Pope Alexander VIII was transferred to its final resting-place, opened, and the dead man's features were easily recognizable. The eleven cardinals and a notary were present, and Pietro kissed the hands of his uncle (he had every reason to do so).

On 31 March 1706 an oratorio by Ottoboni was performed, dedicated to Filippo Neri (father of the oratorio form) and taken from the Psalms of Jeremiah; it included six muted trumpets. The walls were covered in black velvet, diffused light streamed from vases of porphyry and the musicians' lamps were covered with paper shades painted with scenes from the Passion.

Handel is known to have participated in the great *feste* given by Ottoboni, but his name is never mentioned in the Valesio Diary. On 7 January 1708 Valesio informs us that 'today Wednesday there are to begin the weekly series of cantatas which are given in the theatre of Ottoboni's Cancelleria and will continue until the following Carnival'. We also hear that the Cardinal tended to spoil his favourite castrato singer, Andrea Adami, known as 'Bolsena'. On 8 April the Cardinal tried to have 'the Bolsena' made a canon, and when this was sabotaged by the other canons he secured him a benefice in S. Maria Maggiore, and in Venice had him created a citizen 'first class' to be addressed with 'Illustrissimus'; 'that castrone', adds Valesio. But on 11 June 1709, we hear that Ottoboni, newly returned from Florence, was displeased because the Grand Duke would not address 'the Bolsena' as befitted a *gentiluomo*: the Grand Duke had invited the castrato to sing and gave him as a fee only six flasks of wine.

Half a year before Handel arrived in Rome, on 17 May 1706 Carlo Colonna (1665–1739) the former Papal major-domo was created a cardinal. Although Colonna's relationship to Handel is well documented in Mainwaring, it was not until 1959 that the late James S. Hall, in a valuable article,[5] suggested a more than probable connection between a large part of Handel's Latin choral compositions of 1707 (some dated in autograph), the Cardinal and the Carmelites.

The article proposes that Handel composed a huge set of Vespereal Offices for the Feast of Our Lady of Mount Carmel in the church of S. Maria di Monte Santo in the Piazza del Popolo, which were performed there in the afternoon and evening of 16 July 1707. This was then followed by a grand Mass (not by Handel). The clue for all this came from a manuscript score of the Carmelite Motet 'Saeviat tellus', praising the Order ('Sub tantae Virginis tutela, Carmelitae, triumphate'); this manuscript, which came from the Colonna Library in Rome, is now in the British Library.[6] Dr Hall was unable to prove the connection between Cardinal Colonna and the Carmelites or the church of S. Maria, but now we have independent assistance from Valesio's Diary, which does not mention the event for 1707 but devotes the following description to the services of 1708: 'Si celebrò hoggi la festività della Madonna del Carmine nella chiesa di Monte Santo con Solenne musica fatta alle spese del cardinal Colonna, ma non furono fatti gli archi, come è consueto, a vi fu poca illuminazione e concorso.' 'Today is celebrated the Festival of the Madonna del Carmine in the church of Monte Santo with solemn music given at the expense of Cardinal Colonna, but they did not erect the arches, as they usually do, and there was little illumination and not many people.'[7]

Handel's participation in the Vespers seems to have included the following:

First Vespers

Motet 'Saeviat tellus' (scoring: Sop. Solo, oboes, str., b.c.).

First Antiphon: 'Haec est regina virgineum' (Ms. formerly in Colonna Library in Rome, sold 1878: for Sop. Solo, str., b.c.).

Second Antiphon: 'Te decus virgineum' (ditto; for Alto Solo, str., b.c.).

Second Vespers

Psalms 'Dixit Dominus' (scoring: five-part voices SSATB, soli and choral, str. and b.c.) Aut., British Library, signed Rome, April 1706–7 (for dating see p.75, n.1).

'Laudate pueri' (scoring: sop. solo, five-part choir SSATB, 2 ob., str., b.c.) Aut., British Library, signed Rome, 8 July 1707.

'Laetatus sum' (lost?)

'Nisi Dominus' (scoring: ATB Soli, double choir (SSAA TTBB), double string orch., b.c.) Aut. (now lost) dated Rome, 13 June 1707.

The copy from the Colonna Library, now in the British Library (Eg. 2458), mentions this work as forming part of the Carmelite Vespers.

'Lauda Jerusalem' (lost?)

That the Psalms for the Second Vesper Offices in Handel's setting were conceived cyclically might have occurred to anyone studying the sources, for there are no fewer than three British manuscript scores which contain the 'Dixit Dominus', 'Laudate pueri' and 'Nisi Dominus' in conjunct order; and of these at least one, from the library of Handel's librettist Charles Jennens (now Manchester Public Library Ms. 130 Hd4, v. 205), lays claim to a certain authenticity. The others belonged to the double-bass player Dragonetti, later Vincent Novello (now Royal College of Music, London Ms. 248). The fact that neither 'Laetatus sum' nor 'Lauda Jerusalem' is included may indicate either that Handel was not the composer or that they are lost (perhaps the most likely explanation) or that they were performed in Gregorian chant. But it is becoming ever clearer that the last word on Handelian sources for his Italian sojourn has yet to be spoken;[8] and perhaps the interest which was generated by the tercentenary of his birth may provide further discoveries.

James S. Hall thought the beautiful *Salve Regina* might have belonged to the Vespereal Offices, but since then, it has been discovered that the work was copied for the Ruspoli family in Vignanello Castle in June 1707 (see below); so its first performance was apparently then (though its use in the subsequent Carmelite ceremony in July is not precluded by the Vignanello performance). It has been suggested that it is this tremendous Vespers cycle that may have enabled Handel to move freely in Catholic Rome and to make his debut in St John Lateran, which Dr Hall rightly describes as 'the Pope's own cathedral as Bishop of Rome, and the mother Church of the Universal Church'. Having Cardinal Colonna as a powerful sponsor in the Sacred College was the way in which the difficulties were overcome.

If Handel's first protector in Rome was, chronologically, Cardinal Colonna, the third one listed here, Benedetto Pamphilj (1653–1730) provided him with his most important sacred Italian text of this period (apart from those taken from the Bible): the Oratorio *Il trionfo del*

Tempo e del Disinganno (hereafter *Il trionfo*) performed, possibly at the Cancelleria, in Lent of 1707 (copyist's score dated 14 May 1707, Rome). He also wrote other texts, among them a farewell cantata for Handel ('Hendel non può mai Musa') which the composer considered silly flattery (see p.70).

Now that the leading ecclesiastical participants in Handel's Roman triumphs have been introduced, we must turn to an Italian nobleman who was to prove to be Handel's principal patron: Marchese Francesco Maria Ruspoli (1672–1751), known to music scholars as the great Roman patron of Antonio Caldara,[9] and now, since the brilliant research by Ursula Kirkendale, revealed to have been Handel's principal Roman patron during the years 1707–9. He was married to Isabella Cesi del Duca d'Acquasparte. In the autumn of 1706, Ruspoli inherited the two rich estates of Vignanello (near Viterbo) and Cerveteri, which increased his income considerably and enabled him to enlarge his musical establishment, fortunately just as Handel emerged on the Roman scene.

The old Ruspoli palace in Rome (during Handel's sojourn there) was known as the Palazzo Bonelli on the Piazza del SS Apostoli, formerly rented by the Imperial Ambassador; Marchese Ruspoli rented it in the period under consideration, later moving into the present Palazzo Ruspoli on the Corso. It was in the Palazzo Bonelli – now the Prefettura – that Handel's new Oratorio *La Resurrezione* was performed in 1708.

At the time that Handel was a member of the household, Ruspoli was hoping to be made a prince, and immense pains to flatter Pope Clement were made to that end: for example, the performance in March 1708 of the *Oratorio di San Clemente*. But Ruspoli considered, no doubt rightly, that more than flattering oratorios was needed to raise him from the marquisate to a princeling, and on 8 July 1708 he offered to raise a regiment of 500 well-armed men provided the Pope would consent to install Ruspoli's eleven-year-old son as Colonel (perhaps Ruspoli thought this honour would help soften the fact that his older son and heir was impotent). The Pope had no objections, and at the Palazzo Bonelli on 9 September the young Ruspoli gave a luncheon for his officers, all in wine-red uniform with gold braid, their hats adorned with white feathers and white and turquoise cockades. At eleven in the evening the Regiment marched to receive the papal blessing. On 3 February, Ruspoli was made Prince of Cerveteri (his estate on the Mediterranean some fifty kilometres from Rome), and on 27 March another son was born, securing the line. At the end of that summer, 27 August, there was a great *festa* at the Palazzo Bonelli, at which was given the Serenade by Antonio Caldara, 'Chi s'arma di virtù vince ogni affetto'. All the windows facing the Piazza were lighted with torches, and painted railings and *trompe l'oeil* effects highlighted the musicians' loggia, protected from the windy weather by glass windows that reflected the candle light. The Serenade ended late at night, and the new Princeling caused 'copious and excellent refreshment' to be distributed in the piazza – which was thronged with Romans as well as carriages (without their horses), which could hardly budge until morning. The other cardinals who were invited included Pamphilj, Colonna and Ottoboni. Antonio Caldara had replaced Handel as the principal Ruspoli composer, 'il Sassone' meanwhile having settled in Florence.

What were the business arrangements that Handel had with Ruspoli, or indeed with his other Roman patrons? Curiously, in all the detailed Ruspoli account-books (now in the Vatican Library), there is never a mention of any fee being paid to Handel, and yet he must have needed cash during these years.

The inexplicable fact is, moreover, that Handel was expected to provide music, and especially Italian cantatas, for the Sunday morning concerts not only in Rome but also at Vignanello. There are bills for Handel's meals, and those of his 'companion', possibly a certain Herr von Binitz (the name is known to us from the writings of Handel's German friend and colleague, Johann Mattheson),[10] also of expenses such as music paper and a bed rented for him while he was rehearsing and producing the Oratorio at the Palazzo Bonelli in 1708 – but no salary. Perhaps, as with Prince Nicolaus Esterházy and Haydn sixty years later in Hungary, rewards in gold were made to 'il Sassone'. The same may apply to Handel's three cardinal patrons gathered at the *festa* given by his fourth patron that August night in 1709. But the total absence, up to now, of any evidence of Handel's finances is slightly mysterious.

By May 1707 Handel was composing Italian cantatas for Ruspoli, and he continued to do so during several periods: May to October

1707, February to May 1708, July to November 1708 and the beginning of 1709 (though the evidence for Handel's actual presence with the court in 1709 is not clear). Foremost among the soloists was Margarita Durastanti, soprano, for whom Handel wrote numerous soprano cantatas, performed at the Sunday *conversazioni*. Handel later called her to London, together with the nucleus of the Ruspoli instrumentalists: the violinists Domenico and Pietro Castrucci (father and son) and the cellist Filippo Amadei (see below p. 117). Most of Handel's Italian cantatas were for voice and basso continuo (cello and/or *violone*, double bass, and keyboard instrument, usually harpsichord). Apart from the performers listed by name above, there was also a double bass (*violone*) player, Bartolomeo Cimapane; and of course Handel directed from the harpsichord (or in the case of church cantatas, of which there were several including the famous *Salve Regina* given at Vignanello, the organ). If larger numbers of strings or additional instruments were required (such as the trumpet for the Cantata *Diana cacciatrice*, performed at Vignanello in May or June of 1707), they were specially engaged. For chamber music, the typical *sonata da camera* or *sonata da chiesa* could be performed (two violins, cello and/or *violone*, harpsichord or organ). Of course the *Diana* Cantata was part of a special genre called 'della caccia' – hunting cantatas – used in conjunction with the hunting season at Vignanello (there are many bills dealing with hunting equipment, porters and so on in the Ruspoli documents).

A harpsichord tuner had to adjust the Roman cembalo to be sent to Vignanello: obviously the local artisans did not include such an exotic man; there are, moreover, bills for refreshments given to the hungry and thirsty musicians. Also, Ursula Kirkendale has found a bill (dated June 1707) for jewellery sent up from Rome to Vignanello apparently as a special reward for the music given in the church for the celebrations of S. Antonio, at which the *Salve Regina*, sung by Signora Durastanti, was first performed. A ring with six little diamonds (says the bill) was the reward for the song of the star-studded Queen of Heaven, and it would seem there was a ring with an amethyst (or another with a hyacinth stone) for 'il grande Sassone'.

Handel was now in close contact with all the leading musicians of Rome, and constantly exposed to the greatest music – except opera, of course – that the Holy City could provide. Mainwaring tells of an entertaining contretemps, all resolved in a friendly and civilized way (as befitted the two protagonists) between the great Corelli and Handel, and a kind of contest between Domenico Scarlatti and Handel. Both took place in the friendly Palazzo della Cancelleria of Cardinal Ottoboni, who also presented 'il Sassone' to Domenico Scarlatti's father, the great Alessandro. Mainwairing continues:

> . . . We are now to relate his reception at Rome. The fame of his musical achievements at Florence and at Venice had reached that metropolis long before him. His arrival therefore was immediately known, and occasioned civil enquiries and polite messages from persons of the first distinction there. Among his greatest admirers was the Cardinal Ottoboni, a person of a refined taste, and princely magnificence. Besides a fine collection of pictures and statues, he had a large library of music, and an excellent band of performers, which he kept in constant pay. The illustrious CORELLI played the first violin, and had apartments in the Cardinal's palace. It was a customary thing with his eminence to have performances of Operas, Oratorios, and such other grand compositions, as could from time to time be procured. HANDEL was desired to furnish his quota; and there was always such a greatness and superiority in the pieces composed by him, as rendered those of the best masters comparatively little and insignificant. There was also something in his manner so very different from what the Italians had been used to, that those who were seldom or never at a loss in performing any other music, were frequently puzzled how to execute his. CORELLI himself complained of the difficulty he found in playing his Overtures.[11] Indeed there was in the whole cast of these compositions, but especially in the opening of them, such a degree of fire and force, as never could consort with the mild graces, and placid elegances of a genius so totally dissimilar. Several fruitless attempts HANDEL had one day made to instruct him in the manner of executing these spirited passages. Piqued at the tameness with which he still played them, he snatched the instrument out of his hand; and, to convince him how little he understood them, played the passages himself. But CORELLI, who was a person of great modesty and meekness,

wanted no convicing of this sort; for he ingenuously declared that he did not understand them; i.e., knew not how to execute them properly, and give them the strength and expression they required. When HANDEL appeared impatient, *Ma, caro Sassone* (said he) *questa Musica è nel style Francese, di ch'io non m'intendo!*

A little incident relating to CORELLI, shows his character so strongly, that I shall be excused for reciting it, though foreign to our present purpose. He was requested one evening to play, to a large and polite company, a fine Solo which he had lately composed. Just as he was in the midst of his performance, some of the number began to discourse together a little unseasonably. CORELLI gently lays down his instrument. Being asked whether anything was the matter with him? Nothing, he replied, he was only afraid that he interrupted conversation. The elegant propriety of this silent censure, joined with his genteel and good-humoured answer, afforded great pleasure, even to the persons who occasioned it. They begged him to resume his instrument, assuring him at the same time, that he might depend on all the attention, which the occasion required, and which his merit ought before to have commanded.

Hitherto HANDEL has chiefly been considered, if not wholly, in the quality of Composer. We shall now have occasion to enter into his character as a Player or Performer. And it must not be forgot, that, though he was well acquainted with the nature and management of the violin; yet his chief practice, and greatest mastery was on the organ and harpsichord.

When he came first into Italy, the masters in greatest esteem were ALESSANDRO SCARLATTI, GASPARINI, and LOTTI. The first[12] of these he became acquainted with at Cardinal OTTOBONI's. Here also he became known to DOMINICO [*sic*] SCARLATTI, now living in Spain, and author of the celebrated lessons. As he was an exquisite player on the harpsichord, the Cardinal was resolved to bring him and HANDEL together for a trial of skill. The issue of the trial on the harpsichord hath been differently reported. It has been said that some gave the preference to SCARLATTI. However, when they came to the Organ there was not the least pretence for doubting to which of them it belonged. SCARLATTI himself declared the superiority of his antagonist, and owned ingenuously, that till he had heard him upon this instrument, he had no conception of its powers. So greatly was he struck with his peculiar method of playing, that he followed him all over Italy, and was never so happy as when he was with him.

HANDEL used often to speak of this person with great satisfaction; and indeed there was reason for it; for besides his great talents as an artist, he had the sweetest temper, and the genteelest behaviour. On the other hand, it was mentioned but lately by the two PLAS [the famous Haut-bois] who came from Madrid, that SCARLATTI, as oft as he was admired for his great execution, would mention HANDEL, and cross himself in token of veneration.

Though no two persons ever arrived at such perfection on their respective instruments, yet it is remarkable that there was a total difference in their manner. The characteristic excellence of SCARLATTI seems to have consisted in a certain elegance and delicacy of expression. HANDEL had an uncommon brilliancy and command of finger: but what distinguished him from all other players who possessed these same qualities, was that amazing fulness, force, and energy, which he joined with them. And this observation may be applied with as much justness to his compositions, as to his playing.

While he was at Rome he was also much and often at the palaces of the two Cardinals, COLONNA, and PAMPHILII. The latter had some talents for Poetry, and wrote the drama of IL TRIONFO DEL TEMPO, besides several other pieces, which HANDEL set at his desire, some in the compass of a single evening, and others extempore . . . One of these was in honour of HANDEL himself. He was compared to Orpheus, and exalted above the rank of mortals. Whether his Eminence chose this subject as most likely to inspire him with fine conceptions, or with a view to discover how far so great an Artist was proof against the assaults of vanity, it is not material to determine. HANDEL's modesty was not however so excessive, as to hinder him from complying with the desire of his illustrious[13] friend. [Mainwaring pp. 54–64]

It is not clear with whom Handel first stayed at Rome when he made that spectacular appearance at St John Lateran's on 14 January, nor which of his illustrious patrons was at that moment specially caring for his welfare; but if we assume that Cardinal Colonna was the key figure at the beginning of Handel's Roman career, it may be that the crucial commission for the Carmelites was not the first sacred duty which the young composer took upon himself. In the so-called Santini Library in the episcopal palace at Münster (Westphalia), there are two important Handel Cantata scores in Latin from Rome – Abbate Fortunato Santini (1778–1862) was an avid collector and musical antiquarian – including what may be Handel's first Roman composition of significance, the Cantata 'Donna che in ciel'.[14] The source is entitled '. . . [composed for] Anniversario della Liberatione di Roma dal / Terremoto nel giorno dell. Purif.^{e} della Beat.^{ma} V[irgin]^{e}'. The feast of the Blessed Virgin's Purification takes place on 2 February, and although no date is given on the Santini Ms., one circumstance suggests 1707 (rather than 1708 or 1709) as the year of composition: by February 1708, Handel was working regularly for Ruspoli, and in their account books there is no sign of such a Cantata which, in any case, requires a choir, normally beyond the scope of the court performances. Perhaps, indeed, Ottoboni was responsible for this Handelian Cantata – the records and account books of the Cardinal remain to be investigated. In any case, Valesio tells us of the circumstances:

> Wednesday 2 [February] . . . In celebration today of the Feast of the Blessed Virgin's Purification, the Papal Choir assembled in the Vatican, and with the usual distribution of candles, sang the *Te Deum* in thanksgiving to the Lord God for having saved the city from the earthquake of the year 1703. [III, p.761]

Handel's magnificent Cantata also provides us – if our assumption of its chronology is correct – with the first evidence of a large-scale instrumental piece of the Roman period: the *Ouverture* or *sinfonia* in the French (Lully-an) style with which the work opens. Its bold, sure touch is astonishing. Perhaps Handel had before composed instrumental works that reflected this kind of complete mastery, but none is known to us;[15] here we have Handel, just turned twenty-two, showing that he had completely assimilated the French and Italian styles of instrumental (orchestral) music. Indeed, Handel's ability to assimilate 'foreign' styles is almost unique: only Mozart later had the ability to this uncanny extent. And as for the rest of this amazing work, Handel has proceeded to conquer the world of the Italian chorus with the same breathtaking mastery displayed in the fiery Overture. Perhaps the most startling section is the final piece of the Cantata, which begins in the minor and turns (as appropriate to a piece of thanksgiving) to the major; but what is special is the exchange between soprano soloist and choir, her ejaculations 'Maria!' being seized upon by the choir and commented upon with dramatic, almost operatic fervour. Stylistically there are many hints of the music to come: the typical upward progressions, and the deft writing for the choir (a heritage of his background, but made to sound, in some magical way, thoroughly Italian). It was a *tour de force* and in one explosive gesture it established Handel as the leading composer in Rome.[16]

The major work with which Handel was now involved – apart from the Psalm 'Dixit Dominus' (the second Carmelite cycle) – was the Lenten Oratorio *Il trionfo del Tempo e del Disinganno* (later known, in revised versions, as *Il trionfo del Tempo e della Verità* and just before Handel's death as *The Triumph of Time and Truth*), the text by Cardinal Benedetto Pamphilj, in whose household accounts the bill for copying the Oratorio and an Italian Cantata *Il delirio amoroso* (opening words 'Da quel giorno fatale', perhaps also supplied by the creative Cardinal?) of 14 May 1707 has survived.[17]

Handel used a great deal of his successful Italian music in later works for London, including an odd adaptation of the 'Dixit Dominus' in *Deborah* – unlike most of these borrowings, this is not an improvement – and none more thoroughly than *Il trionfo*. Nowadays, we are less impressed with it than with the Latin church music, which is rightly enjoying a spectacular revival. There are marvellous touches in Handel's first Oratorio: the suave and sophisticated handling of the orchestra, the attractive vocal writing, and the clever structure. But the libretto does not contain much material of a kind to fire the young composer's imagination, such as the part of Lucifer in *La Resurrezione*. Also we lack the choruses and the dramatic force of the church music, especially of the 'Dixit Dominus'. Yet there is one breathtaking exception: a little 'sonata' for *obbligato* organ and orchestra, a miniature organ concerto which looks forward in a quite remarkable way to the great organ concertos of the London years. Its rushing strings are set off by the delicious interplay of the solo instruments (a kind of gigantic Corellian *concertino*, or solo group, with oboes, solo violin and of course 'il Sassone' himself at the organ). In its small, condensed form it also looks forward to the later concertos, many movements of which are constructed along these lines rather than in the more conventional *ritornello-solo* form as we know it in Vivaldi and Bach. Here again is a completely formed model for later Handel, in miniature but of an amazing structural and musical perfection.

And now to the work which seems to sum up in one fell swoop the bold genius of the twenty-two-year-old Handel: the 'Dixit Dominus'. There are, basically, two features which are immediately arresting. The first is historical: Handel's sure ability to assimilate the musical language of the country in which he was working. Just as he at once grasped the beauty and, for him, the usefulness of the Purcellian English anthem, Handel at once saw and understood the new *concerto grosso* style of Corelli, Torelli and Antonio Vivaldi (Handel's slightly older contemporary, some of whose new concertos for the Pietà in Venice, where he had been engaged in 1704, Handel could have easily heard either in Florence, Rome or elsewhere: Ms. copies of what would be the famous *L'Estro Armonico*, published in Amsterdam in 1711, were circulating four years earlier). The very beginning of the 'Dixit', with its echoing cascades of broken arpeggios rolling majestically, seems to be the epitome of the Italian concerto spirit, while the chorus – of staggering technical difficulty, displaying immediately the excellence of Roman choirs at the beginning of the century – following the instrumental *ritornello* is of a power which stuns even today. Connoisseurs would have relished the second feature in the overall stylistic picture, its novelty: for example, the wildly unexpected D flat in bar 3 (which sets the tone for the jagged harmonies that make the work so interesting); while the men of the purple would equally have relished the *cantus firmus*,[18] an old Roman plainchant (which, however, very clever musicians with real knowledge of Protestant chorales might have recognized as containing elements of 'Wachet auf' as well – an example of the 'dry humour' which Johann Mattheson noted as part of Handel's language in Hamburg?). This striking psalm tone appears in both soprano parts' unison at bar 51, and it is a brilliant stroke to have brought it in again at the very end of this long work, to underline literally the words of the Doxology, 'sicut erat in principio' ('As it was in the beginning'). The *cantus firmus* technique, being more German than Italian, would have struck many in Rome as a very bold and original inspiration – which it is, even today.

Another aspect of the work's stylistic novelty is a trait encountered in the end of the Cantata 'Donne che in ciel', written for the deliverance from the earthquake of 1703: the combination of a vocal soloist with the choir, the deliberate juxtaposition in vocal terms of the *concertino* and *ripieno* techniques of the Italian *concerto grosso*. Here in the 'Dixit' this principle is vastly expanded to include the confrontation of five solo voices with the choir. In No. 7 comes the most spectacular moment in the Psalm. It concerns the text 'Judicabit in nationibus, implebit ruinas: conquassabit capita in terra multorum' ('He shall judge among the heathen; he shall fill the places with the dead bodies; and smite in sunder the heads over diverse countries'). Handel sweeps the music aside in a half cadence, with the word 'ruinas' and then changes metre to illustrate, in a menacing and powerful sequential entry, the word 'conquassabit', with a chorus chanting over and over again the 'sa' syllable of the word. Cleverly, this chilling effect is not maintained for more than a few bars. And where did Handel get the inspiration for the extraordinarily Vivaldian 'night music' sound at the beginning of 'De torrentis in via bibet' ('He shall drink of the brook in the way')? Actually, one should, perhaps, say Italian rather than Vivaldian, for the effect is found in other concertos and *concerti grossi* of the period *c.* 1700. Wherever Handel drank of the brook, he made it his own! No wonder that Felix Mendelssohn, when first visiting England in 1829, borrowed the 'Dixit' and made a fair copy; and when he returned the autograph he kissed it before it was put back on the shelf.

Of the remaining sections of the Great Vespers, one might single out the unpublished and highly original Motet 'Saeviat tellus', with its vigorous tone painting, and the stupendous conclusion – another Doxology – for double choir and double string orchestra, of the 'Nisi Dominus', which was not published complete in full score until 1928 (Tokyo, ed. S. Tsuji). This stirring music was later incorporated into the Coronation Anthem 'The King Shall Rejoice'. What is now urgently needed is a publication of the complete Carmelite Vespers, as far as we have them: they would make up a fascinating and rewarding evening on their own, whether in concert or church performance.

In the first Ruspoli period (16 May to 14 October 1707), the court had just returned from the newly-won estate of Cerveteri on 6 April. Lent was spent in Rome, but in the middle of May the whole court, including Handel and the musicians, went to Vignanello for three weeks. After another interlude in Rome, the court returned to Vignanello for Pentecost, where there was a ceremony in honour of St Anthony of Padua. Among the works which were composed for this spring and summer was the famous *L'Armida abbandonata* (Cantata 'Dietro l'orme fugaci', with strings and *basso continuo*), the parts copied in June. This was a work which J.S. Bach considered so highly that he copied it entirely in his own hand. The *Diana cacciatrice* (copied in May) has been mentioned (see p. 51). During June there was the Pentecost ceremony at Vignanello, which included new religious music by Handel. A new altarpiece by Michelangelo Geruti, depicting St Anthony above the clouds, was installed in the church, and on 13 June Handel's new Motet 'In festo S. Antonij de Padua . . . 1707' with the text 'Coelestis dum spirat aura' (soprano solo, strings, b.c., first published by R. Ewerhart, Cologne 1957) was the musical highlight of the Feast. Pentecost Sunday was the day before, 12 June, and for it Handel composed his Motet 'O qualis de coelo sonus' (again Margarita Durastanti, soprano, with strings and organ continuo, played of course by Handel himself). At one of these two feasts, the new 'Salve Regina'[19] was first sung by Signora Margarita, and the work includes a movement with organ solo for its composer. This 'Salve Regina' is altogether a milestone in Handel's Italian career, and the work in which his attraction to the Catholic Church is most dramatically felt. There is something mystic, dark and gripping about Handel's utter and total commitment to the rapturous text, which has fascinated Catholic composers for centuries. If this music is any proof (and it must be considered as such), Handel was clearly almost ready for conversion. No Catholic composer ever penned a concluding section so meltingly beautiful, austere, and darkly rich.

During the rest of the season in Rome Handel produced cantatas for Marchese Ruspoli, including a huge 'Cantata a tre con Violini', the score in two volumes (beginning text: 'Cor fedele'), with parts for Clori, Tirsi (both soprano), Filena (alto), 2 recorders, 2 oboes, strings and archlute with *basso continuo*. Only part of this giant work – the score contains 564 pages – has ever been printed.[20] It is a major Roman work and high time to have it available; the fine overture was later used in the Handelian pasticcio *Oreste* (1734). Handel also composed Cantatas for Ruspoli in French and Spanish that summer and autumn ('Sans y penser' and 'Nò se emendera jamás'; the latter's fragmentary autograph was sold at Sotheby's in 1954). But 'il Sassone' was already involved in a much larger project and one close to his heart: a new opera, and for the city of Florence.

Previously, the information about this work was scanty and so inaccurate that it was seriously doubted whether it was actually performed; it was variously placed in the autumn of 1707, or in 1708. Mainwaring calls the new work *Rodrigo* and says Handel received for it a service of plate and 100 sequins, and that the leading soprano, Vittoria Tarquini, became Handel's mistress.[21] As we shall see (p. 73), the whole story, previously dismissed as fancy, was well known in Hanover when Handel arrived there in 1710.

Some years ago a German scholar discovered the printed libretto in no fewer than two copies in the Museo Civico in Bologna. Not even the title was found to be correct: it was *Vincer se stesso è la maggior vittoria*, not *Rodrigo* (who was the protagonist, however) and the libretto is further described as 'drama [*sic*] per musica rappresentato in Firenze nell' autunno Dell'Anno 1707 sotto la protezione del Serenissimo Principe di Toscana'. The cast is, fortunately, given in this newly-discovered word-book:[22]

> RODRIGO Re delle Spagne – Il Sig. Stefano Frilli. ESILENA sua Moglie – La Sig. Anna Maria Cecchi detta la Beccarina. FLORINDA Sorella di Giuliano Conte di Ceuta – La Sig. Aurelia Marcello. GIULIANO Conte de Ceuta, e fratello di Florinda – Il Sig. Francesco Guicciardi, EVANCO figlio di Vitizza già Re d'Aragona – La Sig. Caterina Azzolina detta la Valentina. FERNANDO Generale di Rodrigo – Il Sig. Giuseppe Perini. Un Bambino che non parla, figlio di Rodrigo, e di Florinda.

The names of the composer and librettist are not given, but it is thought that Antonio Salvi may have been responsible for reworking an older libretto entitled *Il duello d'amore, e di vendetta* (by Francesco Silvani, music by M.A. Ziani, Venice 1700) into Handel's new book. Handel probably met Salvi in the late autumn of 1706 at Florence or Pratolino, where his Opera *Il gran Tamerlano* with music by Alessandro Scarlatti was being given with none other than Vittoria Tarquini, grand ducal mistress. At any rate Handel was to set several librettos by Salvi (*Rodelinda, Scipione, Sosarme, Ariodante, Berenice*). Of the cast of *Vincer*, three (Marcello, Cecchi and Azzolina) were at the Mantuan court and had been forced to flee because of the war; Handel later tried to lure to London Guicciardi, the tenor who was afterwards (in 1719) to become famous. It is not certain where Handel's Opera was given: the Teatro del Cocomero and the Pitti Palace would appear to be the two possibilities.

Vincer has survived only in fragmentary form (lacking the beginning and the end), but enough is there for us to see that it is partially taken from *Almira* of Hamburg days, and that in turn it served as a useful source for *Agrippina* (for example, the protagonist's Aria 'Dolce amor' which becomes 'Ingannata un sol volta' in *Agrippina* and was obviously such a success that Handel plundered it again for *Il pastor fido* in London). The theory that *Vincer* was produced privately in the Pitti Palace rather than as a public entertainment at the Teatro del Cocomero gains credence from the fact that it made no impact on the Italian operatic world at all, contrary to the great success of *Agrippina*. We have no Florentine reaction to the grisly tale of 'battle, murder and sudden death' (Streatfeild, p. 225) – a pity, because the surviving music is of a very high standard, particularly Handel's treatment of Esilena, a foretaste of the extraordinary understanding of female psychology that would find such moving documentation in his later operas and oratorios. We shall in future refer to the work by its old title *Rodrigo*. The Overture is followed by a string of pretty dances so extended that one almost glimpses a ballet.

From Florence, Handel appears to have journeyed northwards to Venice, where he spent the winter of 1707–8. Mainwaring's journals are again the main source for Handel's two visits to Venice but, as has been pointed out (Streatfeild p. 37, n. 3), Mainwaring was notorious for his inaccuracy with regard to times and seasons, so much so that he telescoped the two visits into one in his account: the first, in the winter of 1707–8; the second and more significant in 1709–10, when *Agrippina* was composed and staged to a rapturous public (see pp. 71f). The following extract relates to the first visit:

> The nature of his design in travelling made it improper for him to stay long in any one place. He had stayed near a year at Florence, and it was his resolution to visit every part of Italy, which was any way famous for its musical performances. VENICE was his next resort. He was first discovered there at a Masquerade, while he was playing on a harpsichord in his visor. SCARLATTI happened to be there, and affirmed that it could be no one but the famous Saxon, or the devil. Being thus detected, he was strongly importuned to compose an Opera. But there was so little prospect of either honour or advantage from such an undertaking, that he was very unwilling to engage in it. [Mainwaring, pp. 51f.]

Apart from this report about Scarlatti, in the wording of which is the faint suggestion that the Italian recognized Handel's style of playing (from the contest at Cardinal Ottoboni's in Rome, no doubt), it has been very plausibly suggested by Streatfeild (pp. 36f.) that it was on the occasion of this first stay in Venice that Handel was introduced to Prince Ernst August of Hanover, brother of the elector (later George I of England), who was in Venice between 30 September and the end of November 1707. Another contact of great importance was Cardinal Vincenzo Grimani, who owned the celebrated Teatro San Giovanni Gristosomo there and was to write the word-book of *Agrippina*. But perhaps the most significant meeting for Handel's future was with Charles, fourth Earl (later first Duke) of Manchester, who was Ambassador Extraordinary at Venice from July 1707 to October 1708, and who according to Mainwaring was struck by the young composer's talents and invited him to England, an invitation which Handel could not immediately accept, but which 'turned his thoughts in the direction of England' (Streatfeild, p. 39). While at the Venetian Carnival of 1708, Handel could have heard two interesting operas, Alessandro Scarlatti's *Mitridate Eupatore* and Caldara's *La Partenope*, given at San Giovanni Gristosomo; Caldara was also a fugitive from the 'Serenissima di Mantova' who after the

Gonzaga's collapse took up service with Cardinal Grimani at Naples. In 1730, Handel was to compose his own opera *Partenope* (libretto by Stampiglia), based largely on the Venetian setting he had heard in 1708.

The first Sunday in Lent Handel returned from Venice to Rome and the Ruspoli court, which gave Alessandro Scarlatti's Oratorio, *Il giardino di rose*, as the first work of the oratorio season in the conversazione of that day, 26 February. But Handel also contributed a new solo cantata, probably for Margarita Durastanti, at the beginning of the day (Kirkendale, p. 231), as well as composing another Cantata 'Lungi dal mio bel nume' a few days later (autograph: 3 March). He now needed the rest of the Lenten season to compose what would be the most spectacular oratorio performance ever mounted by the Ruspoli family: *La Resurrezione*, the crowning event of the 1708 Lenten season at Rome, to be given at the Palazzo Bonelli on Easter Sunday. Fortunately, the documents from the family archives make it the best documented Handel oratorio in existence.

The bills are revealing. On 18 March we read of 'payment for transport of the bed and other things for Monsù Endel' (Kirkendale, p. 256; Deutsch, p. 21), and later 'payment to the Jew for a month's hire of the said bed and linen coverlets' (ditto), and on 20 March 'payment for music paper, quills and strings for the harpsichord, as per list' (Kirkendale, p. 256). Since the Ruspolis rented the Palazzo Bonelli, they seem to have had to furnish Handel's room with a rented bed from 'the Jew'.

The stage and decorations were originally planned for a room (*stanzione – stanzone* in modern Italian) on the second floor but apparently the crowds were so numerous that it had to be transferred to a larger room on the floor below. There were on the stage four rows of seats for the orchestra (who, contrary to the practice in many petty German courts where the musicians played standing, remained seated here), sloping upwards to the back wall. There were twenty-eight music stands, their legs shaped like fluted cornucopias: on half of them were the coat-of-arms of the Marchese, on the other half those of his wife. There was a separate, raised podium for the 'concertino de' violini', thus preserving for this vocal work the Corellian division for the concerto grosso of 'concertino' (solo violinists and solo cello) and 'ripieno' (the main body). The back of the stage had a large painted canvas, the Ruspoli arms in the four corners, a picture of the Resurrection of Our Lord with a 'gloria of *putti* and cherubims', the angel announcing the event to the two Marys (Magdalene and Cleopha). John the Evangelist was shown near a mountain, and demons were falling into the abyss. Damasks, red and yellow taffeta, huge candelabra and a curtain in front of the stage (which would be ingeniously raised and lowered) combined to create a vast Baroque spectacle, the whole supervised by Giovanni Battista Contini, who built the cathedral of Vignanello (under Ruspoli patronage) and the library of prints at Montecassino, and who was a protégé of the Marquis. The 'Stanzione delle Accademie' (where the work was to have been given) had been hastily decorated, and when the audience climbed upstairs to have their 'rinfreschi' in the interval, they could see in the adjacent room a waterfall that cascaded down to a bathing scene (fountains were another of Contini's specialities). [Kirkendale, pp. 233–35]

The orchestra can be reconstituted exactly. Arcangelo Corelli was the leader and there were 22 (23?) violins, 4 violas, 6 *violoni* (bass viols), 6 double basses, 4 oboes, 2 trumpets and one mysterious 'trombone' player who turns out to have played the bassoon part required in the score (where there is no trombone). Contrary to the usual delicate distribution of the strings at the Ottoboni concerts, where the numbers of the violins equalled the number of all the other strings,[23] Handel required quite a different and in any case much larger ensemble. Possibly the size of the hall suggested the heavy bass section (whereby some of the twelve players must have played cello; the score's viola da gamba part was played by a 'house musician' and is therefore not listed in the bills, nor are the flute and two recorder parts, presumably played by some of the four oboe players).

The first (public) rehearsal was held on Palm Sunday in the 'Stanzione delle Accademie' on the second floor of the Palazzo, they then moved downstairs to the 'Salone al Piano Nobile' for the second rehearsal; the third was on Holy Saturday. Marchese Ruspoli caused no fewer than 1,500 word-books to be printed, which were distributed at the five performances – three rehearsals and two concerts. Valesio (op. cit. IV, p. 57) even reports the event on Easter Sunday and adds, 'Many of the nobility and a few cardinals were present.' The role of Maddalena was taken by Margarita Durastanti, and when the Pope heard of it, he had Ruspoli called to Cardinal Paolucci and given a severe dressing-down for employing a female singer. She had to be replaced for the performance on Easter Monday by a castrato named Filippo, borrowed from the Queen of Poland, Maria Casimira. This event, too, was reported by Valesio: it must have been a scandal of considerable proportions. But the 'damage' had been done, and the most famous air of the Oratorio, 'Hò un non so che nel cor', became associated with Signora Margarita (who as matters turned out was to sing it again in *Agrippina* the following year, Handel's brilliant stroke which made the opera almost a guaranteed success). Apart from providing delicious refreshments in the intervals of the Oratorio, the Marchese distributed some valuable rings, ('rose-diamond ring, with rubies and diamonds', 'another ring, with diamonds and aquamarine', 'another, with diamonds of large size', and so on; Deutsch p. 23, Kirkendale p. 258) for the singers, perhaps for Corelli, and certainly for 'Monsù Endel', conducting from the harpsichord.

Now that Rudolf Ewerhart has discovered the conductor's score of *La Resurrezione*,[24] which fortunately includes the hitherto unknown overtures[25] to both parts as well as the rewritten music for the opening, we can see that, in the course of rehearsals, considerable alterations had to be introduced *vis-à-vis* the autograph manuscript (mostly King's Library, now British Library). Here the beautifully printed libretto is also of great assistance in showing us what the Roman audiences actually heard in April of 1708.

The Oratorio is perhaps the major Handelian rediscovery of our age. Once again, the long-playing record rather than the printed score has been of crucial importance, from the first recording, conducted by Dr Ewerhart for Vox productions in 1961, to the one by Christopher Hogwood for Decca (1982). All of a sudden, the music has come alive with its brilliant orchestration – again with the Handelian 'enlarged' concept of the *concerto grosso* technique – its beautiful vocal writing, and its joyous, vigorous message. Except for the Vespers, it is the principal work of Handel's Roman years and at the same time a convenient place to take stock of his achievements.

The way in which Marchese Ruspoli introduced the Oratorio to Roman society shows that the focal point of the form had moved from the church into the salon. But not only that: Handel and his contemporaries obviously regarded such an Oratorio as thinly disguised opera, which was of course forbidden in the papal city. Recently it has been demonstrated that real opera was infiltrating Rome increasingly under the disguise of 'rehearsals' (no 'performances', as it were, being given). The Vatican only objected to Margarita Durastanti participating in the first 'performance' of *La Resurrezione*, on Easter Sunday, not in the previous three rehearsals, even though they had been public and obviously attended by a large throng.

The non-existence of opera in Rome was certainly a pressing reason for young Handel to want to extricate himself from the friendly clutches of Marchese Ruspoli and all the well-meaning cardinals. They could do all manner of kindnesses for their German protégé but they could never satisfy his devouring ambition, namely, to compose and produce operas. Ultimately, then, Rome failed to provide Handel with the one thing he most wanted in the world, and that was why he was happy to leave it.

The leading part in *La Resurrezione* – not surprisingly if one had been able in 1708 to peer into Handel's future – is the figure of Mary Magdalene (Signora Durastanti). Her music is not only the most striking and beautiful, but also Handel's attention to her part shows even at this early stage his ability to project himself into female roles. Her rendition of 'Hò un non so che nel cor' may have been the public's favourite number, but in fact her grand entrance earlier in Part One is possibly the most beautiful music in the whole work. After a short accompanied recitative 'Notte, notte funesta' ('night, sorrowful night') comes an extraordinary aria 'Ferma l'ali, e sui miei lumi / Non volar, o sonno ingrato' ('Fold thy wings and fly not over my eyes, ungrateful sleep'), scored with two flutes in their lowest register. By using a gigantic pedal point which lazily unfolds during the whole of those first two lines and their repetition, Handel instantly creates a hypnotic mood of sleep, one of his many evocations of 'night music', rivalled in effectiveness only by those of Vivaldi's concertos (which all seem to postdate *La Resurrezione* by several years at least). One thinks ahead to the description of the rising moon at the beginning of Act II in *Ariodante* of 1735 (based on Antonio Salvi's *Ginevra* which, as will be seen, Handel may have heard at Pratolino a few months after the production of *La Resurrezione*). Technically, the pedal point is a literal description of 'ferma' (the English translation inevitably loses some of the imagery).

Although the large and sumptuous orchestra took second place in the hierarchy of the Oratorio's construction, the instrumental part of the work proved to be no less grand than the vocal. Here, only the introductory 'sonata' and 'introduzione', which begin Parts One and Two respectively, show us that Handel was still pursuing the lines he had explored in the organ 'sonata' of his first Oratorio, *Il trionfo*. This kind of orchestration might be called the 'permanent obbligato', in which almost every section of the orchestra is, occasionally, used in the 'concertino' (to use the Corellian term from the *concerto grosso*). Handel is said, in his youth, to have preferred the oboe to all other instruments; and certainly the extraordinary opening of the first orchestral introduction ('sonata') with its brilliant writing for solo oboes, not only supports the story but even now conveys something of the excitement of the whole Roman period. Such a 'sonata' must have seemed the epitome of instrumental music, a kind of supernatural *scuola italiana*. It is a wonder that the dignified and gentle Corelli felt no jealousy towards the boundless energy and superb craftsmanship evident in this Oratorio, where there are even echoes of Corelli's Op. 6 Concerti Grossi. Ursula Kirkendale thinks, with every justification, that Handel's great work had been conceived as part of a joint operation between Cardinal Ottoboni and Marchese Ruspoli: 'Alessandro Scarlatti's *Passione*,' she writes (op. cit. p. 238) 'performed on Wednesday of Holy Week at Cardinal Ottoboni's, in the Cancelleria, and Handel's *Resurrezione* must have been planned together, as a sequence . . . The sequence of Passion and Resurrection in this genre is . . . unique.'

A final and rather amusing bill from the Ruspoli Archives shows that Ruspoli had engaged a 'dispensatore' named Francesco Maria de Golla to provide Handel's meals and wine; his bill 'per Ciberie per Monsù Endel e Com:° [compagno] come per lista S[cudi]38.75'. Compared to a monthly salary of 20 scudi for Signora Margarita, this amount of food and wine for Handel and (one presumes) Herr von Binitz suggests opulent meals with the wine flowing freely, 'making' as Ursula Kirkendale suggests (p. 239) 'the marble tables bend'.

'Il Sassone' now journeyed to Naples where he remained for about two-and-a-half months and where, on 16 June 1708, he completed another large-scale work: this was the Cantata or Serenade (Serenata) *Aci, Galatea e Polifemo* 'Sorgi il di', supposedly composed for the wedding of the Duca d'Alvito (whose name was added by Handel to the end of the autograph) with Donna Beatrice Sanseverino, daughter of the late Prince di Monte-Miletto, on 19 July 1708. Mainwaring tells us that in Naples, 'as in most other places, he had a palazzo at his command, and was provided with table, coach, and all other accommodations' (p. 67). It is supposed that Cardinal Grimani was responsible for the Neapolitan invitation: as one of the leading diplomats in Imperial service, he was in disgrace at the Vatican after Field Marshal Count Daun had taken Naples in the summer of 1707, and when Handel arrived a year later, he was, as Viceroy of Naples, one of the principal opponents of Pope Clement XI. So deeply involved in the political tensions of the war was he that he was hardly in a position to do more than wish his young German protégé well.

Apart from *Aci*, Handel also composed a new large Cantata, 'Se tu non lasci amore' (2 sop., bass) in Naples: The autograph is dated 14 July. Recently it has been doubted whether he stayed for the first performance of *Aci* on the 19th, in view of another substantial food bill presented by the victualler Golla 'per Cibarie del Sassone' (food for the Saxon) for the amount of 13 scudi 37, i.e., at Ruspoli's in July. (Food for Handel and his companion for two months was 38.75; if Handel stayed at Naples for *Aci* and left on the 20th, he cannot have been in Rome before that evening, and 13 scudi for ten days of food, even of Handelian dimensions, seems impossible.) Possibly the Serenata was performed earlier, and not at the marriage. It would have been very unusual for Handel to complete a large-scale work on 16 June when the performance was scheduled for 19 July. Probably *Aci* was first given at another festive occasion (a party at the ducal house?).

Aci is a subject which fascinated Handel all his life. In 1718 he composed a beautiful English work on the subject at Cannons, the stately home of the Duke of Chandos, revising it in 1732 (and later) and continuing to perform it until 1742. In the later versions, parts of the original Italian *Aci* were incorporated, and indeed Handel was right to think highly of it. As we have now come to expect, the orchestration (with recorders, oboe, trumpet and two obbligato violoncelli, apart from the solo voices, soprano, alto and bass, with strings and harpsichord continuo) is enchanting. It is in fact an enlarged chamber cantata of the kind that Handel was now composing with consummate mastery.

Back in the oppressive heat of Rome, we find the Ruspoli household supplying two large, used curtains lined with wooden slats 'for the windows of M: Endel by order of Sig^{re} Cauliere [Cavaliere] S[cudi] 3.90' (Kirkendale, p. 265). Handel was now composing music for a rather odd occasion. There was in Rome an institution called the Arcadians, founded by followers of Queen Christina of Sweden in 1690, which consisted largely of the nobility such as Ruspoli (who had the Arcadian name of 'Olinto'), men of the purple such as Cardinal Ottoboni, and a few non-aristocratic artists and musicians, such as Alessandro Scarlatti ('Terpandro'), Corelli ('Arcimelo'), Benedetto Marcello and the organist Pasquini. (Handel was too young to be a member, not having arrived at the requisite age of twenty-four, but the statutes say this consideration could have been waived.) In the summer of 1708, Ruspoli was the Arcadian host in his 'bosco' (wood) south of San Matteo in Merulana, and Cardinal Pamphilj proceeded to compose a song in Handel's honour entitled 'Hendel non può mia Musa' (we recall that 'Hendel' was the usual spelling in Italy), which may first have been improvised as a 'cantata' by 'il Sassone'. We have a delightful report of an 'Arcadian Academy' by G.M. Crescimbeni[26] when it was being held at the Cancelleria, at which time (1712) Alessandro Scarlatti and G.B.F. Zappi, the poet, improvised a cantata together.

Perhaps Handel and the Cardinal offered a similar performance in the summer of 1708 at the 'bosco'. Recently Charles Jennens's copy of Mainwaring's biography has been discovered,[27] and in the margin of the passage discussing Cardinal Pamphilj, Jennens has added a delightful anecdote. Mainwaring (pp. 62f) writes:

> The latter had some talents for Poetry . . . [for the full quotation see above p. 46]. [Jennens adds:] Cantata the 19th in my collection;

> which contains only 51: [in fact 50: the collection is now in the Manchester Public Library, *ex coll.* Flower] in all. Handel told me that the words of Il Trionfo &c were written by Cardinal Pamphili, and added 'an old Fool!' I ask'd 'why Fool? because he wrote an Oratorio? Perhaps you will call *me* fool for the same reason!' He answer'd 'So I would, if you flatter'd me, as He did.'

Since Christmas could not be celebrated at the proper time as it was too cold to take refuge in an Arcadian 'bosco', they celebrated it in the summer, and Handel contributed a Christmas Cantata 'Arresta il passo' (2 sopranos, strings, continuo) for their meeting on Saturday, 14th July (Kirkendale, p. 240f.) All during this Roman summer Handel produced large numbers of cantatas for the Ruspoli conversazioni, including the celebrated *Il Tebro* ('O come chiare e belle') for 2 sopranos, alto, trumpet and strings with continuo, the trumpet being required for the words 'voglio altro stile, cangiare in tromba la zampogna umile', meaning that Ruspoli the warrior-hero must exchange the rustic shawm (his previous shepherd's existence) for the martial trumpet. The soprano role to whom this passage is entrusted is 'Olinto' (Ruspoli's Arcadian name): all this is connected with Ruspoli's soldiers and the Pope's secret meetings in September 1708 to finance his mobilizations. This is one of the very few secular cantatas for which Ruspoli had a libretto printed in an edition of 300 copies. As Handel was sweating in the heat of a Roman September, the major domo caused to be delivered to 'Monsù Endel' forty-five pounds of 'neuaiolo', crushed ice or 'snow', in which to cool his bottles of wine and water (Kirkendale, p. 243). The final food bill of the period defines precisely when Handel left: 12 September.

Handel's movements between mid-September 1708, when he appears to have left not only Rome but anything like a permanent connection with the Ruspoli family, and Boxing Day of 1709, when the première of *Agrippina* is supposed to have taken place in Venice are in fact rather obscure. There is really no evidence at all, from documents now available to us, that Handel ever returned to Rome at all in the coming months, and no evidence except hearsay that he actually met the composer Agostino Steffani, (who was also priest and diplomat in the service of Johann Wilhelm, Elector Palatine at Düsseldorf) at Cardinal Ottoboni's in the spring of 1709. Steffani was in Rome, on a diplomatic mission for his master, between October 1708 and June 1709. Yet Handel's description to Hawkins of his meeting[28] Steffani in Germany in the spring of 1710 does not sound as if they had met earlier: 'I was acquainted with the merits of Steffani, and he had heard of me' (V, p. 267). Certainly there are documents, discovered by the late Mario Fabbri,[29] to show that Handel was in Tuscany between March and November 1709, though perhaps not continuously. He is reported in a diary by Francesco Mannucci (Archives of San Lorenzo in Florence) to have been at Siena on Good Friday 1709 where a sacred Cantata *Il pianto di Maria* 'Giunta l'ora fatal' was performed on the orders of Prince Ferdinando de' Medici. And a final piece of evidence: in the autumn season of 1709 at Pratolino, one of the operas was by the redoubtable team of Salvi and Perti: *Berenice*, given on 30 September, the word-book of which Handel later (1737) set to music himself. But we know of no compositions of this period other than the (apparently dubious) *Il pianto di Maria*. In view of the sparse documentation for this period, we shall now follow Handel to Venice in the late autumn for the rehearsals and performance of his greatest Italian triumph: *Agrippina*.

Handel was always a swift worker, and *opera seria* in those days was composed at great speed, revised quickly and subject to a variety of last-minute substitutions that required composers to be expert pragmatists. *Rodrigo*, now that we have the original libretto, shows signs of having been adapted at the last minute to local exigencies, and the same applies to *Agrippina*. It was obviously put together hastily, and a good portion[30] borrowed from earlier works which were not known in Venice (or at least outside Rome or Naples) and which Handel considered might also be best-sellers in Venice. 'Hò un non so che nel cor' from *La Resurezzione*, for example, was even to be sung by the same agile soprano, Signora Margarita. Handel was right. The aria was taken to London by another of the *Agrippina* cast, Francesca Vanini-Boschi, who inserted it in Alessandro Scarlatti's opera *Pirro e Demetrio* where it was also a marked success – probably the first extract of a Handel opera heard in London.

The principal source for Handel's stay in Venice in the winter of 1709–10, apart from the autograph score and printed libretto of *Agrippina*, is Mainwaring. After the passage quoted above (p. 62) about the young composer being detected *en masque* at the harpsichord by Domenico Scarlatti, our source continues:

> At last, however, [during his second visit to Venice, 1709–10] he consented [to compose an opera] and in three weeks he finished his AGRIPPINA, which was performed twenty-seven nights successively; and in a theatre which had been shut up for a long time, notwithstanding there were two other Opera-houses open at the same time; at one of which GASPARINI presided, as LOTTI did at the other. The audience was so enchanted with this performance, that a stranger who should have seen the manner in which they were affected, would have imagined they had all been distracted.
>
> The theatre, at almost every pause, resounded with shouts and acclamations of *viva il caro Sassone!* and other expressions of approbation too extravagant to be mentioned. They were thunderstruck with the grandeur and sublimity of his style: for never had they known till then all the powers of harmony and modulation so closely arrayed, and so forcibly combined.
>
> This Opera[31] drew over all the best singers from other houses. Among the foremost of these was the famous VITTORIA, who a little before HANDEL'S removal to Venice had obtained permission of the grand Duke to sing in one of the houses there. At AGRIPPINA her inclinations gave new lustre to her talents. HANDEL seemed almost as great and majestic as APOLLO, and it was far from the lady's intention to be so cruel and obstinate as DAPHNE.

On 26 December then (the date has not been positively confirmed) *Agrippina*, with the composer at the harpsichord, was produced for the first time at the Teatro San Giovanni Crisostomo. The cast was as follows:

> Claudio – Signor Antonio Francesco Carli, bass
> Agrippina – Signora Margherita[32] Durastanti (alternating with Elena Croce, soprano)
> Nerone – Signor Valeriano Pelegrini (called Valeriano), soprano
> Popea – Signora Diamante Maria Scarabelli, soprano

Otone – Signora Francesca Vanini-Boschi, contralto
Pallante – Signor Giuseppe Maria Boschi, bass
Narciso – Signor Giulano Albertini, alto
Lesbo – Signor D. Nicola Pasini, bass
Giunne – ? (contralto)

Whether its fame brought the seductive Vittoria Tarquini (known as 'La Bombace' or also 'Bombragia') into Handel's bed or not must remain an open question. In the correspondence of the Electress Sophie of Hanover, however, there is interesting corroboration of this flirtation; writing to her grand-daughter, the younger Sophie Dorothea, from Herrenhausen Castle on 14 June 1710, the Electress says:

> Here there is no news except that the Elector has taken into his service a Kapellmeister named Händel, who plays the harpsichord marvellously to the enjoyment of the Electoral Prince and Princess. He is a good-looking man and there is talk that he was the lover of Victoria . . . [ed. G. Schnath, *Briefwechsel der Kurfürstin Sophie von Hannover mit dem Preussischen Königshause*, Berlin & Leipzig 1927; see Hicks, op. cit. p. 83]

This is yet another instance where the Mainwaring biography should be taken far more seriously than has often been the case. What is more important, however, is the presence of la Durastanti from the Ruspoli Court in Rome, who alternated with la Croce in the title role. Copies of the score circulated as far as Vienna and the German courts. It was not a typical *opera seria* of the period – but then, Handel's operas rarely were. In Rome, the younger composer had been attached to courts closely associated, and politically allied, with the papal cause in the War of the Spanish Succession. In 1709 Handel had even set, in his last known cantata texts for Marchese Ruspoli, words actually connected with papal/French, anti-Habsburg sentiments. The Cantata 'Ah, che troppo ineguali' dedicated to the Blessed Virgin Mary, with the Aria 'O del ciel Maria regina', is considered by Reinhard Strohm (op. cit. 171f.) to refer to the battles between papal (with Ruspoli) troops against Imperial forces in the winter of 1708–9, while the large Cantata a cinque (five parts) 'Io languisco fra le gioie' refers to the peace treaty between the Pope and the Emperor and glorifies King Carlo III of Spain. With Cardinal Grimani Handel was consorting with the papal enemy, and the figure of Claudio in *Agrippina*, who sings a vain and silly Aria 'Io di Roma il Giove son' ('I'm the Jove of Rome'), is thought to be a persiflage on His Holiness. Altogether scholars have tended to see the opera as a satire on the vicious habits of court life, and more particularly life at the Vatican under Clement XI. Handel was thus treading a very thin line in his musical loyalties: the super pragmatist, musically speaking, of the period. Perhaps 'il Sassone' was not altogether unhappy to shake the dust (and mud, in the Veneto in the winter of 1710) from his shoes and look to his laurels in other cities such as Hanover and London.

There are, unfortunately, few sources which reveal many details of Handel's private life during this period. However, the Diary of Francesco Mannucci, written in 1711 and mentioned above, records a conversation of 15 February between Prince Ferdinando de' Medici, the composer Perti and other Florentine musicians, in which they refer to Handel's sacred Cantata 'Il pianto di Maria' for Holy Friday at Siena two years before, but more interestingly the musicians also mention Handel's 'borrowings' – which were, even then, not so unnoticed as scholars sometimes like to believe and hope – as well as his 'malizzia'. It was later said that Handel had a violent temper and swore like a coachman in several languages; but, at least in later years, he was never accused of being malicious. Perhaps it was a youthful bile, later sweetened. The one portrait (although painted later) which faintly suggests the eruptive young man of twenty-one freshly arrived in Italy is that by Sir James Thornhill.

During his Italian sojourn Handel's musical knowledge had been greatly enhanced, as had his social education in the way civilized people at court lived, ate and drank, and made conversation; indeed, Handel was later reported to be a welcome addition to any dinner table, but one needed a knowledge of four languages to appreciate his trenchant wit. Also, most significantly, he acquired and developed an appreciation of painting, something he learnt at once and retained all his life, being one of the very few *settecento* composers apart from Corelli to do so.

Handel's chief languages while in Italy had been Latin and Italian; his Italian may have had a hideous German accent, but there can be little doubt that he became extremely fluent in both languages. This aspect of Handel's four years in Italy, then, was clearly of crucial importance for that part of his career which he always regarded as his most important interest: the composition of *opera seria*. An almost fabulous amount of new music had flowed from that fertile Saxon mind: an enormous Latin Vesper cycle, over a hundred Italian cantatas, some of vast length, chamber music duets and trios, two operas, two oratorios and *Aci, Galatea e Polifemo*: a list over which a lesser man would have worked for at least a decade. But the great and encouraging success of *Agrippina* must have persuaded him that his future lay primarily as a composer of Italian operas. To pursue that goal must have seemed considerably easier in 1710, with Florence and Venice now singing his operatic praises, than when he left Germany those four long years earlier.

The chief characteristic of all the works of this Italian period is power. The bold personality of the man leaps forth in almost every movement: his tremendous innovative strength, his ability to create a mood in an instant. But coupled with this all-pervasive sense of power there is also a reflective, tender side in which he reveals an ability to penetrate the innermost secrets of the human mind, male or female. For choral strength there is little to equal the high-points of the 'Dixit Dominus'; for quiet, loving understanding of the female mind, Handel never surpassed the music for Mary Magdalene and Agrippina (sometimes identical). In short, 'he arrived in Italy a gifted but crude composer with an uncertain command of form,' writes Winton Dean with his usual perspicacity (*New Grove*, p. 11) 'and left it a polished and fully equipped artist'.

NOTES

1 There is however the possibility that Handel was using what is known as the 'old calendar', which ran from 25 March to 24 March and in which the first twelve weeks of a given year (say 1707) would be written 1706 (or 1706/7). The autograph of the 'Dixit Dominus' which Handel was to write three months after his arrival in Rome is signed: S[oli] D[eo] G[loria] / G F Hendel / 1706['6' to '7'] / li [blank] D'Aprile / Roma. Perhaps the work was begun in March, when the change-over from '1706/7 to '1707' would have occurred. This 'old-style' calendar is not to be confused with the eighteenth-century British system, in use until 2 September 1752, whereby Britain was eleven days behind the Continent. In this book, the Continental calendar is used until Handel's arrival in England, in the

autumn of 1710, following which the British dating is used: when Handel was again on the Continent the British date is used, the Continental following in parentheses.

2 F. Valesio, *Diario di Roma*, vols. III & IV, ed. G. Scano & G. Oraglia, III (1978), pp. 754ff.; referred to hereafter as 'Valesio' and citing the volume and page number of the modern edition.

3 U. Kirkendale, 'The Ruspoli Documents on Handel', *Journal of the American Musicological Society*, XX (1967), p. 224, n. 12.

4 P. M. Young, *Handel*, 1946.

5 'Handel among the Carmelites', *Dublin Review* (1959) no. 233, pp. 121ff.

6 E.g. 2458, written on paper with the same watermarks as those of many Handel autographs of 1707–8.

7 Valesio: IV, 114, 16 July 1708 (Monday). This of course shows beyond doubt the Cardinal's connection with the ceremony. The motet is not dated, but the other pieces are partly dated 1707, and in 1708 Handel was busily writing cantatas for the Ruspoli family and returned to Rome from Naples only after July 12, when he completed (at Naples) his Cantata 'Se tu mi lasci'. In Valesio's note, the fact that the ceremony had taken place in previous years is clearly suggested.

8 Such a Vespers might have included a *Magnificat*, and that brings us to the vexed question of the so-called Erba *Magnificat* and Urio *Te Deum*. To reduce an extremely complicated matter to its simplest, the question is whether two obscure composers, Diongi Erba and Francesco Antonio Urio composed the music in question, or whether Handel in fact wrote them in northern Italian towns called Erba and Urio. In any case he certainly copied them and used them extensively, with revisions, in *Israel in Egypt*. Possibly Handel used the Erba *Magnificat* in the Roman Vespers, but since the evidence for Handel's authorship is so tenuous (also for the *Te Deum*) I have preferred to ignore the works in connection with the Carmelite Vespers. Whatever their origins, it is valuable to have two pieces if only as evidence of a flourishing choral tradition nurtured in northern Italy by such obscure composers. Larsen (*Handel's Messiah*, Copenhagen 1957, p. 43) sums up the matter when he writes, 'But whether Handel composed them or only copied them, we may view these works also as evidence of Handel's close connection with Italian choral traditions.' The copy of the Erba *Magnificat* in the Royal College of Music is of British origin (watermarks: 'J WHATMAN', 'G R' with lyre, etc.), Cat. 185.

9 *Antonio Caldara: Sein Leben und seine venezianisch-römischen Oratorien*, Graz & Cologne, 1966; and Kirkendale, op. cit., pp. 222–73, 518.

10 *Grundlage einer Ehren-Pforte*, Hamburg 1740, p. 95.

11 The Overture for IL TRIONFO DEL TEMPO was that which occasioned CORELLI the greatest difficulty. At his desire therefore he made a symphony in the room of it, more in the Italian style. [Original footnote.] In a brilliant piece of research, Anthony Hicks (op. cit., p. 83) has identified with considerable certainty the original, discarded 'Ouverture' in the French style for *Il trionfo*: it is the Overture in B flat (vol. xlviii, 108–II of the *HG*) which Walsh published, a year before Handel's death, *Overtures* 11th collection (1758). It shares its main theme in the Allegro with that of *Il trionfo* which in turn, with the addition of trumpets, was rewritten as the 'Sonata' that opens *La Resurrezione* (1708). The unknown 'Sonata a 6' for solo violin and strings (*HG* xxi, pp. 108–16) is also written on paper of the same time as that used for the 'Dixit' and must therefore have been composed in 1707.

12 This person (i.e. the elder *Scarlatti*) was the author of an Opera entitled, *Principessa Fidele*, which is reckoned a chef-d'oeuvre in its kind. He also made several Cantatas very highly esteemed by the judges of Music. [Original footnote.] [*La Princepesse fedele* was first produced at Naples on 8 February 1710.]

13 This expression will not be thought too strong by those who know what sincere esteem and cordial regard he attracted from persons of the highest distinction. [Original footnote]

14 See Rudolf Ewerhart, 'Die Händel-Handschriften der Santini-Bibliothek in Münster', *Händel-Jahrbuch* VI (1960), pp. III–50. Dr Ewerhart has made editions not only of 'Donna che in ciel' but also 'O qualis de coelo sonus' (Cologne 1959 and 1957) and has also made excellent recordings including the first of *La Resurrezione* (1961).

15 The overture to Handel's Hamburg opera *Almira* of 1705 has survived and is its composer's first known orchestral work; it is competent, indeed attractive, but lacks the bold force of the Roman cantata.

16 This chronological position is also proposed by A. Hicks, op. cit., p. 87.

17 Lina Montalto, *Un Mecenate in Roma barocca: il Cardinale Benedetto Pamphili (1653–1730)*, Florence 1955, pp. 325 and 335.

18 The opening of the 'Nisi Dominus' also incorporates an old plainchant (Fifth Psalmtone). But which Roman plainchant is used in the 'Dixit'? The truth of the matter is extraordinary: no one has ever identified it. Chrysander (Vol. 1, p. 462) maintain that it comes from the Easter services, but the Italian scholar Paolo Isotta, who has subjected this 'Dixit' to a thorough study. ('Dixit Dominus Domino Meo . . . Struttura e Semantica in Haendel e Vivaldi', *Rivista Internazionale de Musica Sacra* Arno 2, No. 3 [1981] pp. 247–359, esp. p. 270 n. 9), has been unable to find any trace of the cantus firmus in plainchant sources. Dr Isotta wonders if the *cantus firmus* is not Handel's own, in a 'psalmodizing' fashion. I consider it, however, entirely possible that Handel made use of a plainchant *cantus firmus* which is no longer in general use (i.e., missing in the *Liber usualis*) and therefore very difficult to locate. On this subject, too, the last word has not been spoken.

19 The copyist Antonio Giuseppe Angelini, who was in Vignanello, wrote a bill for which receipt was acknowledged on 30 June (the bill also has Margarita's signature as a control), including 'Per due Mottetti con V.V.' (violin) and 'Per una Salue [Salve] parte e V.V.e Violone'. Kirkendale, op. cit. 254.

20 *Händel-Gesellschaft*, op. cit. liiiB, pp. 99ff.

21 *Vittoria*, who was much admired both as an Actress, and a Singer, bore a principal part in this Opera [not true, H.C.R.L.]. She was a fine woman, and had for some time been much in the good graces of his Serene Highness. But, from the natural restlessness of certain hearts, so little sensible was she of her exalted situation, that she conceived a design of transferring her affections to another person. HANDEL's youth and comliness, joined with his fame and abilities in Music, had made impressions on her heart. Tho' she had the art to conceal them for the present, she had not perhaps the power, certainly not the intention, to efface them. [Mainwaring, pp. 50f.]

22 Reinhard Strohm: 'Händel in Italia: nuovi contributi', *Rivista italiana di musicologia* IX (1974), pp. 152-74.

23 S. H. Hansell, 'Orchestral Practice at the Court of Cardinal Pietro Ottoboni', *Journal of the American Musicological Society* (1966), XIX, pp. 398–403.

24 'New Sources for Handel's *La Resurrezione*', *Music and Letters* XLI (1960),

pp. 127–35. The score is in the Santini Collection at Münster (Westphalia).

25 The first was a thorough reworking of the Overture to *Il trionfo* of 1707.

26 *Breve Notizia dello stato antico, e moderno dell'adunanza degli Arcadi publicata l'anno 1712 (L'Istoria della volgar Poesia)*, 3rd ed., vol. VI, Venice 1731, pp. 313f.

27 Winton Dean, 'Charles Jennens's Marginalia to Mainwaring's Life of Handel', *Music & Letters*, LIII (1972), pp. 160–4. It has been assumed that Handel went to Florence (Pratolino) for the coming season, where he could have seen the latest work by Salvi, *Ginevra, principessa di Scozia* (music by Giacomo Antonio Perti); though there are no documents to support this theory, Handel used the libretto as the basis for his *Ariodante* in 1735. Ruspoli, on the other hand, may have first taken Handel to one of his country estates. At any rate, there was another large cantata ready for performance at Rome on 28 October, *Il duello amoroso* for soprano and alto soloists with string orchestra and harpsichord continuo. Margarita Durastante sang the part of the nymph Amarilli and the contralto Pasqualino (who had sung in *La Resurrezione*) the part of Dalisio the shepherd. Dr Ewerhart found the lost score in Münster, and it was seen that two of the arias, Amarilli's 'Placer che non si dona' and Daliso's 'È vanità' were used in *Agrippina* as arias by Poppea and Ottone. This cantata was regarded as a special event in the Ruspoli court and invitations were delivered by messenger; but there is the possibility that Handel was not present (the parts had been copied before the end of August, which meant that the score was ready before Handel left Rome in September). The same applies to two continuo cantatas 'di M.[u] Handel' for which the copyist was paid on 24 November. It seems unlikely that Handel was in Rome after mid-September 1708.

28 Mainwaring (pp. 69f.) states that Handel met Steffani in Venice: see chapter III, p. 7.

29 *Alessandro Scarlatti e il Principe Ferdinando de' Medici*, Florence 1961, pp. 24f. and 'Nuova luce sull'attività fiorentina di Giacomo Antonio Perti, Bartolomei Cristofori, e Giorgio F. Haendel' in *Chigiana* XXI (1964), pp. 148f.

30 Seven numbers from Keiser's *Octavia*, three from *Rodrigo*, two from the Cantata *Il Duello amoroso* of 1707, three from *La Resurrezione* and also borrowings from the Cantata *Arminta e Fillide* ('Arresta il passo') of 1708. Harris, p. 182.

31 It seems that French Horns, and other wind-instruments as little known to the *Italians*, were introduced on this occasion. I believe they never had heard them before, as accompaniments to the voice. [Original footnote]

32 She signs herself 'Margarita' on all the autograph signatures of the Ruspoli documents.

III
Kapellmeister in Hanover & the first British sojourn 1710–1714

WITH THE CHEERS of the Venetian audiences ringing in his ears, Handel set off in February 1710, journeying northwards. He had been highly recommended to various courts in Austria and Germany, including Tyrol, to whose Governor, Carl, Prince von Neuburg, Handel had been suggested in a letter of 9 November 1709 from the Crown Prince of Tuscany. Although he stopped in Innsbruck at the beginning of March, the composer's goal was a greater court in northern Germany: Hanover, where Georg Ludwig (later King George I of England) was Elector. His consort was Princess Sophie Dorothea of Zell, a pathetic woman despised by her husband (see below p. 125).

Mainwaring tells us of his arrival there (though not the date of his contract – 16 June 1710 – nor the precise terms: 1,000 Thaler):

> HANDEL having now been long enough in Italy effectually to answer the purpose of his going thither, began to think of returning to his native country. Not that he intended this to be the end of his travels; for his curiosity was not yet allay'd, nor likely to be so while there was any musical court which he had not seen. HANOVER was the first he stopped at. STEFFANI [Agostino Steffani, the composer: see previous chapter] was there and had met with favour and encouragement equal, if possible, to his singular desert. This person (whose character is elegantly sketched by a lover of his Art and friend to his memory) he had seen at Venice, the place of his nativity. Such an acquaintance he was glad to renew: for STEFFANI's compositions were excellent; his temper was exceedingly amiable; and his behaviour polite and

genteel. Those who are inclined to see a fuller account of him, may consult those Memoirs of his Life, consisting indeed of a very few pages, but sufficient to do him great honour. We shall soon have occasion to mention him again, and therefore shall only add at present, that he was Master of the Chapel to his late MAJESTY, when he was only Elector of Hanover. This was an office and title highly creditable there, tho' far inferior to those which he afterwards bore.

At Hanover there was also a Nobleman who had taken great notice of HANDEL in Italy, and who did him great service (as will appear soon) when he came to ENGLAND for the second time. This person was Baron KILMANSECK [Johann Adolf, Baron von Kielmansegg]. He introduced him at court, and so well recommended him to his Electoral Highness, that he immediately offered him a pension of 1500 Crowns per annum as an inducement to stay. Tho' such an offer from a Prince of his character was not to be neglected, HANDEL loved liberty too well to accept it hastily, and without reserve. He told the Baron how much he owed to his kind and effectual recommendation, as well as to his Highness's goodness and generosity. But he also expressed his apprehensions that the favour intended him would hardly be consistent either with the promise he had actually made to visit the court of the Elector Palatine, or with the resolution he had long taken to pass over into England, for the sake of seeing that of LONDON.[1] Upon this objection, the Baron consulted his Highness's pleasure, and HANDEL was then acquainted, that neither his promise nor his resolution should be superseded by his acceptance of the pension proposed. He had leave to be absent for a twelve-month or more, if he chose it; and to go whithersoever he pleased. On these easy conditions he thankfully accepted it.

To this handsome pension the place of Chapel-master was soon after added, on the voluntary resignation of STEFFANI. He thought such an office not perfectly consistent with the high titles of Bishop and Ambassador, with which he was now invested. And he was glad of this, or any other opportunity of obliging HANDEL. Notwithstanding the new favour conferred upon him, he was still in possession of the privilege before allowed him, to perform his engagements, and pursue his travels. He considered it as his first and principal engagement to pay a visit to his Mother at Hall. Her extreme old-age, and total blindness, tho' they promised him but a melancholy interview, rendered this instance of his duty and regard the more necessary. When he had paid his respects to his relations and friends (among whom his old Master ZACKAW [Handel's master, Friedrich Wilhelm Zachau: see first chapter] was by no means forgot) he set out for DUSSELDORP [Düsseldorf]. The Elector Palatine [Johann Wilhelm] was much pleased with the punctual performance of his promise, but as much disappointed to find that he was engaged elsewhere. At parting he made him a present of a fine set of wrought plate for a desert, and in such a manner as added greatly to its value. [pp. 69–74]

Handel's arrival at Hanover is also recorded in an authentic report by Hawkins:[2]

'When I first arrived at Hanover I was a young man . . . I was acquainted with the merits of Steffani, and he had heard of me: I understood something of music, and,' putting forth his broad hands, and extending his fingers, 'could play pretty well on the organ; he received me with great kindness, and took an early opportunity to introduce me to the princess Sophia[3] and the elector's son, giving them to understand, that I was what he was pleased to call a virtuoso in music; he obliged me with instructions for my conduct and behaviour during my residence at Hanover; and being called from the city to attend to matters of a public concern, he left me in possession of that favour and patronage which [he] himself had enjoyed for a series of years.'

Curiously enough, the watermarks of a Handel Cantata, *Apollo e Dafne* ('La terra e liberata'), dated *c.*1708, follow us on this voyage from Italy to Germany. The composer started the work in Venice, using typical Venetian paper (as indicated by watermarks), then changing to Lombard paper, then to German paper, and finally revising and completing the work in England, using British paper (or possibly Dutch, the difference often being impossible to discern).[4] It is one of the composer's finest dramatic cantatas, and is perhaps a summation of his whole Italian experience. It is also the kind of practical, lightly-scored work (flute, 2 oboes, strings and continuo; solo soprano, solo bass voices) that he could have performed easily at any of the local courts through which he travelled.

Handel's favourable reception at Düsseldorf was no doubt in part the result of a warm recommendation from the Crown Prince of Tuscany, who was the Palatine Electress's brother; and indeed, letters have survived from her addressed to her brother in Florence, praising Handel and securing his help in choosing a 'northern' harpsichord (much more complex and refined than contemporary Italian instruments) for the court in Florence.[5] After several weeks at the friendly Düsseldorf court, Handel finally left for England in September 1710, arriving in London late in November or early in December.

What was it like to arrive in the London of Queen Anne on a chilly autumn morning in 1710? The coffee-houses had been full of the good war news: victory after victory over King Louis XIV and his allies. Marlborough, having been a national hero, had since been toppled by the Tories, and France's position was suddenly improved. Henry Lord Bolingbroke was (until 1714) Foreign Minister. The first critical edition of the works of William Shakespeare, by Nicholas Rowe, had commenced publication the previous year. And London looked very prosperous.

For a contemporary bird's-eye view of a typically smoky London, we turn to the diaries written that very year by a German compatriot of Handel's, one Zacharias Conrad von Uffenbach who, one morning, climbed the tower of St Paul's:[6]

> On Saturday morning, 14 June, we drove to St Paul's Church, which is almost in the centre of the city. We first climbed up the tower in order that we might have a prospect of the town from above before the air was full of coal-smoke. One mounts a fine wide stone staircase of a hundred and ten steps to the first gallery and then there is a wooden one, which is not nearly as wide. From the top one can see almost the whole city, especially in the direction of Westminster. The prodigious size and length is amazing, though it is not so very wide. At the bridge called London Bridge it is widest. The tower is certainly very high, though it does

not appear to be so from below on account of its thickness and, chiefly, on account of the height of the church itself. It is open inside, so that one can look down from the dome and up into it from the church, which is an extremely fine sight. . . .

Shortly before, Uffenbach had gone to see the opera in the Haymarket:

[10 June 1710] . . . In the evening we went to the opera 'Hidaspis', which was being given for the last time, because it was summer, when the Lords for the most part reside in the country. The opera house is in Haymarket, which is a large square. It is not at all large but is certainly very massive and handsomely built. The opera was very lovely in all respects, in composition, music and representation. I am sure that, as far as the first two items are concerned, nothing could be better, even in Italy. The singers were few in number but all were excellent, especially the principal and the Director Nicolai, who has already been much admired in Venice but has greatly advanced himself here, because he earns prodigiously large sums of money. The best of the females is Margarite de l'Épine, who has also done very well for herself. The orchestra too is so well composed that it could not be better. They are all foreigners, mostly Germans and then French, for the English are not much better musicians than the Dutch, and they are fairly bad. The conductor is [Johann Christoph] Pepusch[7] from Brandenburg, who is known everywhere for his amazingly elegant compositions. The scenery and properties had all been made expressly for the opera and were very fine, though not as costly as those in Italy; but the costumes were of the finest and the performances were in all things most natural and uncommonly elegant. In especial the representation of the lion with which Hidaspes has to fight was incomparably fine. The fellow who played him was not only wrapped in a lion-skin, but, moreover, nothing could be seen of his feet, which usually betray the fact that a man is hidden within. . . . The singers expressed so well the emotions they must represent that I have never seen the like, above all Nicolini[8], who excels all actors in the world in this respect.

Uffenbach has, obviously, confused 'Nicolai', 'Nicolini' (the singer) and the real manager, Owen Swiney; but the essential message is that the London Opera was very good.

Almost the very day when Handel arrived, his hit tune from Rome (in *La Resurrezione*) and Venice (*Agrippina*), 'Hò un non so che nel cor', was introduced into Alessandro Scarlatti's *Pirro e Demetrio* at the Haymarket Theatre by the singer Francesca Vanni-Boschi, who had created the role of Ottone in *Agrippina*. Now the Aria had English words, ''Tis not your wealth, my dear', and shortly thereafter it appeared in print, first without (but later, when he was famous, with) Handel's name. A few months later it was parodied as a 'famous mock song', wherein we read:

> Another King most stout
> Turn'd English Op'ras out,
> Which Britains first admired,
> But now alas are tired.

And later in the poem, Nicolini's exploits with the lion in *Hydaspes* are also glorified:

> He kill'd so Brazen faced,
> A Lion which amazed,
> The mob for whom twas fit,
> And scar'd them from their wit.
> [Deutsch, pp. 40ff.]

It has recently been shown that another popular tune from *Agrippina*, 'La mia sorte fortunata' was introduced in a potpourri entitled *Etearco*, given in London on 10 January 1711. It turned out to be one of those tunes that travelled far in Handel's *œuvre*: from its place in Handel's Venetian triumph it had come from the composer's Neapolitan success, *Aci, Galatea e Polifemo* of 1708, as 'Che non può la gelosia' and, having found its way to *Agrippina* and the potpourri *Etearco*, it continued as 'Damero la tua fierezza' in *Giulio Cesare* and finished in the great, tragic *Jephtha* as 'Freedom now once more possessing'. It is one of the more extreme cases of Handel's self-borrowings.[9]

Handel played for Queen Anne and astonished the court with his flamboyant writing for the trumpet: he was an instant success, with the public and with the Queen. Mainwaring supplies us with an interesting note on the state of music in England when Handel arrived there:

> Excepting a few good compositions in the church style, and of a very old date, I am afraid there was little to boast of, which we could call our own. At this time Operas were a sort of new acquaintance, but began to be established in the affections of the Nobility, many of whom had heard and admired performances of this kind in the country which gave them birth. But the conduct of them here, *i.e.* all that regards the drama, or plan, including also the machinery, scenes, and decorations, was foolish and absurd almost beyond imagination. The last Pope but one was so exceedingly entertained with Mr ADDISON'S humorous account of this curious management, that on reading his papers relating to it, he laughed till he shook his sides. Mr ADDISON seems, a little unfairly, to impute this vitiated taste to the growing fondness for every thing that was Italian. It is far from impossible, that the Manager might have found his taste established here, and have been obliged to conform to it. Who or what the Composers were, we are not informed;[10] nor is it very material to enquire. For, from the account of the commencement of the Italian Opera here, as we find it in the 18th N° of the SPECTATOR, it is plain, that, what with the confusion of languages, and the transposition of passions and sentiments owing to that cause, the best Composer could hardly be distinguished from the worst. The arrival of HANDEL put an end to this reign of nonsense.
>
> The report of his uncommon abilities had been conveyed to England before his arrival, and through various channels. Some persons here had seen him in Italy, and others during his residence at Hanover. He was soon introduced at Court, and honoured with marks of the Queen's favour. Many of the nobility were impatient for an Opera of his composing. To gratify this eagerness, RINALDO, the first he made in England, was finished in a fortnight's time. . . . [pp. 76–8]

Handel's introduction to London was immeasurably helped by the assistant manager of the Haymarket Theatre, John Jacob Heidegger, a Swiss of German descent, whose house with its eighteenth-century frescoes of operatic scenes, still stands on Richmond Green.[11] Heidegger was Handel's collaborator for the next few decades and proved to be a good and reliable manager. His ugliness was famous (for a story in which Heidegger figures, see below p. 89).

The word-book for *Rinaldo* was on sale at 'Rice's coffee-house by the Playhouse in the Hay-market' (*Daily Courant*) on 13 February 1711. In it, there was the entire Italian text as well as a complete English translation: the libretto was by Giacomo Rossi, after a sketch by Aaron Hill, and there is a note to say that 'La Musica è del Signor Georgio Frederico Hendel, Maestro di Capella di S.A.E d'Hanover.' The word-book was dedicated to Queen Anne, and Aaron Hill (who signed this dedication), concluded as follows:

> . . . 'twere a publick Misfortune, shou'd OPERA'S for want of due Encouragement, grow faint and languish: My little Fortune and my Application stand devoted to a Trial, whether such a noble Entertainment, in its due Magnificence, can fail of living, in a City, the most capable of *Europe*, both to relish and support it.
>
> Madam,
>
> This Opera is a Native of your Majesty's Dominions, and was consequently born your Subject: 'Tis thence that it presumes to come, a dutiful Entreater of your Royal Favour and Protection; a Blessing, which having once obtain'd, it cannot miss the Clemency of every Air it may hereafter breathe in. Nor shall I then be longer doubtful of succeeding in my Endeavour, to see the *English* OPERA more splendid than her MOTHER, the Italian.

And Hill also provided a preface to the word-book which is sufficiently interesting and important to be quoted at length:

> When I ventur'd on an Undertaking so hazardous as the Direction of OPERA's in their present Establishment, I resolv'd to spare no Pains or Cost, that might be requisite to make those Entertainments flourish in their proper Grandeur, that so at least

it might not be my Fault, if the Town should hereafter miss so noble a Diversion.

The Deficiencies I found, or thought I found, in such ITALIAN OPERA's as have hitherto been introduc'd among us were, *First*, That they had been compos'd for Tastes and Voices, different from those who were to sing and hear them on the *English* Stage; And *Secondly*, That wanting the Machines and Decorations, which bestow so great a Beauty on their Appearance, they have been heard and seen to very considerable Disadvantage.

At once to remedy both these Misfortunes, I resolv'd to frame some Dramma, that, by different Incidents and Passions, might afford the Musick Scope to vary and display its Excellence, and fill the Eye with more delightful Prospects, so at once to give Two Senses equal Pleasure.

I could not chuse a finer Subject than the celebrated Story of *Rinaldo* and *Armida*, which has furnish'd OPERA's for every Stage and Tongue in *Europe*. I have, however, us'd a Poet's Privilege, and vary'd from the Scheme of Tasso, as was necessary for the better forming a Theatrical Representation.

It was a very particular Happiness, that I met with a Gentleman so excellently qualify'd as Signor *Rossi*, to fill up the Model I had drawn, with Words so sounding, and so rich in Sense, that if my Translation is in many Places to deviate, 'tis for want of Power to reach the Force of his Original.

Mr *Hendel*, whom the World so justly celebrates, has made his Musick speak so finely for its self, that I am purposely silent on that Subject; and shall only add, That as when I undertook this Affair, I had no Gain in View, but That of the Acknowledgement and Approbation of the Gentlemen of my Country; so No Loss, the Loss of That excepted, shall discourage me from a Pursuit of all Improvements, which can be introduc'd upon our *English* Theatre. [Deutsch, pp. 32f.]

In this extravagant work-book, even Giacomo Rossi had his say, in which he refers to 'Mr *Hendel*, the *Orpheus* of our century' having composed the whole Opera in a fortnight, scarcely giving Rossi 'the time to write'.

And so, on Handel's twenty-sixth birthday, *Rinaldo*, with its stunningly large orchestra including four trumpets and kettledrums, was given its première at the Haymarket Theatre with the world-famous Nicolini (Nicolò Grimaldi) in the title role. It was a resounding success, partly no doubt because of the spectacular staging and effects, among which a flock of live sparrows was let loose, to the delight of the audience and the critical fury of men like Joseph Addison, who ridiculed the elaborate staging in The *Spectator*.

Rinaldo makes lavish use of Handel's earlier music, mostly that composed in Italy, and often uses the original words. No doubt the splendid war music with its trumpets (see Appendix) was composed after the success he had enjoyed with those instruments at Court; and as in his Roman Vespers, where he had skilfully introduced organ solos for himself, so in *Rinaldo* we find harpsichord solos which excited special attention, as it was not the custom for the continuo instrument to shine from the opera pit. Mainwaring tells us of the general acclaim:

> To return to our account of RINALDO. In this Opera the famous NICOLINI sung. Its success was very great, and his engagements at Hanover the subject of much concern with the lovers of Music. For when he could return to England, or whether he could at all, was yet very uncertain. His Playing was thought as extraordinary as his Music. One of the principal performers here used to speak of it with astonishment; as far transcending that of any person he had ever known, and as quite peculiar to himself. Another, who had affected to disbelieve the reports of his abilities before he came, was heard to say, from a too great confidence in his own, 'Let him come! we'll Handle him, I warrant ye!' There would be no excuse for recording so poor a pun, if any words could be found, capable of conveying the character of the speaker with equal force and clearness. But the moment he heard HANDEL on the organ, this great man in his own eye shrunk into nothing. [pp. 82–4]

Within a month, *Rinaldo* was being given in Dublin, the first Italian opera to be staged in Ireland; it is thought that the head of the company, 'N.G. Nicolini', must mean Niccolò Grimaldi. The contact was to prove prophetic for Handel, who no doubt heard of the work's success there. By April, *Rinaldo* was published by John Walsh, whose name was from this moment to be inextricably linked with Handel's: this was the first announcement of any printed edition of Handel's music, and thus a milestone in both men's careers.

Handel made many friends in England, some of them for life. One such was Mary Granville (later Mrs Pendarves and still later Mrs Delany), who was ten years old when she met the great man in 1711.

> In the year '10 I first saw Mr Handel who was introduced to my uncle [Sir John Stanley, a commissioner of customs] by Mr Heidigger, the . . . most ugly man that was ever formed. We had no better instrument in the house than a little spinet of mine, on which the great musician performed wonders. I was much struck with his playing, but struck as a child, not a judge, for the moment he was gone, I seated myself at my instrument and played the best lessons I had then learnt. My uncle archly asked me if I thought I should ever play as well as Mr Handel. 'If I did not think I should,' cried I, 'I would burn my instrument!' Such was the innocent presumption of childish ignorance. [Deutsch, p. 31]

Seventy years later, in 1784, the year of the first great Handel Commemoration at Westminster Abbey, there was a musical soirée to which Mrs Delany was invited. A witness writes, 'I was so enchanted with the song of "I know that my Redeemer liveth" that I was going to desire Sir W[illia]m [Hamilton] to play it again, but looking towards dear Mrs Delany I forbore [as] the tears were trickling down her venerable cheeks' (Deutsch, p. 824). Handel may have made implacable enemies – all in the theatre inevitably do – but he made friends early in his career who loved and admired him all their lives. It was also during his first visit to London that Handel made the acquaintance of the musical coal merchant, Thomas Britton, whose rooms were in Clerkenwell. There Britton held weekly music parties which Handel is known to have attended.

Mainwaring now informs us of Handel's return to the Continent:

> He had now been a full twelve-month in England, and it was time for him to think of returning to Hanover. When he took leave of

> the Queen at her court, and expressed his sense of the favours conferred on him, her Majesty was pleased to add to them by large presents, and to intimate her desire of seeing him again. Not a little flattered with such marks of approbation from so illustrious a personage, he promised to return, the moment he could obtain permission from the Prince, in whose service he was retained. [p. 84]

In June 1711, Handel went to Düsseldorf, where he was again received with joy by the Elector Palatine, who wrote two letters to Hanover excusing Handel's delay in arriving there: one to the Elector and one to the Dowager Electress, both dated 6 (17) June (Deutsch, p. 43). To Georg Ludwig the Palatine Elector wrote, entreating that he 'not deign to interpret amiss this delay, occurring against his [Handel's] will, and not to lay it to his charge, but to grant him your continuing grace and *protection* . . .'

His return to Hanover is chronicled by Mainwaring:

> Soon after his return to Hanover he made twelve chamber Duettos for the practice of the late Queen, then electoral Princess. The character of these is well known to the judges in Music. The words for them were written by the Abbate MAURO HORTENSIO, who had not disdained on other occasions to minimise to the masters of harmony.
>
> Besides these Duettos (a species of composition of which the Princess and court were particularly fond) he composed a variety of other things for voices and instruments. [p. 85]

On 12 (23) November 1711 Handel was in Halle for the christening of his niece, Johanna Friderica Michaelsen, who was to become the composer's favourite. Presumably Handel also visited his elderly and infirm mother.

But Handel was again drawn to England, and (writes Mainwaring)

> Towards the end of the year 1712, he obtained leave of the Elector to make a second visit to England, on condition that he engaged to return within a reasonable time. [pp. 85f.]

Handel's patrons, apart from the Opera, were this time a Mr Andrews of Barn-Elms in Surrey, who also had a house in town, and Richard, Earl of Burlington. Some time in 1713 or 1714 the composer moved into Burlington House, Piccadilly, as Lord Burlington's permanent guest. Here, he seems to have lived in the same manner as at the house of Ruspoli in Rome, though (as with the Ruspoli family) we know nothing of any financial arrangements.

Meanwhile Handel's old favourite of Ruspoli days, Margarita Durastanti, had arrived in London and was to sing Eurilla in *Il pastor fido* (The Faithful Shepherd), Handel's new opera based on the then-famous pastoral play by Battista Guarini of 1585 but with a new word-book by Rossi. It was not a great success during its first season (seven performances) but proved to be very popular when Handel revived it in 1734 (eighteen performances). The work contains beautiful music and it was first made known to twentieth-century audiences in a suite made before the Second World War by Sir Thomas Beecham. Among the cast of the first performance at Queen's Theatre on St Cecilia's Day (22 November) 1712 was Valeriano Pellegrini (Handel's first Nerone in *Agrippina*) and Richard Leveridge, the British bass singer.

Handel's third Opera for London, *Teseo*, was first given at Queen's Theatre on 10 January 1713 with Margarita Durastanti, Valeriano Pellegrini and Leveridge. It received thirteen performances (the last one with additions) and was thus a solid success; but Handel never revived it again and it was not performed for over 250 years. Hardly had *Teseo* been presented when Swiney (as a contemporary reports) 'Brakes & runs away & leaves ye Singers unpaid ye Scenes & Habits also unpaid for. The Singers were in Some confusion but at last concluded to go on with ye operas on their own accounts, & divide ye Gain amongst them' (*Coleman's 'Opera Register'*). From this grim situation the solid Heidegger took over and became the manager of Queen's Theatre and Handel's faithful impresario.

The next major composition was the short opera *Silla* which was staged privately at Burlington House, Piccadilly, on 2 June 1713. This appears not to have been considered a particularly important work although the opera may have made a brief appearance at the King's Theatre, Haymarket. The missing libretto has now been found[12] from which we can see that Rossi again supplied Handel with the text.

Despite the operatic setbacks – the first of many that would beset Handel for the next several decades – Handel's position in the country was more secure than ever before. Mainwaring sums it up:

> The great character of the Operas which HANDEL had made in Italy and Germany, and the remembrance of RINALDO joined with the poor proceedings at the Haymarket, made the nobility very desirous that he might again be employed in composing for that theatre. To their applications her Majesty was pleased to add the weight of her own authority; and, as a testimony of her regard to his merit, settled upon him a pension for life of 200 *l. per Annum*.
>
> This act of the royal bounty was the more extraordinary, as his foreign engagements were not unknown. . . .
>
> The time had again elapsed to which the leave he had obtained, could in reason be extended. But whether he was afraid of repassing the sea, or whether he had contracted an affection for the diet of the land he was in; so it was, that the promise he had given at his coming away, had somehow slipt out of his memory. [pp. 88 ff.]

When he had been in Hanover, Handel wrote to a friend in London, 'J'ai fait, depuis que je suis parti de vous, quelque progrès dans cette langue [anglaise]' ('Since I left you I have made some progress in this language') (Deutsch, p. 44) and now he began to compose large-scale works to English-language texts. The first to be performed was his *Ode for the Birthday of Queen Anne* which was given at Court on 6 February 1713; among the singers was the vivacious and handsome girl Anastasia Robinson, later the Countess of Peterborough, who would become a famous Handelian soprano in the course of the next decade. But the most important piece of English church music was the Utrecht *Te Deum*, completed on 14 January, followed shortly thereafter by the *Jubilate*. The Treaty of Utrecht was not actually signed until the end of March but Handel's new music was given a public rehearsal (with paid tickets) at the Banqueting House in Whitehall on 19 March, and this was followed by the official performance at St Paul's on 7 July. In composing all these English anthems, Handel made a close study of the music of Henry Purcell, and indeed in the coming years Handel's *Te Deum* and Purcell's setting were performed alternately until 1743, when Handel's Dettingen *Te Deum* superseded both (an exception was in 1721, it seems; Deutsch, p. 61). The assimilation of the Purcellian spirit into Handel's English anthem style marks a significant watershed in the composer's musical life, and was to prove of decisive importance in the (as yet unborn) Handelian oratorio form. Later reports, such as Mainwaring's, also give these celebratory works for the Peace of Utrecht a position of unique significance:

> It was not many months after his arrival at LONDON that the peace of Utrecht was brought to a conclusion. Each year of this memorable reign had been so crowded with heroic achievements and grand events, that the poets and painters of our island seem to have sunk, as it were, under the load of matter, which had been heaped upon them. And had our musicians been thought equal to the task, a foreigner would hardly have been applied to for the song of triumph and thanksgiving, which was now wanted. The illustrious family which had taken HANDEL into its patronage, had not only been deeply concerned, but highly distinguished, in the course of the war. The military talents, and personal bravery of its members had contributed to its prosperous issue. And not only the august house of Hanover, but most of the protestant Princes of the country to which he was indebted for his birth and education, had concurred in the reduction of that overgrown power, which long had menaced their religion and liberty. These circumstances produced that particular sort of interest and attachment, which, when joined to the dignity and importance of a subject, dispose an artist to the utmost exertion of his powers. No performance can be thoroughly excellent, unless it is wrought *con amore*, as the Italians express it. HANDEL, it must be owned, had all these advantages. And it is not too much, perhaps it is too little to say, that the work was answerable to them. But let the grand TE DEUM and JUBILATE speak for themselves! Our business is not to play the panegyrist, but the historian. [Mainwaring, pp. 86ff.]

We now come to an interesting document, written by Heidegger about the middle of 1713, and giving us some insight into the monies earned by Handel and the singers of the Queen's Theatre. It seems that for the seasons 1711 and 1712 the composer earned £811.00., a huge sum by the standards of the day. In 1713 Margarita Durastanti earned £400, Mrs Barber £300, Mr Handel:

	£	s.	d.	
In the first division	86	0	0	
In the second	26	17	0	
His benefitt day	73	10	11	
Remains due	243	12	1	
	£430	0	0	[Deutsch, pp. 58f.]

While the others earned: Valeriano Pellegrini £645, Signora Pilotti Schiavonetti £500, Valentino Urbani £537.10.0, and Signora Manina (who had a small part in Handel's *Teseo*) £100. It can be seen that although Handel did not command the huge sums of the Italian singers, nevertheless his fee was a substantial one.

Handel's benefit concert was a performance of *Teseo* on 16 May, and (says *Coleman's 'Opera Register'*) 'Here ended ye Operas for this season.'

On 1 August 1714, Queen Anne died and George I of Hanover was proclaimed King. Handel must have realized that he was now in a very embarrassing position, having treated in a cavalier manner his patron's generosity and forbearance. The manner of Handel's reception by his new royal patron, and the origin of the famous *Water Musick*, are the subject of the next chapter.

NOTES

1 It seems he had received strong invitations to England from the Duke of Manchester. [original footnote]

2 Hawkins, Sir John, *A General History of the Science and Practice of Music*, London 1776, vol. v p. 267.

3 The Dowager Electress Sophie, whose daughter was Sophie Charlotte, Queen of Prussia when Handel was in Berlin. The elector's son was to become George II of England in 1827. [H.C.R.L.]

4 Autograph in British Library, King's Collection, R.M. 20 e. I. Venetian paper showing three crescents with siglum 'SS'; Lombard paper like Eineder 643, 'CV' (there: 1715); German paper is unicorn springing; British or Dutch paper: crown with fleur-de-lis and fragments of letters 'LVG'.

5 G. Schnath (ed.), *Briefwechsel der Kurtürstin Sophie von Hannover mit dem Preussischen Königshause*, Berlin & Leipzig, 1927, p. 189.

6 W.H. Quarnell and M. Mare (trans. & eds.), *London in 1710 From the Travels of Zacharias Conrad von Uffenbach*, London 1934, pp. 17f., 31f.

7 Pepusch (1667–1752) was born in Berlin and came to Britain in 1700, establishing the Academy of Antient Music in 1710. In 1718 he married Francesca Margherita de l'Epine, who was sensationally ugly but an excellent artist; she was to sing for Handel in 1712 and 1713 (*Rinaldo*). Pepusch is, of course, best known as the composer of *The Beggar's* Opera. He was organist and composer to the Duke of Chandos at Cannons in 1712, where he was succeeded by Handel.

8 Niccolò Grimaldi (called 'Nicolini'), the soprano castrato who would sing the title role at the première of Handel's *Rinaldo* in 1711.

9 J. Merrill Knapp, 'Handel's Second Song on the London Stage', *Musical Times* cxxiii (April 1982), pp. 251f.

10 The composers included M.A. Bononcini (three complete operas and pasticcios), A. Scarlatti (one complete opera, three pasticcios), F. Parini, F. Conti, etc. A complete list in Deutsch, p. 47. [H.C.R.L.]

11 When I worked there, as part of a BBC team in 1958, it belonged to the late Edward Croft-Murray of the Prints and Drawings Department, British Museum. Mr Croft-Murray subsequently proved to be of invaluable help to me on many occasions.

12 M. Knapp, 'The Libretto of Handel's "Silla"', Music & Letters I (1969), pp. 819ff.

IV
The Water Musick years

ENGLAND'S NEW KING, George I, landed at Greenwich on 18 September 1714 and continued to London where he moved into St James's Palace on the 20th. On the 26th, Sunday morning, 'His Majesty went to His Royal Chappel at St James's . . . [A] *Te Deum* was sung, composed by Mr Handel, and a very fine Anthem was also sung . . .' (*Post Boy*, 28 September).

Even if Handel was in disgrace his music, at any rate, was not. In fact, the new king may have been thoroughly annoyed at the man while continuing to love his music. Here is the account of the composer's situation as related by Mainwaring:

> On the death of the Queen in 1714, his late Majesty came over. HANDEL, conscious how ill he had deserved at the hands of his gracious patron, now invited to the throne of these kingdoms by all the friends of our happy and free constitution, did not dare to shew himself at court. To account for his delay in returning to his office, was no easy matter. To make an excuse for the non-performance of his promise, was impossible. From this ugly situation he was soon relieved by better luck than perhaps he deserved. It happened that his noble friend Baron Kilmanseck was here. He, with some others among the nobility, contrived a method for reinstating him in the favour of his Majesty; the clemency of whose nature was soon experienced by greater persons on a much more trying occasion.
>
> The King was persuaded to form a party on the water. HANDEL was apprised of the design, and advised to prepare some Music for that occasion. It was performed and conducted by himself, unknown to his Majesty, whose pleasure on hearing

> it was equal to his surprise. He was impatient to know whose it was, and how this entertainment came to be provided without his knowledge. The Baron then produced the delinquent, and asked leave to present him to his Majesty, as one that was too conscious of his fault to attempt an excuse for it; but sincerely desirous to attone for the same by all possible demonstrations of duty, submission, and gratitude, could he but hope that his Majesty, in his great goodness, would be pleased to accept them. This intercession was accepted without any difficulty. HANDEL was restored to favour, and his Music honoured with the highest expressions of the royal approbation. As a token of it, the King was pleased to add a pension for life of 200 *l.* a year to that which Queen ANNE had before given him. Some years after, when he was employed to teach the young Princesses, another pension of the same value was added to the former by her late Majesty. [pp. 89–92]

That the famous 'water party' actually took place is confirmed by three contemporary reports – not, however, in the year 1715 but two years later. The first two accounts are in British newspapers:

> On *Wednesday* the 17th of *July*, in the Evening, the King, attended by their Royal Highnesses the Prince and Princess of *Wales*, and a numerous Train of Lords, Gentlemen, and Ladies, went up by Water to *Chelsea*, and was entertain'd with an excellent Consort of Musick by Count *Kilmanseck*; after which, His Majesty and their Royal Highnesses supp'd at the Lady *Catherine Jones*'s, at the House of the late Earl of *Ranelagh*'s; and about Three a Clock in the Morning, return'd by Water to *Whitehall*, and thence to St *James*'s Palace. [*The Political State of Great-Britain*, 1717; Deutsch, p. 76].

> On Wednesday Evening [the 17th], at about 8, the King took Water at Whitehall in an open Barge, wherein were also the Dutchess of Bolton, the Dutchess of Newcastle, the Countess of Godolphin, Madam Kilmanseck, and the Earl of Orkney. And went up the River towards Chelsea. Many other Barges with Persons of Quality attended, and so great a Number of Boats, that the

> whole River in a manner was cover'd; a City Company's Barge was employ'd for the Musick, wherein were 50 Instruments of all sorts, who play'd all the Way from Lambeth (while the Barges drove with the Tide without Rowing, as far as Chelsea) the finest Symphonies, compos'd express for this Occasion, by Mr Hendel; which his Majesty liked so well, that he caus'd it to be plaid over three times in going and returning. At Eleven his Majesty went a-shore at Chelsea, where a Supper was prepar'd, and then there was another very fine Consort of Musick, which lasted till 2; after which, his Majesty came again into his Barge, and return'd the same Way, the Musick continuing to play till he landed. [*Daily Courant*, 19 July 1717]

While the third, and most interesting, is a report from the Prussian Resident, Bonet, to Berlin. It will be noted that certain details in this latter document differ from those of the printed sources (who was the hostess, and the presence or absence of the Prince and Princess of Wales); but for our purposes, these differences are immaterial:

> [London, 19th (30th) July 1717.]
>
> A few weeks ago the King expressed to Baron Kilmanseck His desire to have a concert on the river, by subscription, similar to the masquerades this winter which the King never failed to attend. The Baron accordingly applied to Heidecker, a Swiss by origin, but the cleverest purveyor of entertainments to the Nobility. The latter replied that, much as he would wish to comply with His Majesty's desires, he must reserve subscriptions for the great events, namely the masquerades, each of which brings him in three or 400 guineas net. Observing His Majesty's chagrin at these difficulties, M. de Kilmanseck undertook to provide the concert on the river at his own expense. The necessary orders were given and the entertainment took place the day before yesterday. About eight in the evening the King repaired to His barge, into which were admitted the Duchess of Bolton, Countess Godolphin, Mad. de Kilmanseck, Mrs Were and the Earl of Orkney, the Gentleman of the Bedchamber in Waiting. Next to the King's barge was that of the musicians, about 50 in number, who played on all kinds of instruments, to wit trumpets, horns, hautboys, bassoons, German

> flutes, French flutes, violins and basses; but there were no singers. The music had been composed specially by the famous Handel, a native of Halle, and His Majesty's principal Court Composer. His Majesty approved of it so greatly that he caused it to be repeated three times in all, although each performance lasted an hour – namely twice before and once after supper. The [weather in the] evening was all that could be desired for the festivity, the number of barges and above all of boats filled with people desirous of hearing was beyond counting. In order to make this entertainment the more exquisite, Mad. de Kilmanseck had arranged a choice supper in the late Lord Ranelagh's villa at Chelsea on the river, where the King went at one in the morning. He left at three o'clock and returned to St James' about half past four. The concert cost Baron Kilmanseck £150 for the musicians alone. Neither the Prince nor the Princess [of Wales] took any part in this festivity. [Deutsch, p. 77]

(Handel lost a real friend and protector when Baron Kielmansegg, himself an amateur composer, died a few months later, on 15 November.)

These 'water parties' were extremely popular and it seems probable that there were others as well as those that are documented. The extent to which Handel's music was involved, is also open to conjecture, but the fact that the *Water Musick* comprises three distinct suites, in three different keys (F, D, G), might indicate that there were three separate entertainments at least.

An interesting variant to the royal reconciliation is provided by Hawkins (v, p. 239), who relates the story of the *Water Musick* and then adds the following circumstance: Francesco Geminiani, the celebrated Luccan violinist and composer, arrived in London in 1714 as a protégé of Baron Kielmansegg, now Master of the King's Horse, to whom Geminiani two years later dedicated a set of violin sonatas which he now introduced (in manuscript) at court. The composer insisted on being accompanied by Handel, and the performance was so brilliant that the King at once forgave Handel. Perhaps both stories are true. At any rate, on 17 October 1714 he received half his annual salary from the Hanover *Staatscassa*, so he can never have been in total disgrace.

The *Water Musick* is, together with Bach's 'Brandenburg' Concertos and Vivaldi's *The Four Seasons*, the most popular instrumental music of the first half of the eighteenth century. Although Handel's sophisticated and delightful music never plumbs the depths of Bach's slow movements (for example 'Brandenburg' Nos. 1 or 6) – how could it, being conceived as genuine alfresco music? – nevertheless the *Water Musick* is a milestone in the *settecento*'s orchestral literature. Like the 'Brandenburg' Concerto No. 1, Handel introduces a pair of horns in the F major suite, and it is now thought that it marked one of the first times these instruments were heard by British audiences. As with Bach's concerto, it is believed that the horns were probably played by itinerant Bohemian musicians: the Bohemians were the great exponents of the horn in those days, carrying their highly specialized craft throughout Europe.[1]

It seems that there are at least three *Water Musick* suites: one in F with French horns; one in D with trumpets; and a softer one in G with flutes suitable for performance at the 'choice supper in the late Lord Ranelagh's villa at Chelsea,' where 'there was another very fine Consort of Musick, which lasted till 2 [a.m.] . . .'

Until after the Second World War, the *Water Musick* was known to the general public only in the suites cleverly arranged and re-orchestrated by Sir Hamilton Harty; but in the 1950s, musicians and scholars began to examine new manuscript sources for the music, some of it hardly known even to Handelians. The principal result of all this scholarly activity was, first, to establish the original orchestration, and secondly, to work out the three groups of suites that are now commonly played. (It is, of course, not necessary to perform the music in the order in which it was composed and/or performed, ending with the delicate chamber-music-like Suite in G; but it is essential to recognize that there was some kind of master-plan in Handel's mind when he wrote the various suites, and that the whole is not so haphazard a collection of pieces as was once thought.)

The results of this scholarship can be seen conveniently in the miniature score edited by Roger Fiske in the Edition Eulenburg (1308, published in 1973) which is taken from the principal sources, manuscript and printed; for easy reference, readers may like to have here a thematic guide of the three suites (see Appendix).

Apart from the splendidly extrovert trumpet and horn suites, this extraordinary music reveals another facet of Handel's art of diplomacy; for there is no questioning the distinctly *English* quality of many of the dance movements – and not just the titles (such as 'Hornpipe'). This peculiarly British quality of the music is particularly noticeable in the G minor suite. Handel had already assimilated the musical tradition of his adopted country to an amazing extent: he *was* in many respects a British composer, but with far more than the usual international flair (and experience) – a remarkable fusion of solid German upbringing, Italian training (and a predilection for Italian opera), and a thorough acquaintance with French taste and English tradition.

The *Water Musick* proved to be immensely popular: it was played in the taverns and in public gardens, in the aristocratic halls and in the London and Bristol and Edinburgh town houses; it was arranged for small band, for solo harpsichord, for flute (a characteristic *settecento* instrument of the cultivated amateur); in short, it conquered England.

Handel's aspirations still centred round the opera house, and the next work of this *genre* he produced was *Amadigi di Gaula* (King's Theatre, 25 May 1715) with Nicolini in the title role and Mrs Robinson as Oriana. The work enjoyed a modest half-dozen performances but was revived in 1716 (in one of those performances Handel introduced two new 'Symphonies' or orchestral pieces) and 1717, and may be accounted something of a success. Handel composed it, as Heidegger's dedication of the libretto to the Earl of Burlington shows, in the comfort of Burlington House in Piccadilly ('. . . as it is compos'd in Your own Family . . .'). (The word-book of Handel's previous Opera, *Teseo*, had been likewise dedicated to Burlington by the librettist.) *Rinaldo* was also being revived and the King attended two performances in July 1715, but shortly thereafter 'ye Rebellion of ye Tories and Paptists [*sic*]', or the 'Jacobite alarm' as it was usually called, stopped the production of operas, 'ye King and Court not liking to go into such Crowds these troublesome times' (*Coleman's 'Opera Register'*).

In fact the Haymarket Theatre was not re-opened until February 1716, and *Amadigi* was given as a benefit for Mrs Robinson on 3 March – she had been sick and forced to relinquish the role the previous year.

In July King George went to Hanover and Handel followed him after the season's last performance of *Amadigi* on 12 July, at which Handel's old friend from Berlin days, Attilio Ariosti, played a solo on the viola d'amore between the acts; Ariosti had just arrived in town and was to stay in England for twelve years.

In Germany Handel visited his family at Halle, and in the autumn of 1716 he went to Ansbach where he persuaded his old university friend Johann Christoph Schmidt to give up the wool trade and to become Handel's principal copyist and the head of the soon-famous 'Smith' (his anglicized name) scriptorium. John Christopher Smith and his young son of the same name became Handel's intimate friends as well as business partners.

Upon Handel's return to London, late in 1716, he took in hand a new revival of *Rinaldo* with considerable changes for a new singer, Gaetano Berenstadt (5 January 1717). The composer was now persuaded to join the household of James Brydges, the Earl of Carnarvon (from 1719 first Duke of Chandos) as composer in residence. Handel stayed for the most part at Cannons, a handsome new estate near Edgware, where the Earl kept a small but excellent group of singers and instrumentalists. By 25 September 1717, the Earl was writing to John Arbuthnot that 'Mr Handle [*sic*] has made me two new Anthems very noble ones & most think they far exceed the two first.' Probably one of these new Chandos Anthems, as they are now called, was the magnificent 'As pants the hart' which soon became the most popular of the series. The Earl suggested to Dr Arbuthnot that 'You had as good take Cannons in your way to London' (Deutsch, p. 78). Mention of Dr Arbuthnot recalls the following note in Mainwaring:

> The Poet [Alexander Pope] one day asked his friend Dr ARBUTHNOT, of whose knowledge in Music he had a high idea, What was his real opinion in regard to HANDEL as a Master of that Science? The Doctor immediately replied, 'Conceive the highest that you can of his abilities, and they are much beyond any thing that you *can* conceive.' [p. 93]

To this we may add Mainwaring's slightly reticent description of Handel at Cannons:

> The remaining two years he spent at CANNONS, a place which was then in all its glory, but remarkable for having much more of art

> that nature, and much more cost than art. . . . Whether HANDEL was *provided* as a mere implement of grandeur, or *chosen* from motives of a superior kind, it is not for us to determine. [p. 95f.]

Handel's vocal music composed at Cannons was largely in the English language, which perhaps was significant in laying the foundations of his later career as a composer of oratorios. Of the many small but sophisticated works written for or at Cannons, the most significant are the two English masques, *Acis and Galatea* (spring 1718) and the first setting of *Esther* (1718?). Both contain strong Purcellian overtones, and *Acis* especially is of a particularly radiant freshness and beauty – the finest English 'Little opera' (as it was termed by a member of the audience) since Purcell's *Dido and Aeneas. Acis* is more effective than *Esther*, but in the choruses of the latter there is a strong sense of greatness soon to come. If *Esther* is the gateway to Handel's later oratorio style, *Acis* must have caused many in the audience to wish that Handel could have seen his way to composing more English-language operas of this outstanding excellence.

It must have been about 1716 that Handel composed his last major work in the German language, the so-called *Brockes Passion*, the word-book having been written by Senator Barthold Heinrich Brockes of Hamburg, who had printed it there in 1712. Handel's old friend Mattheson wrote in his *Ehren-Pforte* (op. cit.) that Handel 'had composed the Passion in England, and had sent it in an uncommonly closely-written score by post' to Mattheson, who caused it to be performed in the refectory of Hamburg Cathedral on 23 March 1719, during Holy Week; this event may, however, have been preceded by another performance at Hamburg three years earlier (a libretto of that date, while not mentioning Handel's name, incorporates at least one textual variant known only in his setting). Apart from Handel's, the *Brockes Passion* was also set by Keiser, Telemann, and Mattheson, and Bach used part of it in his *St John Passion* as well as copying out the whole of Handel's setting (score now in the Berlin State Library).

Handel's setting of the Passion was widely respected in his lifetime, and several contemporary manuscript copies of the score have survived in Germany. It is thought that Mattheson encouraged Handel to compose it with a specific view to performing four different settings in Hamburg during the year 1719, returning to the old custom of performing settings of all four Gospel accounts of the Passion during Holy Week. Whatever the real reason for the work's existence, Handel was by now out of practice in setting the German language and there are several incorrect syllabic stresses that he allowed to creep into his score; and of course there were the usual borrowings from earlier works (for example, the Utrecht *Te Deum*). What people thought of this confrontation of the four settings in 1719, we do not know; Senator Brockes apparently liked them all so much that he was undecided 'to whom to award the palm'. Handel's setting was full of his vigorous style but one could hardly say that the text, with its overtones of German pietism, inspired the composer to give of his best.

NOTES

1. See Horace Fitzpatrick, *The Horn and Horn-playing and the Austro-Bohemian Tradition from 1680 to 1830*, London 1970.

V
The Alpine Faun & the Royal Academy 1719–1728

HANDEL'S FRIENDS AND admirers must have seen that the regular production of Italian opera in London was at best a precarious venture: when successful the income was huge but, financially, a great deal of capital was required and there was considerable risk involved. In Mainwaring's report the figure of £40,000 has been queried, but by February 1720 Sir John Vanbrugh stated that nearly £20,000 had been raised by subscription.

> During the last year of his residence at Cannons, a project was formed by the Nobility for erecting an academy at the Haymarket. The intention of this musical Society, was to secure to themselves a constant supply of Operas to be composed by HANDEL, and performed under his direction. For this end a subscription was set on foot: and as his late Majesty was pleased to let his name appear at the head of it, the Society was dignified with the title of the Royal Academy. The sum subscribed being very large,[1] it was intended to continue for fourteen years certain. But as yet it was in its embrio-state, being not fully formed till a year or two after. [Mainwaring, pp. 96–8]

We now come to interesting contemporary memoirs about Handel by one of his aristocratic patrons, the fourth Earl of Shaftesbury (Anthony Ashley Cooper):

> The method of this Subscription [for the Academy of Music] was, for each Subscriber to sign a Bond for £200, which Sum was to answer, all calls that might be made, upon the Subscribers for

> Expences in carrying on the Opera's exceeding the Sums collected each night at the House. And a sett of Directors were Elected, for carrying on the Affairs of the Academy; which was Incorporated by a Charter. The Directors were for the most part Persons of Distinction. [Deutsch, p. 844]

Whatever the true subscription was, the figure early in 1720 was a considerable one, enabling the Royal Academy to launch its first opera, Porta's *Numitore*, on 2 April of that year. This was succeeded by Handel's Opera *Radamisto* on 27 April (see below p. 109).

In the administration of the Academy, Heidegger was the manager, Handel the musical director and Paolo Rolli the librettist and secretary for the Italian affairs of the institution. Rolli was a great intriguer, and his amusing correspondence with Abbate Giuseppe Riva (the Modenese Representative usually in London but often abroad on holiday or on business) is in the Campori Collection at the Biblioteca Estense in Modena, and makes entertaining reading. Rolli was no friend of Handel's and refers to the composer as 'l'uomo' or 'il Proteus alpino' or 'L'Alpestre Fauno' ('The Alpine Faun'). The correspondence was discovered by Streatfeild and published complete by Deutsch. Like all intriguers, Rolli soon gained a poor reputation and Handel trusted him not at all (and rightly so): 'I am amused that he [Handel] should suspect me and not trust my most polite manners in his majestic Faunlike presence,' writes Rolli to Riva on 18 October 1720 (Deutsch, p. 115).

Handel was empowered by the directors to go abroad and engage the finest singers:

> WARRANT AND INSTRUCTIONS FOR HANDEL, ISSUED BY THOMAS HOLLES, DUKE OF NEWCASTLE, THE LORD CHAMBERLAIN, AS GOVERNOR OF THE ROYAL ACADEMY OF MUSIC, 14th May 1719
>
> Warrant to M[r] Hendel to procure Singers for the English Stage,
>
> Whereas His Majesty has been graciously Pleas'd to Grant Letters Patents to the Severall Lords and Gent. mention'd in the Annext List for the Encouragement of Operas for and

during the Space of Twenty one Years, and Likewise as a further encouragement has been graciously Pleas'd to Grant a Thousand Pounds p.A. for the Promotion of this design, And also that the Chamberlain of his Ma^{ts} Houshold for the time being is to be always Governor of the said Company. I do by his Majesty's Command Authorize and direct You forthwith to repair to Italy Germany or such other Place or Places as you shall think proper, there to make Contracts with such Singer or Singers as you shall judge fit to perform on the English Stage. And for so doing this shall be your Warrant Given under my hand and Seal this 14th day of May 1719 in the Fifth Year of his Ma^{ts} Reign.

To Mr Hendel Master of Musick . . .

Holles Newcastle.

Instructions to Mr Hendel.

That Mr Hendel either by himself or such Correspondenc^{s} as he shall think fit procure proper Voices to Sing in the Opera.

The said Mr Hendel is impower'd to contract in the Name of the Patentees with those Voices to Sing in the Opera for one Year and no more.

That Mr Hendel engage Senezino as soon as possible to Serve the said Company and for as many Years as may be.

That in case Mr Hendel meet with an excellent Voice of the first rate he is to Acquaint the Govr and Company forthwith of it and upon what Terms he or She may be had.

That Mr Hendel from time to time Acquaint the Governor and Company with his proceedings, Send Copys of the Agreem^{ts} which he makes with these Singers and obey such further Instructions as the Governor and Company shall from time to time transmit unto him.

Holles Newcastle.
[Deutsch, pp. 89f.]

The composer decided to start his search at the court of Dresden, where the King of Saxony, Friedrich August I (who was also August II, King of Poland) kept a magnificent opera company. One of his leading composers was later J.A. Hasse. Mainwaring supplies the basic information:

> HANDEL therefore, after he quitted his employment at Cannons, was advised to go over to DRESDEN in quest of Singers. Here he engaged SENESINO and DURISTANTI, whom he brought over with him to ENGLAND. [pp. 97f.]

Handel played harpsichord at the Dresden court and was paid one hundred ducats; en route he visited the Palatine court at Düsseldorf (May 1719) and then went to Halle to visit his family; there he is said to have just missed J.S. Bach, coming from Cöthen (Chrysander II, pp. 18f.).

Francesco Bernardi ('Senesino' or the little Sennese) was a celebrated soprano castrato; his salary in London was £2,000, while Margarita Durastanti, who was also at Dresden, received £1,600. (Rolli immediately began his web of intrigue: 'Oh! What a bad choice for England! I shall not enter into her singing merits but she really is an Elephant'; Deutsch, p. 94).

As befitting its most august subscriber, Handel dedicated the word-book of his new opera, *Radamisto*, to the king. It was, as we have seen, the second work for the Academy and was given, of course, at the King's Theatre, Haymarket:

HANDEL'S DEDICATION OF THE LIBRETTO OF *Radamisto*, [27th April] 1720

To the
KING'S
Most Excellent Majesty

Sir,

The Protection which Your Majesty has been graciously pleased to allow both to the Art of *Musick* in general, and to one of the lowest, tho' not the least Dutiful of your Majesty's Servants, has embolden'd me to present to Your Majesty, with all due Humility and Respect, this my first Essay to that Design. I have been still the more encouraged to this, by the particular Approbation Your Majesty has been pleased to give to the Musick of this *Drama*:

Which, may I be permitted to say, I value not so much as it is the Judgment of a Great Monarch, as of One of a most Refined Taste in the Art: My Endeavours to improve which, is the only Merit that can be pretended by me, except that of being with the utmost Humility.

SIR,

Your Majesty's
Most Devoted,
Most Obedient
And most Faithful
Subject and Servant,
GEORGE-FREDERIC HANDEL.
[Deutsch, p. 103]

A contemporary diary records briefly the huge success: 'At Night, *Radamistus*, a fine opera of Handel's making. The *King* there with his Ladies. The *Prince* in the Stage-box. Great crowd.' [Diary of Mary, Countess Cowper, Lady of the Bedchamber to the Princess of Wales] Mainwaring describes the event in more detail:

In the year 1720, he obtained leave to perform his Opera of RADAMISTO. If persons who are now living, and who were present at that performance may be credited, the applause it received was almost as extravagant as his AGRIPPINA had excited: the crowds and tumults of the house at Venice were hardly equal to those at LONDON. In so splendid and fashionable an assembly of ladies (to the excellence of their taste we must impute it) there was no shadow of form, or ceremony, scarce indeed any appearance of order or regularity, politeness or decency. Many, who had forc'd their way into the house with an impetuosity but ill suited to their rank and sex, actually fainted through the excessive heat and closeness of it. Several gentlemen were turned back, who had offered forty shillings for a seat in the gallery, after having despaired of getting any in the pit or boxes.

But, it may be thought, that the great excellence of SENESINO, both as to voice and action, might have a considerable share in the wonderful impressions made upon the audience. For, by virtue of great advantages in the representation, many performances of little

> or no value, have not only passed, but been well received. – To the ladies especially, the merits of SENESINO would be much more obvious, than those of HANDEL. – Perhaps they would. That *all* depended on the Composer, I am as far from asserting, as I am from believing that any other person could have shewn such a singer to equal advantage. Let any impartial and competent judge consider, whether it is likely that the whole musical world could have afforded a composer besides himself, capable of furnishing SENESINO with such a song, as that of Ombra Cara in the very Opera before us. [pp. 101f.]

Handel took out a copyright privilege for fourteen years and gave the score of *Radamisto* to Richard Meares to print. The copyright was in principle an astute idea but it could not prevent rival publishers from issuing pirated editions, especially of 'favourite songs'.

Later in the year, Senesino arrived together with the tenor Matteo Berselli and the composer Giovanni Bononcini. Handel's *Radamisto* was revived to include these spectacular new singers. Matters were complicated when Durastanti became pregnant (her husband, Casimiro Avelloni, was with her in England), but she managed to sing a different part (Zenobia) at the revival on 28 December.

Bononcini and Handel were now joined by a third composer, Filippo Amadei. Each composer had his adherents and the Academy found an amusing way in which to settle the arguments as to their relative merits. Mainwaring relates the story:

> The great success of it matur'd the project before concerted for establishing an academy. For it could not be effected at once, as a considerable number of great persons had been instrumental in bringing over BUONONCINI and ATTILIO.[2] And these foreigners they were the more unwilling to abandon, because they really had abilities in their profession. Perhaps the contents ran as high on both sides, as if the object of them had been much more important. Yet I cannot agree with some, who think them of no importance, and treat them as ridiculous. Those who thought their honour engaged to support the old Composers; who really preferred them to HANDEL; or fancied that it was a defect

of humanity, or an act of injustice to discard them, not because they were unfit for their office, but because another foreigner was come, who was thought to be fitter; – had surely a right to interest themselves warmly in their defence, at a time when they were so much in want of assistance . . . .

Such then was the state of things in the year 1720, at the time RADAMISTO was performed. The succeeding winter brought this musical disorder to its crisis. In order to terminate all matters in controversy; it was agreed to put them on this fair issue. The several parties concerned were to be jointly employed in making an Opera, in which each of them was to take a distinct act. And he, who by the general suffrage, should be allowed to have given the best proofs of his abilities, was to be put into possession of the house. The proposal was accepted, whether from choice, or necessity, I cannot say. The event was answerable to the expectations of HANDEL's friends. His act was the last, and the superiority of it so very manifest, that there was not the least pretence for any further doubts or disputes. I should have mentioned, that as each made an overture, as well as an act, the affair seemed to be decided even by the overture with which HANDEL's began. The name of the Opera was MUZIO SCÆVOLA. [pp. 101f., 104f.]

Handel could now book another operatic triumph to follow *Radamisto: Floridante*, adapted by Rolli from an older libretto by Silvani, *La costanza in trionfo*. When it was given at the King's Theatre on 9 December 1721, Senesino was in the title role and there were no fewer than fifteen performances followed by another seven at the beginning of the subsequent season (at which time several arias were added); it was revived, without much success, in 1727 (two performances).

We now enter a long period in which Handel was almost entirely taken up with directing the musical affairs of the Academy and composing operas for it. But the rival composer Bononcini soon became more popular with his simpler, more tuneful scores. During the first two years of Bononcini's stay in London, he could boast of sixty-three performances against only twenty-eight of Handel's.

In the latter part of 1722, the famous soprano Francesca Cuzzoni arrived to sing for the Academy. She was immediately given the leading role (Teofane) in Handel's new opera *Ottone*, but she refused to sing the great aria composed especially for her, 'Falsa imagine', whereupon Handel seized her and threatened to thrust the shrieking soprano out of the open window until she agreed to sing it: the aria became the success of the season (as Handel predicted), but she now loathed the composer. Here are the contemporary documents concerning *Ottone*'s prodigious success:

FROM THE *Daily Courant*, 12 January 1723

At the King's Theatre . . . this present Saturday . . . will be presented, A New Opera call'd OTHO, King of Germany. Pit and Boxes to be put together and in Regard to the Increase of the Numbers of the Subscribers, no more than Three Hundred and Fifty Tickets will be deliver'd out this Day, at Mrs White's Chocolate-House in St James's street, at Half a Guinea each. N.B. No Tickets will be given out at the Door, nor any Persons whatever admitted for Money. Gallery 5s. By Command, no Directors, Subscribers, or any other Persons will be admitted behind the Scenes. To begin exactly at Six a-Clock.

CAST OF *Ottone*, 12 January 1723

Ottone – Signor Senesino, alto
Teofane – Signora Cuzzoni, soprano
Emireno – Signor Boschi, bass
Gismonda – Signora Durastanti, soprano
Adelberto – Signor Berenstadt, bass
Matilda – Mrs Robinson, soprano

FROM *Colman's 'Opera Register'*, January 1723

Anno 1722 Decr Sigra Faustina Cuzzoni first sung at ye Theatre above sd [in the Haymarket] towards ye end of this year in the Opera called Ottone – & was extreemly admired & often performed Sigra Durastanti Sigr Senesino Mrs An^a Robinson sung also in ye said Opera & pleased much.[3]

MONSIEUR DE FABRICE TO COUNT FLEMMING
(Translated)

London, January 15th, 1722–23.

. . . In the end the famous Cozzuna [*sic*] not merely arrived but even sang in a new opera by Hendell, called Othon – the same subject as the one at Dresden – with enormous success; the house was full to overflowing. Today is the second performance and there is such a run on it that tickets are already being sold at 2 and 3 guineas which are ordinarily half a guinea, so that it is like another Mississippi or South Sea Bubble. Over and above that, there exist two factions, the one supporting Hendell, the other Bononcini, the one for Cenesino [*sic*] and the other for Cossuna [*sic*]. They are as much at loggerheads as the Whigs and Tories,[4] and even on occasion sow dissension among the Directors.

FROM THE *London Journal*, 19 January 1723

His Majesty was at the Theatre in the Hay-Market, when Seigniora Cotzani [*sic*] performed, for the first Time, to the Surprize and Admiration of a numerous Audience, who are ever too fond of Foreign Performers. She is already jump'd into a handsome Chariot, and an Equipage accordingly. The Gentry seem to have so high a Taste of her fine Parts, that she is likely to be a great Gainer by them.

FROM THE *Daily Courant*, 22 January 1723 (*Ottone* repeated)

. . . Whereas it has been usual to deliver out the Opera Tickets at White's Chocolate-House, the Royal Academy have judged it more Convenient that they for the future be delivered out at their Office in the Hay-Market . . . Upon Complaint to the Royal Academy of Musick, that Disorders have been of late committed in the Footmen's Gallery, to the Interruption of the Performance; This is to give Notice, That the next Time any Disorder is made there, that Gallery will be shut up. [Deutsch, pp. 146–8]

Handel's popularity was now completely restored, though his next opera, *Flavio*, with Senesino, Cuzzoni, Mrs Robinson and Durastanti, was much less successful. Nevertheless, the 'new Opera Tickets are very high . . . They are traded in at the other End of the Town, as much as Lottery Tickets are in Exchange-Alley' (*London Journal* for 2 March 1723; Deutsch, p. 150). Apart from Cuzzoni's temperamental outbursts (see above p. 112), there must have been many others.

One such occurred during the rehearsal of Flavio: the English tenor, Gordon, had apparently threatened to jump on the harpsichord, to which Handel is said to have replied: 'Let me know when and I will advertise it, for more people will come to see you jump than to hear you sing.'

A new composer, Attilio Ariosti, now joined the Academy but could hardly dent the popularity of Handel and Bononcini. London was now the operatic centre of the world, with the finest singers and the greatest living opera composer (though many contemporaries ranked Bononcini nearly as high if not higher).

It was Bononcini who opened the Academy's fifth season with *Farnace* (27 November 1723), followed by a revival of *Ottone*. But everyone's attention was now focused on Handel's new work, *Giulio Cesare in Egitto*, the first of a series of three great and noble *opere serie* in the grandest heroic tradition; the librettist, Nicola Francesco Haym, dedicated the word-book to Caroline, Princess of Wales, who was to be an affectionate patroness of Handel's. The cast included Senesino (Caesar), Durastanti, Mrs Robinson and Cuzzoni (Cleopatra); and the first performance, on 20 February 1724, was another triumph for all concerned:

MONSIEUR DE FABRICE TO COUNT FLEMMING
(Translated)

London, March 10th, 1724.

. . . The opera is in full swing also, since Hendell's new one, called Jules César – in which Cenesino [*sic*] and Cozzuma [*sic*] shine beyond all criticism – has been put on. The house was just as full at the seventh performance as at the first. In addition to that the squabbles, between the Directors and the sides that everyone is taking between the singers and the composers, often provide the public with the most diverting scenes.

MR. LECOQ TO GRAF ERNST CHRISTOPH
MANTEUFFEL[5] IN DRESDEN (Translated)

. . . The passion for the opera here is getting beyond all belief. It is true that the music is beautiful and varied. There are three composers, including the famous Handel, each of whom writes two operas every winter. The orchestra, by and large, is of high quality

> and good care is taken to produce new voices at the theatre from time to time. Durastante [*sic*], whom you know, retired on the day of her benefit with a cantata in praise of the English nation. She said that she was making way for younger enchantresses. That one day brought her more than a thousand pounds sterling. Her benefit last year brought in nearly as much, not to mention her salary of 1200 guineas a year. Have you ever heard, Monseigneur, of prodigality and favour to equal this towards a woman [already] old, whose voice is both mediocre and worn out? That is what the English are like . . .
> London, March 31, 1724. [Deutsch, p. 160]

And so Handel's much beloved Signora Margarita retired from the London stage, and for the moment from Handel's life. But she was to return yet again, nine years later, as a mezzo-soprano.

His opening opera of the next season was *Tamerlano* (31 October 1724) with Cuzzoni and Senesino. The new castrato, Andrea Pacini, had the title role, but the sensation of the evening was the new tenor, Francesco Borosini, as Bajazet. Lady Bristol, in the audience that night, went home and wrote to her husband, 'The new man takes extremely, but the [new] woman [Anna Dotti as Irene] is so great a joke that there was more laughing at her than at a farce . . . The Royal family were all there, and a greater crowd than ever I saw . . .' (Deutsch, pp. 174f.). As was customary, the score was immediately published, 'Corrected and Figur'd by his [Handel's] own Hand . . . And to render the Work more acceptable to Gentlemen and Ladies, every Song is truly translated into English Verse . . .' (Deutsch, p. 175).

Handel's next contribution was *Rodelinda*, with Cuzzoni, Senesino and Borosini in the cast (13 February 1725); it was another great success, especially Cuzzoni in the title role, whose brown silk costume was the talk of the town (Dean, *New Grove*, p. 32). *Rodelinda* was a success from the outset, and Senesino's Aria 'Dove sei, amato bene?' (for the part of Bertarido) became widely admired. It is a work about conjugal love and Cuzzoni shone in the title role. There was a spectacular revival in London in 1959 with Joan Sutherland and Janet Baker, and many Handelians regarded *Rodelinda* as containing in its libretto and in its music the seeds of a genuinely popular stage piece for modern audiences. *Rodelinda, Regina de' Longobardi*, as the full title reads, ran for fourteen performances in 1725 and enjoyed two revivals, each with eight performances, in 1725 and 1731.

1725 was also the year in which a famous epigram about Handel and Bononcini was 'composed' by John Byrom; for some time it was falsely attributed to Swift:

> Some say, compar'd to Bononcini,
> That Mynheer Handel's but a Ninny;
> Others aver, that he to Handel
> Is scarcely fit to hold a Candle:
> Strange all this Difference should be
> 'Twixt Tweedle-dum and Tweedle-dee!
> [Deutsch, p. 180]

In 1726, after considerable negotiation, the Academy succeeded in engaging the beautiful and brilliant soprano, Faustina Bordoni. She had been the toast of Vienna and her salary in London, like Cuzzoni's and Senesino's was £2,000 p.a. She became the wife of the celebrated opera composer Johann Adolph Hasse in 1730. Her first appearance at the King's Theatre, Haymarket, was in Handel's *Alessandro* on 5 May 1726, at which the incredible cast included no less than Senesino in the title role as well as Faustina *and* Cuzzoni. Of course it was almost unheard of for two primadonnas to appear together and, just as opposing factions had grown up around the two principal composers, the Academy's choice of these two singers caused a sensation and created a similar situation. Handel and his librettist also had to overcome the considerable problem of providing both sopranos with parts of equal importance, an impossible task which seemed doomed to fail, as indeed it did during a performance of Bononcini's *Astianatte* (see below p. 118). In the first month *Alessandro* was given eleven times and although it was as successful as the directors had hoped, the huge salaries involved were now causing serious financial problems. *Alessandro* has been preceded by Handel's *Scipione* (12 March), again with Senesino and Cuzzoni, which enjoyed thirteen performances but was only revived for six further performances in 1730. Perhaps the singers were beginning to mean much more than even Handel's finest music, for *Alessandro*, once the original cast had dispersed, was only revived for one season (1732).

The composer now produced another great work for his inimitable vocal trio, *Admeto*:

> MRS. PENDARVES TO HER SISTER, ANN GRANVILLE
>
> January 26th, 1726–7.
>
> Mrs Legh is transported with joy at living once more in 'dear London', and hearing Mr Handel's opera performed by Faustina, Cuzzoni & Senesino (which was rehearsed yesterday for the first time) that she is *out of her senses* . . . Miss Legh is fallen in love with the *Basilisk*, and says he is the most charming man of the world; he happened to commend Handel, and won her heart at once.[6]

The great German music theorist and composer, Johann Joachim Quantz, was in London for the event and reported in his autobiography:

> On 10 March [1727] I left Paris; and arrived safely in London via Calais on the 20th of the same month . . . At that time Italian opera in London was in full flush. *Admetus*, composed by *Händel*, was the latest, and had magnificent music. *Faustina, Cuzzoni* and *Senesino*, all three virtuosi of the front rank, were the chief performers in it, the rest were middling . . . The orchestra consisted for the greater part of Germans, several Italians, and a few Englishmen. *Castrucci*, an Italian violinist, was the leader. All together, under *Händel's* conducting, made an extremely good effect.
>
> The second opera which I heard in London was by *Bononcini*; it was not, however, so greatly acclaimed as the first . . . [Deutsch, p. 754]

The cast of *Admeto* on 31 January 1727 was as follows:

Admeto – Signor Senesino, alto
Alceste – Signora Faustina, mezzo-soprano[7]
Ercole – Signor Boschi, bass
Orindo – Signora Dotti, contralto

Trasimede – Signor Baldi, counter-tenor
Antigona – Signora Cuzzoni, soprano
Meraspe – Signor Palmerini, bass

The season's further activities are registered in a contemporary newspaper, the *Flying Post*, 4 February 1727:

> The Directors of the Royal Academy of Musick have resolved, that after the Excellent Opera composed by Mr Hendel, which is now performing; Signior Attilia shall compose one: And Signior Bononcini is to compose the next time after that. Thus, as this Theatre can boast of the three best Voices in Europe, and the best Instruments; so the Town will have the Pleasure of having these three different Stiles of composing: And, as Musick is a part of Mathematicks, and was always both by the Ancient Jews, and the Heathens, in the most Polite Courts, &c. esteemed a very rational and noble Entertainment; this Polite and Rich Nation will by Collecting what is perfect out of various Countries, become the Place where all Travellers will stay to be diverted and instructed in this Science, as well as in all others.

The two works were Bononcini's *Astianatte* (6 May) and Ariosti's *Teuzzone* (1 November), the last two operas these composers wrote for London.

The Academy was now the subject of lampoons in rival theatres:

FROM THE SONG, 'THE RAREE SHOW', SUNG BY MR. SALWAY IN LEWIS THEOBALD'S PLAY, *The Rape of Proserpine*, MUSIC BY JOHN ERNEST GALLIARD, AT LINCOLN'S INN FIELD THEATRE,
13th February 1727

And for de Diversions, dat make a de Pleasure,
  For dis Great Town,
Dey be so many, so fine, so pleasant, so cheap
  As never was known;
Here be de Hay-Market, vere de Italien Opera
  Do sweetly sound,

Dat cost a de brave Gentry no more as
Two hundred thousand Pound.

(Chorus)

A very pretty Fancy, a brave gallante Show;
Juste come from France toute Noveau.
[Deutsch, p. 202]

Handel, despite his marked German accent mocked in the above broadsheet, was nonetheless a staunch British subject; but technically he was an alien. He therefore decided to apply for naturalization; the documents read in part as follows:

HANDEL APPLIES FOR NATURALIZATION,
13 February 1727

To the Right Honourable The Lords Spiritual and Temporal in Parliament assembled,

The Humble Petition of George Frideric Handel
Sheweth, –
That your petitioner was born at Hall in Saxony, out of His Majestie's Allegiance, but hath constantly professed the Protestant Religion, and hath given Testimony of his Loyalty and Fidelity to His Majesty and the good of this Kingdom,
Therefore the Petitioner humbly prays, That he may be added to the Bill now pending, entituled 'An Act for Naturalisating LOUIS SECHEHAYE' And your petitione will ever pray, & c.,

George Frideric Handel.

FROM THE 'JOURNALS OF THE HOUSE OF LORDS', 13 February 1727

Hodie Ia *vice lecta est Billa*, intituled, 'An Act for naturalizing *Louis Sechehaye*.

A Petition of *George Frideric Handel*, was presented to the House, and read; praying to be added to the Bill, intituled, 'An Act for naturalizing *Louis Sechehaye*.'

It is ORDERED, That the said Petition do lie on the Table, till the said Bill be read a Second Time.

FROM THE 'JOURNALS OF THE HOUSE OF LORDS', 14 February 1727

George Frideric Handel took the Oath of Allegiance and Supremacy, in order to his Naturalization.

ORDERED, That the Petition of *George Frideric Handel*, praying to be added to the above-mentioned Bill, which was Yesterday ordered to lie on the Table till the Second Reading thereof, be referred to the said Committee. [Deutsch, pp. 202f.]

The opera house was still full, as *Colman's 'Opera Register'* assures us:

Apr. 4 Easter Tuesday, Admetus again, & was declared for Saturday, but Signa Faustina being taken very ill – no Opera was perform'd – during all this time the House filled every night fuller than ever was known at any Opera for so long together – 16 times.

But there were grave troubles. The leading singers were behaving impossibly, and during the performance of Bononcini's *Astianatte*, the Princess of Wales was a witness to a hair-pulling, screeching fight between Faustina and Cuzzoni, egged on by their respective admirers.

On Tuesday-night last [the 6th], a great Disturbance happened at the Opera, occasioned by the Partisans of the Two Celebrated Rival Ladies, Cuzzoni and Faustina. The Contention at first was only carried on by Hissing on one Side, and Clapping on the other; but proceeded at length to Catcalls, and other great Indecencies: And notwithstanding the Princess Caroline was present, no Regards were of Force to restrain the Rudenesses of the Opponents. [*British Journal*, 10 June 1727]

The deterioration is also discussed by Mrs Pendarves in a letter to her sister, Ann Granville, of 25 November 1727:

I doubt operas will not survive longer than this winter, they are now at their last gasp; the subscription is expired and nobody will renew it. The directors are always squabbling, and they have so

> many divisions among themselves that I wonder they have not broke up before; Senesino goes away next winter, and I believe Faustina, so you see harmony is almost out of fashion. [Deutsch, p. 218]

Handel produced three new operas for the season of 1727/8: *Riccardo Primo* (11 November 1727), *Siroe* (17 February 1728) and *Tolomeo* (30 April 1728), all with the great trio of Cuzzoni, Faustina and Senesino, but meanwhile a new work was conquering London and destroying the Academy: *The Beggar's Opera*, first given to an enchanted audience at Lincoln's Inn Fields on 29 January 1728. It was vulgar and bawdy; there were great tunes by John Christopher Pepusch to witty texts by John Gay; and it was thoroughly English and everyone could understand the words. It was the death knell for Handel's operas and the Italian singers:

> MRS. PENDARVES TO HER SISTER, ANN GRANVILLE
>
> Somerset House, 29th Jan. 1727–8.
>
> Yesterday I was at the rehearsal of the new opera composed by Handel: I like it extremely, but the taste of the town is so depraved, that nothing will be approved of but the burlesque. The Beggar's Opera entirely triumphs over the Italian one . . . [Deutsch, p. 220]

The whole sorry tale of the Academy's demise is summed up by Mainwaring:

> The perfect authority which HANDEL maintained over the singers and the band, or rather the total subjection in which he held them, was of more consequence than can well be imagined. It was the chief means of preserving that order and decorum, that union and tranquillity, which seldom are found to subsist for any long continuance in musical Societies. Indeed, all Societies, like the animal body, seem to carry in their very frame and frabric [*sic*], the seeds of their own dissolution. This happens sooner or later, only as those are forwarded or retarded by different causes.
>
> SENESINO, who, from his first appearance, had taken deep root, and had long been growing in the affections of those, whose right to dominion the most civilized nations have ever

acknowledged, began to feel his strength and importance. He felt them so much, that what he had hitherto regarded as legal government, now appeared to him in the light of downright tyranny. HANDEL, perceiving that he was grown less tractable and obsequious, resolved to subdue these Italian humours, not by lenitives, but sharp corrosives. To *manage* him he disdained; to controul him with a high-hand, he in vain attempted. The one was perfectly refractory; the other was equally outrageous. In short, matters had proceeded so far, that there were no hopes of an accommodation. The merits of the quarrel I know nothing of. Whatever they were, the Nobility would not consent to his design of parting with SENESINO, and HANDEL was determined to have no farther concerns with him. FAUSTINA and CUZZONI, as if seized with the contagion of discord, started questions of superiority, and urged their respective claims to it with an eagerness and acrimony, which occasioned a total dis-union betwixt them.

And thus the Academy, after it had continued in the most flourishing state for upwards of nine years, was at once dissolved.

The late Laureat [Colley Cibber], who, now and then, has some strokes of humour, (for dulness too hath its lucid intervals) diverts himself much on the subject of these musical frays. The unlucky effects of them at the marriage of the late Duke of Parma, he describes with that pert kind of pleasantry, that native *gaillardise* which attended him through life. The fondness for Italian Singers, he thinks unaccountable: the expence and trouble they occasion, exorbitant and ridiculous. He calls them costly Canary-birds; and on their behaviour at the marriage solemnity just mentioned above, laments as follows, 'What a pity it is, that these forward Misses and Masters of music, had not been engaged to entertain the court of some King of MOROCCO, that could have known a good Opera from a bad one! With how much ease would such a Director have brought them to better order?' – But, had he known any thing of the true[8] spirit of HANDEL, he would not have wished them under better government. It is true they mutinied, and rebelled at last. But the slaves of Asiatic and of African Monarchs, have often done as much.

He remained inflexible in his resolution to punish SENESINO for refusing him that submission, which he had been used to

> receive, and which he thought he had a right to demand: but a little pliability would have saved him abundance of trouble. The vacancy made by the removal of such a Singer was not easily supplied. The umbrage which he had given to many of the Nobility, by his implacable resentments against a person whose talents they so much admired, was likely to create him a dangerous opposition. For, tho' he continued at the Hay-market, yet, in the heat of these animosities, a great part of his audience would melt away . . . [pp. 106–12]

To which we may add, by way of a postscriptum, the following note in Shaftesbury's *Memoirs*:

> In the year 1727, Violent Parties were formed, between the 2 famous Singers, Faustini & Cuzzoni; and in the Election for Directors, Faustini's Party carried it. These Animosities were very prejudicial to the Interest of the Academy, and the Houses began to grow thinner upon it. The Beggar's Opera appearing soon after, gave such a Turn to the Town, that Opera's were generally neglected: And as their Expences were great, and their Receipt small, the Sums Subscribed for was determined in the Summer 1728. And tho' the Term of the Charter was then unexpired, yet the Fund for maintaining Opera's being exhausted, they ceased of course, – and the Singers left England. This is the real Cause of the discontinuance of Opera's at that time. [Deutsch, pp. 844f.]

On 1 June 1728 *Admeto* ended the season, and the Academy itself closed. The day before, the following ominous note had appeared in the newspapers:

> The General Court of the Royal Academy of Musick stands adjourn'd till 11 a-Clock on Wednesday the 5th of June next, in order to consider of proper Measures for recovering the Debts due to the Academy, and discharging what is due to Performers, Tradesmen, and others; and also to determine how the Scenes, Cloaths, etc. are to be disposed of, if the Operas cannot be continued . . . [Deutsch, p. 226]

It was the end of an era.

Handel seems to have had a working contract with the Academy and was not much affected by its financial troubles; for on 4 June 1728, we see him purchasing £700 South Sea Annuities (matured 1751). And a few years before, in 1723, he had moved into a handsome house in Brook Street off Grosvenor Square[9] where he would live until his death.

The sordid squabbles of the Italian singers and their adherents did not ultimately damage Handel's great reputation, which was to gain immeasurably by his active participation in the Coronation ceremonies of 1727, as will be seen in the following chapter.

NOTES

1 The KING subscribed 1000 *l.* and the Nobility 40,000 *l.* [original footnote]

2 Attilio Ariosti had arrived in London in 1716 but did not join the Academy until 1723; see pp. 102, 114. [H.C.R.L.]

3 Colman dated Cuzzoni's début too early, entering these notes some time after the first night. He also mixed the names of Cuzzoni and Faustina (Bordoni) who did not appear in London before 1726.

4 Fabrice alludes to Lotti's opera *Teofane*, produced at Dresden on the occasion of the marriage of the Electoral Prince on 2 September 1719. – The Wings were, in fact, Bononcini's patrons, while the Tories favoured Handel.

5 Manteuffel was a Saxon Minister. [Deutsch, p. 160]

6 The opera in rehearsal was *Admeto*. 'Basilisk' was the nickname of Lord Baltimore, the widowed Mrs Pendarves' most ardent suitor. Elizabeth Legh, of Adlington Hall, near Macclesfield in Cheshire, was a very keen amateur musician, a subscriber for much music, and was apparently in love with the inaccessible master himself. She was the daughter of a widower, owner of the old Hall, and sister of Charles Legh who later was on friendly terms with Handel. She never married. [Deutsch, p. 200f.]

7 Lady Cowper, like the Countess of Burlington and Sir Robert Walpole, a partisan of Faustina, wrote in her copy of the libretto, opposite her favourite's name: 'she is the devil of a singer'. [Deutsch, p. 201]

8 Having one day some words with CUZZONI on her refusing to sing *Falsa imagine* in OTTONE; Oh! Madame, (said he) je sçais [sais] bien que Vous êtes une veritable Diablesse: mais je Vous ferai sçavoir, moi, que je suis Beelzebub le *Chéf* des Diables. With this he took her up by the waist, and, if she made any more words, swore that he would fling her out of the window.

It is to be noted, that this was formerly one of the methods of executing criminals in some parts of Germany; a process not unlike that of the Tarpeian rock, and probably derived from it. [original footnote]

9 The house was under threat of demolition, but has now been preserved.

VI
The Coronation Music of 1727

KING GEORGE I set out for his beloved Hanover with its nearby Herrenhausen Castle in June 1727, leaving behind him a prosperous kingdom and a contented people. He was a hearty sixty-seven and no breath of ill-health had been noted by his attentive physicians. But on the highroad to Osnabrück, in a coach with his Private Secretary and Privy Councillor, the king was suddenly paralysed on 11 June 1727. His last words are recorded as 'Drive on, drive on.'[1] The news was rushed to London, where one rumour had it that he died from a surfeit of watermelons; another, less innocent, report stated that his long-suffering wife, Sophia Dorothea, confined to the grim fortress of Ahlden for thirty-two years as a punishment for her (totally unproved) adultery with the Swedish Count Königsmark, had sent a doom-ridden warning to her faithless and profligate husband. The Prime Minister, Sir Robert Walpole, 'well on the way to a new and loftier eminence',[2] was at dinner at his Chelsea house when the news reached him. *En deshabille* he leaped on a horse and rode at such a rate to Richmond that two horses died under him before he reached the Prince of Wales to inform him of the latter's dramatic change of status.

> The Prince was at Richmond in bed with his wife, when the Duchess of Dorset informed him of Sir Robert's presence. Half-dressed, the [new] King told him to go and take his orders from Spenser Compton; twenty-four hours later the Queen had circumvented this act of rash folly, and Sir Robert, who had expressed, not very convincingly, his willingness to occupy any subordinate position about the Court, was back in office, drawing

> up plans for an increased civil list and the discharge of royal debts. [Plumb, op. cit., p. 68]

The previous organist, William Croft, had died at Bath on 14 August, and on 18 August a new candidate, Maurice Green, 'the greatest Music Genius we have' was recommended by the Bishop of Salisbury. Green was appointed on 4 September; his official title was Organist and Composer of the Chapel Royal. The situation with Handel was slightly more complicated. He had been 'Composer of Musick for his Majesty's Chapel Royal' since 25 February 1723, at which time he had still been a German citizen (i.e., an alien) and not entitled to hold office in the Chapel Royal. His duties, writes Donald Burrows in a very instructive article,[3] 'seem to have been concerned with the provision of instrumentally accompanied ceremonial anthems for occasional royal services'. We have no evidence that Handel was on anything like good terms with his new monarch, but one hurdle had been cleared: the composer had been a naturalized British subject since 20 February 1727. Handel had been, of course, a favourite of George I, and in his son's boundless hatred for his father, George II had no particular obligation to Handel; but in the copy of Mainwaring owned by the Royal Library and containing Ms. notes in a hand remarkably like that of George III (a great lover of Handel), we read the following interpolation:

> That wretched little crooked ill-natured insignificant writer, Player and Musician, the late Dr Green, organist and composer to King George II who forbad his composing the Anthems of his Coronation October 22 1727, and ordered that G.F. Handel should not only have that great honour, but, except for the 1st choose his own words. He had but four weeks for doing this wonderful work which seems scarcely credible, as to the first Zadok the Priest it is probably the most perfect if possible of all His superb compositions. [Flower, p. 188]

It is not known by which means Handel ingratiated himself into the new king's (or queen's) favour, but the results of it were soon being spread about the town, and in the newspapers. By the beginning of September, the *Norwich Mercury* wrote that 'Mr Hendel, [*Sic*] the famous Composer to the Opera, is appointed by the King to compose the Anthem at the Coronation which is to be sung in Westminster-Abbey at the Grand Ceremony' (Deutsch, p. 213). When the decision had been made, the Archbishops of Canterbury and York wanted to instruct the foreigner Handel on the choice of the texts suitable for the occasion. 'I have read my Bible very well,' said the proud composer, 'and shall choose for myself.'[4]

Handel, now obviously unhampered by any financial restrictions, engaged a huge orchestra, and – as was the custom in the eighteenth century – a much smaller choir. In *Parker's Penny Post* of 4 October, we read:

> Mr Hendle [*sic*] has composed the Musick for the Abbey at the Coronation, and the Italian Voices, with above a Hundred of the best Musicians will perform; and the Whole is allowed by those Judges in Musick who have already heard it, to exceed any Thing heretofore of the same Kind: It will be rehearsed this Week, but the Time will be kept private, lest the Crowd of People should be an Obstruction to the Performers.

Rumours of the work's magnificence must have spread rapidly throughout London, for the day after the general rehearsal we read in another London paper (*Read's Weekly Journal*) that 'Yesterday there was a Rehearsal of Musick that is to be performed at their Majesties Coronation in Westminster Abbey, where was present the greatest Concourse of People that has been known' (Deutsch, p. 214). Another report gives us the size of the gigantic undertaking:

> [London] *October* 7. Yesterday there was a Rehearsal of the Coronation Anthem in Westminster-Abbey, set to Musick by the famous Mr Hendall: There being 40 voices, and about 160 Violins, Trumpets, Hautboys, Kettle-Drums, Bass's proportionable; besides an Organ, which was erected behind the Altar: And both the Musick and the Performers, were the Admiration of all the Audience. [*Norwich Gazette*, 14 October 1727]

This approximate size is confirmed by notes on Handel's autograph manuscripts, now part of the precious legacy of Handeliana in the

Royal Library (British Library). The editor of the excellent edition for Ernst Eulenburg, Damian Cranmer, writes: 'At the beginning of *The King shall rejoice* the composer has written against the voice parts "C[anto] 12, H[ughes] et 6, Freem[an]et 6, Church et 6, Wheely et 6, Gates et 6." This information is repeated four times in the same anthem, though not in any other.' This makes 35 male singers and 12 boys, a total of 47 singers. For some peculiar reason, everyone seems inclined to doubt this figure, Dr Cranmer saying it 'should perhaps not be taken as an exact record of the number in the choir at the coronation, being more likely a reflection of the composer's intentions before the event'. There seems, however, absolutely no reason whatever to doubt the generally large size of the musical forces which, together with the record of the equally gargantuan band for the *Fireworks Musick* a dozen years later, constitute authentic evidence of Handel's liking for large forces. Probably there was considerable difficulty in keeping these huge forces together. William Wake, the Archbishop of Canterbury, perhaps still miffed at his Handelian rebuff over the choice of the anthem texts (see p. 127), wrote in his Order of Service against *My heart is inditing*: 'The Anthem(s) in Confusion: all irregular in the Music' which Winton Dean (*New Grove*, p. 34) who discovered the entry, piously hopes 'may refer to a rehearsal'. One eye-witness (César de Saussure) on the other hand, wrote 'During the ceremony a band of the most skilful musicians, together with the finest voices in England, performed admirable music, conducted by the celebrated Mr Handel, who had composed the anthems sung at the Divine Service.'[5]

Nothing like it in living memory had ever been seen in the kingdom. On that splendid day of 11 October 1727 the Queen's rather ample figure glittered from head to foot with jewels, not only her own (which were fabulously valuable) but with a large quantity borrowed from all sorts of sources, public and private. The gigantic orchestra and chorus were arranged like an amphitheatre; in future years – when Handel arranged his forces in a similar fashion – the papers would state: 'The Musick to be disposed after the Manner of the Coronation Service' (*Esther*, May 1732; Deutsch, p. 289). Since the chorus of the Chapel Royal numbered only 36 (10 boys, 26 men), it seems that the newspaper announcement of 4 October quoted above, to the effect that there were also Italian singers (i.e., from the opera house), may have been true. Heidegger had his part in the coronation ceremonies, too, though not at the Abbey: he directed the illuminations at Westminster Hall. As to the actual quality of the performance, it may not have been up to the usual Handelian standards.

Possibly, too, the Chapel Royal Choir was itself not very good. It is significant that two independent and private sources suggest that Handel's later performances there also lacked his customary perfection. At the Prince of Wales's marriage to the Princess of Saxe Gotha at the Chapel Royal in St James's Palace (27 April 1736), the Earl of Egmont wrote 'an anthem composed by Hendel [*sic*] for the occasion was wretchedly sung . . .' (Deutsch, p. 405); and at the funeral service for Queen Caroline on 27 December 1737, the Duke of Chandos wrote to his nephew that Handel's Anthem 'was exceeding fine . . . but I can't say so much of the performance' (Deutsch, p. 443). But what is abundantly clear is the huge success of the four anthems, though *Zadok the Priest* has always been a special favourite, having been repeated at every subsequent coronation since 1727.

Donald Burrows, in his afore-mentioned article, has been able to discover interesting new facts about the choir and its insufficiency at the time Handel took charge of the coronation service.

> Five of the ten Chapel Royal boys had gone from the choir with broken voices in June and the pluralism amongst the Gentlemen was such that only one member of the Westminster Abbey choir was not accounted for from the ranks of the Chapel Royal. [op. cit. p. 471]

The list of singers Handel penned at the beginning of *The King Shall Rejoice* therefore seems to represent what the composer could have expected from a full complement of the Chapel Royal and Westminster Abbey choirs. As for the lists of the other anthems, that for *My Heart is Inditing* has been cancelled, and the title pages (covers) of the other two are no longer intact. The instrumentalists were formed round the King's Musick, which included the finest of the court trumpeters and the kettledrum player. Coronation liveries were provided for the Master and 33 orchestral players, of which 24 were traditionally entitled to wear coronation medals.

The records show, moreover, that the Lord Chamberlain paid Bernard Gates 42 guineas for additional female and male (not boy) singers, and Christopher Smith (J.C. Smith Sen.) for 57 'supernumerary' instrumentalists at three guineas each; therefore, Mr Burrows reckons, if the singers were paid at the same rate they must have numbered 14. The exact details (did boy sopranos mix with lady sopranos from the theatre?) can no longer be ascertained, but Handel's total of 47 voices, allowing for the depleted condition of the two choirs, but considering the substitutes and additional paid members, cannot have been all that wrong. As for the startling total of 160 instrumentalists, perhaps that figure referred to the total number of singers and orchestral players. If we put together 34 (Master and 33 musicians) of the King's Musick and 57 of Smith's 'extras' we have an orchestra of 92 which, added to 47 singers, gives us a grand total of 139 participants (as compared to '160' of the newspaper article). Thus there is rather convincing evidence for (including Handel) 140 performers of the 1727 Coronation anthems – an enormous group by any standards including today's.

Although only one rehearsal date (6 October, see above) has been confirmed, the singers were in fact paid for two: perhaps the first was not a public rehearsal, as we know the second to have been. Smith was paid for copying the anthems, and Christopher Shrider received £130 for 'putting up a large Organ in Westminster Abbey for the performance of Mr Handel's Vocal and Instrumental Musick at the Coronation of His Majesty and the Queen' (Burrows, p. 473). Apparently the Abbey authorities were very jealous of their instrument and the erection of a special one for such an event avoided disputes. And as for disputes, Mr Burrows offers the following from the Chapter Minutes of 14 November 1727:

> Order'd. That an Action be brought against Hues [Francis Hughes?] in the Name of the Dean for Assaulting & refusing his L^{dp} Entrance into the Choir the day of the performance of Musick there against their Maj^{ties} Coronation.

The musicians, it seems, were disposed in two pyramidal-shaped, separate galleries, which must have made communication difficult. When William Boyce, at the coronation of George III in 1761, tried to have the upper part of the main altar removed, he noted that 'the Late Mr Handel, who composed the Music [for the 1727 ceremony], often lamented his not having that part of the Altar taken away, as He, and all the Musicians concerned, experienced the bad effect it had by that obstruction' (Burrows, p. 471).

There are two contemporary sources for the order of the service. One is the printed order, based upon the research of Archbishop Wake's, and using:

> the Original Book of Archbishop Sancroft, all written by Himselfe, be Wch he Crown'd King James & Queen Mary. I found that his Grace had taken very great care and pains to examine the antient forms of this Office, & to draw up That wch He made use upon Them. But the King's Religion obliged Him to omit the whole Communion Service . . . My immediate predecessor Archbp Tenison, who Crown'd both Q Anne and his late Matie King George, took great pains to settle this Office and indeed he has succeeded so well in it, that in my Opinion a better form cannot be framed for the Coronation of His Majestie. But in that there is nothing of the Queen's Coronation: That part of the Office therefore may with very little change of some expressions be taken out of Sancroft's form. So that taking One of these for the King, the other for the Queen, the whole may be settled in one hour's time. [Burrows, p. 470]

Handel took *Let Thy Hand* and *Zadok* from the first two anthems of Sancroft's order, but the composer added 'Alleluja Amen' to the second (just as he later added his 'Alleluja' to Jennens' text of *Saul*, much to Jennens' annoyance, see below). This 'order' was delivered to all the participants on 20 September, and read 'The Form and Order of the Service that is to be performed . . . in the Coronation of their Majesties (1727)'; 100 copies were printed, and Handel must have been not a little astonished to see that the first of the Sancroft anthems (*Let Thy Hand*) had been entirely omitted, while there was a much longer version of *Zadok*, derived from the 1702 coronation.

It was proposed that the ceremony take place on 4 October, which meant that Handel really had little time in which to complete the anthems; in fact the date was, fortunately, postponed to the 11th. Since Handel's other two anthems do not use precisely the same texts as Sancroft's 1685 account, nor are they the same as those in the Form and Order of 1727, one may actually suppose that the composer compiled his own texts for them, especially since he 'manipulated' the text of *The King Shall Rejoice* by inserting the words of verse 5 ('Glory and worship hast thou laid upon him') between verses 1 and 2 of Psalm 21; while *My Heart is Inditing* is a shortened version of Purcell's for the 1685 service.

Fortunately we have Archbishop Wake's annotated copy of the 'Form and Order' (1727) in the Lambeth Palace Archives, but also another, which differs in some details from the 'Form and Order'. This second source, which was first published by Burrows (p. 471) is: 'The Order of Performing the Several Anthems at the Coronation of their Majesties King George the Second and Queen Carolina' copied by Jonathan Smith, Clerk of the Cheque, into the Chapel Royal Cheque Book. Burrows notes that 'it is the only contemporary source to present Handel's text for *My Heart is Inditing* accurately' and thus takes on a special authority. 'It can be seen that Wake added the words of *Let They Hand Be Strengthened* at the Inthronization: this is an unusual position for the anthem;

> It is tempting to suppose that, having discovered that Handel had already set this text, Wake inserted it where it least disturbed his numbering of the anthems. In the Cheque Book this anthem appears in its more usual context at the Recognition. The latter seems more likely to have been Handel's intention and may account for the lighter scoring of the anthem. It follows the 'sounding of the Trumpets and the beating of drums' at the acclamations and is the only one of Handel's coronation anthems that does not include these instruments, whose players may not have been available at that moment to the main body of performers [p. 471].'

Handel's anthems have been marked below with an asterisk:

ORDER OF SERVICE (Wake's annotations in *Italics*)	CHAPEL ROYAL CHEQUE BOOK
PROCESSION	
	O Lord, grant the King a long life Full Anthem (text as set by Child)
ENTRANCE	
Anthem I: I was glad *This was omitted and no Anthem at all Sung . . . by the Negligence of the Choir of Westminster*	I was glad *Full Anthem*
RECOGNITION	
*Anthem II: The King shall rejoice *The Anthem(s) in Confusion: All irregular in the Music*	*Let thy hand be strengthened Verse Anthem
LITANY	
The Choir singing the Responses to the Organ. *To shorten the Service let this be read*	The Litany to be read
ANOINTING	
Anthem III: Come Holy Ghost *This Hymn by mistake of the Music not sung: but the next Anthem instead of it*	Come Holy Ghost This Chanted for Shortness Sake
*Anthem IV: Zadok the Priest	*Zadok the Priest Verse Anthem
Anthem V: Behold, O God, our defender	Behold, O God, our defender This Chanted
CROWNING	
Anthem VI: Praise the Lord, O Jerusalem	*The King shall rejoice Verse Anthem
TE DEUM	
Anthem VII: We praise Thee, O God ['Anthem VII' deleted]	Te Deum of Gibbons' was sung

INTHRONISATION	
*Anthem VIII: Let thy hand be strengthened [text in full]	
AFTER HOMAGE	
*Anthem IX: My heart is enditing *[sic]*	*My heart is inditing Verse Anthem
COMMUNION	
The Organ plays and the Choir singeth: Anthem X: Let my Prayers come up into they presence	During Ye Offertory the Organ plays, till the Alms are done Collecting
The Choir sings: Therefore with angels . . .	Sanctus & c Sung in Musick
The Choir sings: Glory be to God on high	The Gloria in Excelsis Sung in Musick

It is tempting to see in both sources description of 'the Organ plays' a unique possibility for Handel to improvise a voluntary such as would have shaken the rafters of the venerable cathedral. The order of the anthems, then, seems to have been:

1. *Let Thy Hand Be Strengthened*
2. *Zadok the Priest*
3. *The King Shall Rejoice*
4. *My Heart is Inditing*

The order of Handel's autographs, however, in his own numberings is 2–1–3–4. Since this latter might seem a better musical sequence in which to perform the works, we have examined the four in the composer's own order.

Handel was by no means ignorant of the great anthem tradition in the country of his adoption, and there are indications that he had studied his predecessors well, especially of course the great Henry Purcell, whose Coronation anthem for James II, *My Heart is Inditing*, was obviously an inspiration for Handel's own choice of the text. (An even stronger case for Purcellian influence was, as we have already seen, the Utrecht *Te Deum* with its relationship to Purcell's *Te Deum and Jubilate for St Cecilia's Day* [1694].) There is no doubt that the composition of these four anthems marks a distinct watershed in Handel's musical life. They became the best known (and also the best loved) of his English settings and appealed to the ordinary man in a way that Italian opera never could. These anthems also used the most popular book in the English language as their basis, and Handel must have noted their profound success, though it can hardly be said that he heeded the message that their popularity showed: write in English and use the Bible. When he finally did understand, albeit unwillingly, that stubborn man had found the key to his permanent popularity with the British public. Thus the four anthems occupy a position in Handel's *œuvre* quite as important as the Latin church music had during the Roman sojourn. And can it be coincidence that, although the music to the coronation ceremony is almost all new, there are two movements of those Roman works, the 'Gloria Patri' from 'Nisi Dominus' and the same movement from 'Laudate pueri', which Handel suddenly quotes? The 'Nisi Dominus' forms the basis of the final fugue ('Alleluja') in *The King Shall Rejoice*; while in the conclusion to 'Laudate pueri', the entrance of the word 'amen' appears as shown in the Appendix, where its transformation in *Zadok the Priest*, can also be seen.

Not only is the running semiquaver line virtually identical in both pieces (in the same key, too: D major), but the stabbing quavers separated by quaver rests appear in the same kind of context. It could serve as a textbook example of the brilliant manner in which Handel was capable of transforming his own music. On another level, the striking arpeggio chains that begin 'Nisi Dominus' (which must have enchanted the Roman audience) become on an epochal scale the most devastating single effect in all the Coronation anthems: the beginning of *Zadok the Priest* with its own staggering series of arpeggios that end, of course, with that shattering choral entry, 'Zadok the Priest and Nathan the prophet anointed Solomon King'.

Even today, at every coronation, the central part of Zadok is, quite simply, awe-inspiring. The crucial moment is prepared by a long half cadence, to accompany the words 'and all the people rejoiced and said:'. Then comes the triple statement, 'God save the king! Long live the king! God save the king.' George II is described by his biographers as being rather stupid; one hardly needed to be a genius, however, to be overwhelmed by that anthem, which is the greatest public ceremonial music of its kind ever composed. It was designed to create an enormous effect in an enormous space, and it succeeded brilliantly.

An interesting feature of all except one (*Let Thy Hand be Strengthened*) of these anthems is the scoring: apart from the two oboes and three trumpets with kettledrums, there are three violin parts; moreover, the chorus is interestingly written in as many as seven parts which are not consistently so used but contracted or expanded at will. Sometimes there are simply five parts (SAATB), more often seven (SSAATBB). Invariably, however, there is only one tenor part.

Zadok the Priest takes place at a crucial juncture in the coronation ceremony. We quote from the description in the *Encyclopaedia Britannica* (Eleventh Edition, 1910–1, VII, p. 186):

> The ceremonies began the day before the coronation, the king being ceremonially conducted in a procession from the Tower of London to Westminster. There he reposed for the night, and was instructed by the abbot as to the solemn obligations of the kingly office. Early next morning he went to Westminster Hall, and there, among other ceremonies, as *rex regnaturus* was elevated into a richly adorned seat on the king's bench, called the Marble Chair. Then a procession with the regalia was marshalled, and led into the abbey church, the king wearing a cap of state on his head, and supported, by the bishops of Bath and Durham. A platform with thrones, & c., having been previously prepared, under the crossing, the king ascended it, and all being in order, the archbishop of Canterbury called for the Recognition, after which the king, approaching the high altar, offered a pall to cover it, and a pound of gold. Then a sermon appropriate to the occasion was preached by one of the bishops, the oath was administered by the archbishop, and the *Veni Creator* and a litany were sung. Then the king was anointed with oil on his hands, breasts, between the shoulders, on the shoulders, on the elbows, and on the head; finally he was anointed with the chrism on his head.

It is just before the anointing ceremony that *Zadok the Priest* is sung, and as the final cadence echoes in the vast cathedral, the Archbishop begins his ritual, 'Be thy head anointed with holy oil; be thy breast anointed with holy oil':

> Thus blessed and anointed, the king was vested, first with a silk dalmatic, called the *solobium sindonis*, then a long tunic, reaching to the ankles and woven with great golden images before and behind, was put upon him. He then received the buskins (*caligae*), the sandals (*sandalia*), and spurs (*calcaria*), then the sword and its girdle; after this the stole, and finally the royal mantle, four-square in shape and woven throughout with golden eagles. Thus vested, the crown of St Edward was set on his head, the ring placed on his wedding finger, and gloves drawn over his hands, and the golden sceptre, in form of an oath and cross, delivered to him. Lastly, the golden rod with the dove at the top was placed in the king's left hand. Thus consecrated, vested and crowned, the king kissed the bishops who, assisted by the nobles, enthroned him, while the *Te Deum* was sung. When a queen consort was also crowned [in 1727 she was, of course, Caroline], that ceremony immediately followed, and the mass with special collect, epistle, gospel and preface was said, and during it both king and queen received the sacrament in one kind. At the conclusion the king retired to a convenient place, surrounded by curtains, where the great chamberlain took off certain of the robes and substituted others for them, and the archbishop, still wearing his mass vestments, set other crowns on the heads of the king and queen, and with these they left the church.

In the time of Elizabeth I, the service had been conducted in Latin, but since the coronation of James I, English had been used.

Let Thy Hand Be Strengthened is a necessary contrast to the D major splendours of *Zadok*: the key changes to G and, of all the four Coronation anthems, this is the only one to dispense entirely with the ceremonial trumpets and kettledrums. The texture is correspondingly lighter, and the chorus is only in five parts (two alto voices):

> Let thy hand be strengthened and thy right hand be exalted.
> Let justice and judgement be the preparation of thy seat;
> Let mercy and truth go before thy face! Alleluja.

'Let justice and judgement . . .' is the most serious movement of the whole Coronation music, as befits the solemn words. It is a gravely beautiful *Larghetto* in E minor (again in Handel's favourite $^3/_4$ time), the only movement in minor key in all four anthems. Even the conclusion 'Alleluja' has a special kind of weight and seriousness to it.

Zadok the Priest has stolen the glory of all four anthems, but in fact the third, *The King Shall Rejoice*, while not having that overwhelming quality of its D major predecessor, is musically just as beautiful:

> The king shall rejoice in thy strength, O Lord.
> Exceeding glad shall he be of thy salvation.
> Glory and (great) worship hast thou laid upon him.
> Thou hast presented him with the blessings of goodness
> And hast set a crown of pure gold upon his head. Alleluja.

Handel had taken the first line and made a movement out of it, in D major and for seven-part choir (SAATBB) with oboes, three trumpets, kettledrums and the new, interesting, three violin parts. One notes that the orchestra is used with a skill as assured as that in *Zadok*: here the trumpets and kettledrums only enter at bar 15, the choir at bar 29; wave after wave of sound is added in the grand Handelian manner. The second movement drops the trumpets and drums and is in A major, with sprightly dotted rhythms, almost dance-like, and with plastic vocal writing rather like a piece of chamber-music. By the time we are in the middle of this glorious anthem, we realize an interesting fact: although much of the writing is polyphonic and there are the usual choral/instrumental imitations, there are no real fugues at all in these pieces. With the huge forces he had at his disposal, Handel experimented with blocks of sounds, and above all with overwhelming effects, in which three of the four anthems abound.

In *The King Shall Rejoice*, the climactic moment comes after movement two: Handel's curious and favourite 'A tempo giusto' is given a second indication 'Non tanto allegro' and, with a massive block of choral sound supported by long-held oboes and trumpets, we hear 'Glory and (great)[6] worship', the violins rushing across the texture in nimble semiquavers. We continue with another characteristic feature of these anthems: a movement in three-quarter time, which imparts a swaying, forward motion to the music. The final movement is one of Handel's 'fugues' which are not real fugues at all but provide a thrilling conclusion: one is reminded of the final chorus in *Messiah*, where the construction is very similar, even to the monumental *Adagio* conclusion: simple, sublime.

The words, slightly compressed, of the Purcell anthem that Handel calls No. 4 are as follows:

My heart is inditing of a good matter:
I speak of the things which I have made unto the King.
King's daughters were among thy honourable women.
Upon thy right hand did stand the Queen in vesture of gold.
Kings shall be thy nursing fathers, and Queens thy nursing mothers.

We are suddenly in another world. Although there are trumpets and drums that enter with characteristic drama only at bar 73, the tone of this anthem is quite different. For one thing, we have extensive use of solo voices, and the whole quality, the fabric of the music has altered: this graceful yet sturdy music was used for that part of the coronation in which Queen Caroline was crowned. With his usual understanding of the difference between the sexes, Handel has created a graceful tribute to a Queen of whom he grew increasingly fond. The end is, of course, suitably monumental. If we perform the works in the order of Handel's autographs – and in this case, also the original position in the 1727 ceremony – this will be the quartet's conclusion. We are left marvelling at Handel's sure-footed grasp of that which was involved, and required, for such a coronation ceremony, and how he ensured that the final result was simple, monumental, and capable of being performed by a chorus and orchestra of about 140 performers. In the music of Handel's German precursors there is nothing to compare with it, for it is very unlikely that he can have seen a copy of the music, possibly composed by H.I.F. Biber, supposedly for the consecration of Salzburg Cathedral in 1628 but now believed to have been composed half a century later, the *Missa Salisburgensis* – to give the work its new title – and Hymnus 'Plaudite tympana' for 16 vocal, 35 instrumental, 2 organ parts and basso continuo; works which are remarkably Handelian in their elemental forces, though both have their firm roots in the *cori spezzati* tradition of St Mark's in Venice. And as for the immediate British tradition, there was only Purcell, perhaps on a different scale but with similar power and, in the case of the Coronation anthem, similar content (but in considering Handel's British precursors, we must remember that it was not fashionable, in the eighteenth century, to recall the musical past with nostalgia: it was Handel himself who created that new tradition, i.e. of a music that continued in the repertoire even after its composer's death). In the Coronation music Handel had rendered great English texts instantly comprehensible to thousands of men and women, and had transported his enormous dramatic abilities away from the opera house into the cathedral. Many people must have found Westminster Abbey a more suitable venue for the composer's talents than Haymarket.

The main purpose of coronation music is, of course, as part of a coronation ceremony; and Handel must have been unhappy that he could hardly expect (as it were) a repeat performance in the foreseeable future. But with his usual zeal, he soon found that the Coronation anthems could be reworked or re-used. When *Esther* was revised in 1732, we have noted that the composer specially drew attention to the Oratorio's being 'disposed after the Manner of the Coronation Service.' Not only 'disposed after' but also 'including': for *Esther* in its revised state encompassed *My Heart is Inditing* complete and the opening and closing of *Zadok the Priest* (omitting, that is, bars 31–62, 'and all the people rejoiced'). The words of *Zadok* were changed to 'Blessed are all they that fear the Lord', with the necessary small adjustments, but Handel, rather curiously, retained the words 'God save the king'. In this new version, the composer employed it again as the final chorus of the Occasional Oratorio (1746). The other two anthems were incorporated into *Deborah* (1733). (The details of the transformations may be seen in the miniature scores of the original anthems [Nos. 1701–4, 1980].) But the works were also repeated in their original guises, sometimes in conjunction with the Utrecht *Te Deum* and *Jubilate*. They have never left the public's consciousness and their popularity is, today, higher than at any time since their composer's lifetime.

NOTES

1 D. Hume, *A History of England*, London 1875, p. 591.
2 H. Plumb, *The First Four Georges*, London 1970, p. 64.
3 'Handel and the 1727 Coronation,' *Musical Times* CXVIII (1977), p. 469ff.
4 This particular anecdote comes from Burney 'Sketch of the Life of Handel', in *An Account of the Musical Performance* (1785), p. 34. The quotation, in context, reads: 'At the coronation . . . HANDEL had the words sent to him, by the bishops, for the anthems; at which he murmured, and took offence, as he thought it implied his ignorance of the Holy Scriptures . . .' There follows the quotation.
5 *César De Saussure, Lettres et Voyages . . . en Allemagne, en Holland et en Angleterre, 1725–1727*, Lausanne 1903, p. 260.
6 The autograph omits the word 'great'.

VII
The second Italian interlude 1729 & the decline of opera in London 1730–1736

A NEW SCHEME was afoot: Handel and Heidegger were to form a partnership; they put their proposition to the Academy in January 1729. A contemporary diary reports:

FROM THE DIARY OF VISCOUNT PERCIVAL,
18 January 1729

I went to a meeting of the members of the Royal Academy of Musick: where we agreed to prosecute the subscribers who have not yet paid; also to permit Hydeger and Hendle to carry on operas without disturbance for 5 years and to lend them for that time our scenes, machines, clothes, instruments, furniture, etc. It all past off in a great hurry, and there was not above 20 there. [Deutsch, p. 234]

Heidegger was already in Italy at the end of 1728, when he fell under the spell of the great castrato Farinelli (Carlo Broschi); he also wanted to retain Cuzzoni and Faustina, but Handel wanted new talent. Arch-intriguer Rolli wrote to Senesino, who had gone to Venice, as follows:

London, 25th [January] 1729.

Heydeger returned and said that he had not found any singers in Italy; he protested that he did not wish to undertake anything without the two ladies; he spoke only of them and proposed Farinello. In the end, hearing that your friends desired you back, he gave way, and you are once more on good terms with him. He was thinking more of a lucrative subscription than of anything else and he was calculating well, for in this way the two parties and your friends in each would be helping to fill up the annual subscription with 20 pounds per head. This was the scheme, on the basis of which, already known to you, I wrote you the first letter. But Handel was not to be duped by such a paltry stratagem. He revealed his rival's rascally deceit: the only aim of his useless and ridiculous voyage was to profit himself alone. So he [Handel] declared that there was need of a change and has renewed the old system of changing the singers in order to have the opportunity of composing new works for new performers. His new plans find favour at Court and he is satisfied. Faustina is not required, but they have lent quite a favourable ear to you. They want Farinello and Cuzzona, if she does not remain in Vienna, and the promoters are such as can pay. Mylord Bingley is at the head of the project, but the theatre has still to be found. So they called in Heydeger and they have granted him 2200 pounds with which to provide the theatre, the scenery and the costumes.

Handel will have 1000 pounds for the composition, whether it will be by himself or by whomsoever else he may choose. The subscription will be 15 guineas per person, and so far it is thought sufficient. A total of 4000 pounds is proposed for the singers – two at a 1000 pounds each with a benefit performance, and the rest, etc. Handel will shortly depart for Italy, where he will select the cast. Three representatives of the subscribers will go with him, in order to examine them, etc. That is the new system. Riva is already suffering from it, for you can well see what a very ill wind is blowing for Bononcino. So do tell Faustina that her dear little Handel will be coming to Italy, but not for her. Have I not already written you that she would after all have found him quite contrary to her opinions?

Poor dear! I am *so* sorry! This treatment – and I say it for all to hear – is well deserved by all who sacrifice their friends, in order to make the most base advances to their enemies. Expenses must, as I fear, now exclude you; otherwise I would not doubt that sooner or later I should find you here once more, in despite of the Man whose aim it has been to prevent your return. Farinello will come, attracted perhaps by the bait of a benefit performance, for no one – except you – has ever refused him [Handel], so brazen is his begging for charity.

I hear that Cuzzona has surmounted all difficulties in Vienna and it is quite probable that she will remain there in regular service. Without a doubt she made a good impression on the Emperor himself and on the Empress; and over there the company of one's own husband makes a better impression than that of someone else's . . . [Deutsch, pp. 235f.]

Where Heidegger failed, Handel thought he might succeed, as he had before, in engaging singers in Italy. He left London at the beginning of February and proceeded to Venice, where he tried, without success, to engage Senesino. Rolli writes to Senesino on 16 May 1734: 'The news . . . concerning Händel's arrival in Venice was that you gave him a cold shoulder and that he was complaining . . . about it, adding that Princes have a long reach . . .' (Deutsch, p. 242). And we have another report:

SIR LYONELL PILKINGTON TO HIS BROTHER-IN-LAW, GODFREY WENTWORTH, AT BURTHWAIT

Paris, 4th (15th) May 1729.

You seem to despair of any more operas in England, but I fancy there are some hopes yet of their returning. Handel is doing his endeavour in Italy to procure singers, and I fancy his journey will be of more effect than Heidegger's, but I'm told Senesino is playing an ungrateful part to his friends in England, by abusing 'em behind their backs, and saying he'll come no more among 'em. A Frenchwoman, whom I never will forgive for supposing we English can have a fault, told me the other day, that Senesino had built a fine house, with an inscription over the door to let the world know 'twas the folly of the English had laid the foundation of it. Is this pardonable? [Deutsch, p. 242]

In his absence, we learn (Mrs Pendarves to her sister, Ann Granville; Deutsch, p. 238) that 'The subscription for the Opera next winter goes on very well, to the great satisfaction of all musical folks' (16 February 1729).

Did Handel take any music of his own to perform en route?

It seems possible that he did: there has long been considerable controversy about the dating of his beautiful Latin Motet 'Sileti venti'; some have placed it in his first Italian visit of 1707–9, some later. The autograph, in the King's Library, reveals that it was written on Dutch or British paper such as Handel used in England.[1] Thus, this spirited and sophisticated music, which in its final 'Amen' includes a revealing quotation from part of the Roman Vespers of 1707, seems to have been composed in England for a trip abroad. We know that from Venice, Handel proceeded to Rome. Does the quotation, in 'Sileti venti', mean that Handel wanted to give it in Rome, where his various friends of the purple would have recognized and remembered the original? Two contemporary reports confirm Handel's presence in Rome, one by Mainwaring:

> On his arrival at Rome, he received a very friendly and obliging letter of invitation from cardinal COLONNA, with a promise of a very fine picture of his Eminence. But, hearing that the Pretender was then at the Cardinal's, he prudently declined accepting both the invitation and the picture. [p. 113]

and one by Shaftesbury:

> In the Spring 1729 a fresh Subscription was on foot for performing Opera's, under the Patronage of The Princess Royal. Fifty Opera's were engaged to be performed, for a Subscription of 15 Guineas a Ticket; and they were to be under the Direction of Mr Heidegger, and Mr Handell, who were joint Partners in the Thing and their Partnership was for 5 Years. To Execute this Scheme, Mr Handell went to Italy, where he hired Strada, Bernachi &c^a^. When at Rome Mr Handell waited on his old Friend, Cardinal Ottoboni, who received him with the greatest marks of Friendship and Esteem. [Deutsch, p. 845]

The new singers included Antonio Bernacchi, a well-known male soprano castrato who had been in London years before and he participated in the revival of *Rinaldo* in 1717 (his salary was now £1,200); Antonia Margherita Merighi, a contralto profundo (£800); Anna Strada (Signora del Pò), soprano (£600); Annibale Pio Fabri, called 'Balino', tenor (£450); and the German bass, Johann Gottfried Riemschneider (£300), who had been Handel's school-mate at Halle (Deutsch, p. 243).

On his way back to London, Handel stopped in Hanover, and by the beginning of July the new cast could be announced in the London *Daily Journal* (2 July 1729):

> Mr Handel, who is just returned from Italy, has contracted with the following Persons to perform in the Italian Opera's, vz.
>
> Signor Bernachi, who is esteem'd the best Singer in Italy.
>
> Signora Merighi, a Woman of a very fine Presence, an excellent Actress, and a very good Singer – A Counter Tenor.
>
> Signora Strada, who hath a very fine Treble Voice, a Person of singular Merit.
>
> Signor Annibal Pio Fabri, a most excellent Tenor, and a fine Voice.
>
> His Wife, who performs a Man's Part exceeding well.
>
> Signora Bartoldi, who has a very fine Treble Voice; she is also a very genteel Actress, both in Men and Womens Parts.
>
> A Bass Voice from Hamburgh, there being none worth engaging in Italy. [Deutsch, pp. 243f.]

On 10 October, some of the new singers 'had the Honour of a private Performance before their Majesties at Kensington; when the Harpsichord was played by Mr Handell, and Their Performances were much approved' (*Norwich Gazette*, 18 October 1729; Deutsch, p. 245).

Handel's new opera was *Lotario*, first given at King's Theatre on 2 December 1729 with Bernacchi in the title role and including Strada, Fabri, Merighi, Bertolli and Riemschneider. We have an entertaining account of the dress rehearsal by Mrs Pendarves in a letter to her sister, Ann Granville:

> [29?] November 1729
>
> Bernachi has a vast compass, his voice mellow and clear, but not so sweet as Senesino, his manner better; his person not so good, for he is as big as a Spanish friar. Fabri has a tenor voice, sweet, clear and firm, but not strong enough, I doubt, for the stage: he

> sings like a gentleman, without making faces, and his manner is particularly agreeable; he is the greatest master of musick that ever sang upon the stage. The third is the bass, a very good distinct voice, without any harshness. La Strada is the first woman; her voice is without exception fine, her manner perfection, but her person *very bad*, and she makes *frightful mouths*. La Merighi is the next to her; her voice is not extraordinarily good or bad, she is tall and has a very graceful person, with a tolerable face; she seems to be a woman about forty, she sings easily and agreeably. The last is Bertoli, she has neither voice, ear, nor manner to recommend her; but she is a perfect beauty, quite a Cleopatra, that sort of complexion with regular features, fine teeth, and when she sings has a smile about her mouth which is extreme pretty, and I believe has practised to sing before a glass, for she has never any distortion in her face.
>
> The first opera is Tuesday next, I have promised Mrs Clayton to go with her. [Deutsch, p. 247]

But in the event *Lotario* was not a success. Mrs Pendarves wrote to her sister that it 'really is not so meritorious as Mr Handel's generally are . . . Bernachi . . . is not approved of . . . [he] does not suit the English ears. Strada and the rest are very well liked.' Rolli wrote to Riva that 'Everyone considers it a very bad opera' (Deutsch, 249); but Handel (reported Rolli) said Strada 'sings better than the two who have left us' (Cuzzoni and Faustina).

> There is a certain Bertolli, a Roman girl who plays men's parts. Oh! my dear Riva, if you could only see her perspiring under her helmet – I am sure you would fall in love with her in your most Modenese fashion! She is a pretty one! There is also a bass from Hamburg [Riemschneider], whose voice is more of a natural contralto than a bass. He sings sweetly in his throat and nose, pronounces Italian in the Teutonic manner, acts like a sucking-pig, and looks more like a *valet* than anything. Oh, he is fine, I can tell you! They are putting on *Giulio Cesare* because the audiences are falling away fast. I think the storm is about to break on the head of our proud *Orso* [Bear]. Not all beans are for market, especially beans so badly cooked as this first basketful. Aeydeger has won great praise for his dresses and not a little for

> his scenery in which at least he never sinks below *mediocrity*. And yet the great public failed to appear on the first night. We shall see what we shall see. [Deutsch, pp. 249f.]

After all the great initial hopes, the Opera was foundering again. Mrs Pendarves writes to her sister.

> Pall Mall, 20 Dec. 1729
>
> The opera is too good for the vile taste of the town: it is condemned never more to appear on the stage after this night. I long to hear its dying song, poor dear swan. We are to have some old opera revived, which I am sorry for, it will put people upon making comparisons between these singers and those that performed before, which will be a disadvantage among the ill-judging multitude. The present opera is disliked because it is too much studied, and they love nothing but minuets and ballads, in short the *Beggar's Opera* and *Hurlothrumbo*[2] are only worthy of applause. [Deutsch, p. 250]

On 24 February 1730, Handel's new opera, *Partenope*, was first given, with Strada in the title role and other parts for Merighi, Bernacchi, Bertolli, Fabri and Riemschneider. In studying Handel's achievements and his failures, we now begin to glimpse the extent of his persistence and dogged attachment to his favourite music-form: this time Handel tried his hand at a type of *opera burlesque* in an almost desperate attempt to find a popular new genre. This too, however, found no success, the only positive development being that Walsh now published the score and became Handel's regular publisher henceforth; Handel's music having been pirated for years, the composer obviously considered it better to join forces with that clever and successful British publisher.

Tolomeo, thoroughly revised with twelve new numbers, was now revived (19 May 1740) and received exactly as many performances – seven – as on its first run in 1728.

Rolli gleefully describes Handel's and Heidegger's failures:

ROLLI TO RIVA IN VIENNA (Translated)

London, 12th June, 1730.

> I shall barely answer you on the matter of that *Coppia Eidegrendeliana* [Heidegger-Handel pair] and their worthless operas. Because in truth they succeed no better than they deserve. The musicians will be paid, and that is all that can be done. I perceive besides that either there will be no operas in the new season or there will be the same Company, which is most certainly going from bad to worse. Strada is liked by the very few who wish to forget Cuzzona – as the rest of the rhyme goes they are after all most similar: *I ask your pardon, Sir*. With respect to my ears you were a thousand times right, but as far as my eyes are concerned, my dear *Signor Giuseppe*, you were a thousand times wrong . . .
>
> Marchetto Rizzi, a few days before his death, sent this man Goupy[3] a caricature of Cuzzona and Farinello singing a duet. Goupy added Eideger in a sitting posture with his face turned up, and it was printed in honour and glory of that great band of rogues – the singers. [Deutsch, pp. 234f.]

Handel realized he must replace Bernacchi with his former castrato lead, Senesino, for the 1730/I season. The London public welcomed back their favourite in a revival of Handel's *Scipione*. 'Senesino being return'd charm'd much' (*Colman's 'Opera Register'*, 3 November 1730; Deutsch, p. 262). *Partenope* was the next Handelian revival (2 December 1730), also with Senesino as Armindo.

A particular and private grief was the death of Handel's mother, Dorothea, on 16 (27) December 1730. In the funeral sermon Georg Friedrich was mentioned as standing 'in especial grace by reason of his exceptional knowledge of music' (Deutsch, p. 265). Altogether Handel was greatly attached to his family and corresponded with them regularly, especially his brother-in-law Michael Dietrich Michaelsen.

The composer had more luck with his next opera, *Poro* (2 February 1731); Senesino was in the title role. The book was based on Metastasio's famous *Alessandro nell'Indie*, and *Poro* ran for twenty performances within the year.

A remarkable revival with which Handel was only marginally connected was *Acis and Galatea*, which was given at the Theatre Royal in Lincoln's Inn Fields on 13 March 1731 (some of the singers had worked with Handel): it was the first performance of the work outside Cannons and was a milestone – though not directly of his undertaking – in the composer's career. It showed the London public what a Handel opera was like sung in English.

Handel and Heidegger next tried their hand at reviving the perennially popular but now revised *Rinaldo* (6 April 1731) with Senesino in the title role: it was a modest success (six performances), and a few weeks later they tried *Rodelinda* again, which also proved to be quite successful (eight performances).

But in all this, Bononcini had somehow lost entirely. The Diary of Viscount Percival for 31 August 1731 relates that Handel's 'fire and spirit' far surpassed his brother musicians and 'gave him the preference over Bononcini with the English. So that after some years' struggle to maintain his throne, Bononcini abdicated . . .' (Deutsch, p. 277).

Handel's first new opera for the 1731/2 season was *Ezio* (15 January 1732) with two new members of the cast, Giovanni Battista Pinacci (tenor) and the formidable bass singer, Antonio Montagnana. The king attended four evenings, sometimes with the royal family, but *Ezio* was nonetheless a disastrous failure and after a fifth performance it disappeared forever from the repertory. *Giulio Cesare*, when revived with Senesino and Strada, was not welcomed (four performances). The next new opera, *Sosarme* (15 February 1732) with Strada, Senesino (title role) and Montagnana, fared considerably better but Handel made slashing cuts in a forlorn effort to please his dwindling public. The connoisseurs relished the new work – Viscount Percival thought it 'one of the best I ever heard' (Deutsch, p. 285) – but *Colman's 'Opera Register'* noted 'for many nights much crowded to some people [*sic*] admiration' (Deutsch, p. 286).

Then came another straw in the wind: a private, staged performance of Handel's old English-language masque, *Esther*, at the Crown and Anchor Tavern on Handel's forty-seventh birthday, 23 February 1732. It is thought the composer attended, though the performance was not of his doing. Viscount Percival considered 'this oratoria [*sic*] of religious opera is exceeding fine, and the company were highly pleased . . .' (Deutsch, p. 286). *Esther* was such a triumph that another (unauthorized) performance was arranged for 20 April. Handel's royal harpsichord pupil, Princess Anne, wanted him to mount his own setting of the work at the King's Theatre. The composer revised the work and enlarged it, and 'the House will be fitted up in a decent Manner for the Audience. The Musick to be disposed after the Manner of the Coronation Service' (Deutsch, p. 289); in other words, they would try to give an operatic gloss to the theatre (where the Bishop of London had forbidden oratorios to be staged like an opera), the forces being arranged in pyramid fashion. The end result was a hasty patchwork, with Italian arias interposed, but the public loved it and Handel used his best singers including Senesino, Montagnana and Strada, as well as British forces.

Hardly had the public excitement about *Esther* died down when another unauthorized performance of *Acis* was announced by members of the English Opera at the New Theatre (Haymarket), opposite the Handel-Heidegger establishment, for 6 May 1732. Handel could hardly take this without a rebuttal; later in May, he put on his own version of *Acis*, fleshed out with extracts from his own Neapolitan *Aci e Galatea* (in Italian!) and *Brockes Passion* as well. There were beautiful costumes and 'backdrops'; the public was enchanted. Shaftesbury reports:

> In this Spring (1732) a 4th Ann^{l} Subscrp^{n} was set on foot for the ensuing Season, upon the same terms, but the Subs^{n} for the 50 Opera's for this Season, having been all performed about the end of May, the Town being yet very full, M^{r} H: perform'd in the Hay Market the Masque of Acis & Galatea; This was perf^{d} in Italian, & some additional Songs were thrown into it, & the Stage was disposed in a pretty Manner. It had happened that the preceding Season, only 49 Opera's had been perform'd instead of 50 Subscribed for, so that the Subscribers Tickets of last Year were admitted to this Performance, as were the Subs^{rs} themselves. This Entertainment was performed at least twice which in reality was to the Subscribers of this Year a present of 2 Performances gratis. And in the Spring it was that M^{r} H: perform'd the Oratorio of Esther in Publick, to which he made considerable Additions. [Deutsch, p. 845]

One would have thought that Handel, who could hardly be called unintelligent, would have received the message his public was giving him: we want English words. But no, Handel's stubborn Saxon mind was still fixed on Italian opera, and his next offering, *Orlando*, perhaps in many ways his greatest, was already finished when he received the following letter from his old partner, Aaron Hill:

Dec. 5, 1732

SIR,

I ought sooner, to have return'd you my heart thanks, for the silver ticket which has carried the obligation farther, than to myself; for my daughters are, both such lovers of musick, that it is hard to say, which of them is most capable of being charm'd by the compositions of Mr *Handel*.

Having this occasion of troubling you with a letter, I cannot forbear to tell you the earnestness of my wishes, that, as you have made such considerable steps towards it, already, you would let us owe to your inimitable genius, the establishment of *musick*, upon a foundation of good poetry; where the excellence of the *sound* should be no longer dishonour'd, by the poorness of the *sense* it is chain'd to.

My meaning is, that you would be resolute enough, to deliver us from our *Italian bondage*; and demonstrate, that *English* is soft enough for Opera, when compos'd by poets, who know how to distinguish the *sweetness* of our tongue, from the *strength* of it, where the last is less necessary.

I am of opinion, that male and female voices may be found in this kingdom, capable of every thing, that is requisite; and, I am sure, a species of dramatic Opera might be invented, that, by reconciling reason and dignity, with musick and fine machinery, would charm the *ear*, and hold fast the *heart*, together.

Such an improvement must, at once, be lasting, and profitable, to a very great degree; and would, infallibly, attract an universal regard, and encouragement.

I am so much a stranger to the nature of your present engagements, that, if what I have said, should not happen to be so practicable, as I conceive it, you will have the goodness to impute it only to the zeal, with which I wish you at the head of a design, as solid and unperishable, as your musick and memory. I am,

Sir,

Your most obliged,

And most humble Servant,
A. Hill.
[Deutsch, p. 299]

To start the 1732/3 season, Handel first put on one of his pasticcios and then revised *Tolomeo* again, adding half-a-dozen new numbers for his new singers (2 January 1733); it received a very modest four performances.

The new opera, *Orlando* (27 January 1733), with Senesino in the title role was much appreciated by the cognoscenti (*Colman's 'Opera Register'* notes 'extraordinary fine & magnificent'), and the king attended on 3 February. But despite critical acclaim, this opera, with its potent magic scenes and supernatural idiom, only ran for ten performances and was never revived. And within Handel's operatic family, dissension seethed: John West, Earl of Delaware, writes to Charles, Duke of Richmond:

> There is a Spirit got up against the Dominion of Mr Handel, a subscription carry'd on, and Directors chosen, who have contracted with Senesino, and have sent for Cuzzoni and Farinelli . . . [Deutsch, pp. 303f.]

In short, a rival opera – mutiny – was being bruited about town, the chief rival composer to be Nicola Porpora (later Haydn's teacher), and the chief patron the Prince of Wales who was in this, as in all things, in opposition to his father in the tried and true Hanoverian tradition. The new organization was to be called the Opera of the Nobility.

Meanwhile Handel had pondered the success of his English masques (*Acis, Esther*), now turned into an opera (of sorts) and an oratorio (of sorts). He therefore concocted a pasticcio which turned out to be a kind of 'artist's retrospective', plundering everything from the 'Roman Vespers' to the Coronation anthems but with a few new and good pieces. Samuel Humphreys furnished the word-book and dedicated it to Queen Caroline, and the first performance of *Deborah*, with mammoth forces – 'near a hundred performers, among whom about twenty-five singers', wrote Viscount Percival on 27 March 1733 (Deutsch, p. 309) – occurred at King's Theatre on 17 March 1733.

For the first night the prices were doubled: the public fumed, the newspapers raged. Shaftesbury wrote:

> In the Spring 1733, Mr Handell finding that the Oratorio of Esther, had been well received, [produced] the Oratorio of Deborah, which he reckoned into the number of the 50 Opera's Subscribed for, and – as he had taken great Pains, and as this was a new kind of Musick attended with some Extraordinary Expence, and more over for his own Benefit, he took double Prices, Viz^{t} a Guinea for Pit & Box's. This Indiscreet Step disgusted the Town, and he had a very thin House; however the great Merit of the Piece prevail'd, so far, that it had a considerable run, and was received with great Applause. [Deutsch, pp. 846f.]

Lady A. Irwin, writing to her friend Lord Carlisle on 31 March, believed that Handel

> thought, encouraged by the Princess Royal, it had merit enough to deserve a guinea, and the first time it was performed at that price, exclusive of subscribers' tickets, there was but a 120 people in the House. The subscribers being refused unless they would pay a guinea, they, insisting upon the right of their silver tickets, forced into the House, and carried their point. I was at this entertainment on Tuesday [the 27th]; 'tis excessive noisy, a vast number of instruments and voices, who all perform at a time, and is in music what I fancy a French ordinary in conversation.' [Deutsch, pp. 309f.]

The influential *Craftsman* now joined the fray in a long article in its issue of 7 April 1733, wherein we read:

> The Rise and Progress of Mr *H-l's* Power and Fortune are too well known for me now to relate. Let it suffice to say that He was grown so insolent upon the sudden and undeserved Increase of both, that He thought nothing ought to oppose his imperious and extravagant Will. He had, for some Time, govern'd the *Opera's*, and modell'd the *Orchestre*, without the least Controul. No Voices, no *Instruments* were admitted, but such as flatter'd his Ears,

> though they shock'd those of the Audience. *Wretched Scrapers* were put above the *best Hands* in the *Orchestre*. No Musick but *his own* was to be allowed, though every Body was weary of it; and he had the Impudence to assert, *that there was no Composer in* England *but Himself*. Even *Kings* and *Queens* were to be content with whatever low Characters he was pleased to assign them, as it was evident in the case of Signior *Montagnana*; who, though a *King*, is always obliged to act (except an angry, rumbling Song, or two) the most insignificant Part of the whole Drama. This Excess and Abuse of Power soon disgusted the Town; his Government grew odious; and his *Opera's* grew empty. However this Degree of Unpopularity and general Hatred, instead of humbling him, only made him more furious and desperate . . .

Handel reacted in a fury, dismissing the mutinous Senesino out of hand; the singer made a farewell speech at the Opera's final performance and then took the whole Italian company, except the faithful Signora Strada, to join the rival opera house, which constituted itself on 15 June 1733.

A recently discovered document shows graphically the precarious financial situation of the Handel-Heidegger opera company during the season 1732/3. The authors[4] who describe this new manuscript's content conclude with the statement that 'At the most optimistic estimates, this company might barely have broken even on its actual expenses . . .' There was certainly a dogged determination about G.F. Handel! As if nothing had happened, he decamped for Oxford at the invitation of the University's Vice-Chancellor; Handel was supposed to receive an honorary doctorate but refused. At the Sheldonian Theatre he gave five oratorio performances, including his new contribution to the events, *Athalia*, which brought him a handsome income; at one concert, 3,700 people were in the audience. *Acis and Galatea* was also given (at Christ Church hall). 'It is computed that the famous Mr Handell cleared by his Musick at Oxford upwards of £2,000', wrote the *Norwich Gazette*. Handel had the Opera orchestra with him, but of the old company only Signora Strada was present.

For his forthcoming season 1733/4, Handel revived *Ottone* (13 November 1733) with many new singers, including the faithful

Margarita Durastanti who was now a mezzo-soprano and had obviously come to help in an emergency. Apart from pasticcios, Handel was now working on a new opera, *Arianna*; but the big social events of the season were at the rival house in Lincoln's Inn Fields, where Porpora was conducting Handel's former singers, now strengthened by the arrival of Cuzzoni. Handel's audience largely decamped to hear the 'modern' music of a leading Neapolitan composer.

Old-fashioned though he may have been considered, *Arianna in Creta*, when it was first produced on 26 January 1732, was a notable success. *Colman's 'Opera Register'* noted 'very good & perform'd very often – Sigr Carestino sung surprisingly well: a new Eunuch . . .' (Deutsch, p. 343). The king remained loyal to Handel ('sitting by himself at the Haymarket', wrote one lady). In fact relations with the whole royal family remained unclouded by operatic squabbles, and Handel was asked to compose a wedding anthem for his pupil, Princess Anne, who married William of Orange on 14 March 1734. On the eve, Handel's *Parnasso in Festa*, a pasticcio largely taken from *Athalia* (as yet unknown in London), was given at the King's Theatre with the royal family in attendance. At the actual wedding ceremony, the now-famous Handel anthem was given.

Nicola Porpora meanwhile had the temerity to attack Handel on home ground with an oratorio (*Davide e Bersabea*). Mrs Pendarves attended at the end of March and wrote to her sister, Ann Granville:

> . . . some of the choruses and recitatives are extremely fine and touching, but they say it is not equal to Mr Handel's oratorio of Esther or Deborah. [Deutsch, pp. 315f.]

And indeed she had a chance to hear *Deborah*, which was revived by Handel in April, with the veteran Durastanti participating. A few days later Mrs Pendarves gave a party, where Handel 'was in the best humour in the world, and played lessons and accompanied Strada and all the ladies that sang from seven o'the clock till eleven.' Mrs Pendarves gave them coffee, tea 'and about half an hour after nine had a salver brought in of chocolate, mulled white wine and biscuits. Everyone was easy and seemed pleased, Bunny staid with me after the company was gone, eat a cold chick with me, and we chatted till one o'the clock' (Deutsch, p. 363).

Both opera houses were limping along, and Porpora's *Iphigenia* failed, though the Earl of Egmont wrote in his Diary for 6 May 1734, 'I think the town does not justice in condemning it' (Deutsch, p. 364). Of the Handelian revivals, *Il pastor fido*, with new additions, proved very successful (18 May), with thirteen performances.

The nobility's Opera closed for the season on 15 June, a fortnight before the last performance of *Il pastor fido* at the Haymarket. Handel's contract with Heidegger had now expired, and the manager let the theatre to the Opera of the Nobility for the forthcoming season. Handel joined forces with John Rich at the Covent Garden Theatre, alternating Rich's plays with Handelian operas. The composer secured the services of the famous French dancer, Maria Sallé, but the rival theatre was able to engage the greatest castrato singer in history – Farinelli. The composer Hasse, asked to join the Nobility's Opera, refused when he heard of the situation but sent the score of his *Artaserse*, to which additions by Riccardo Broschi were made; this was the Nobility's first offering of the new season, and Carlo Broschi, *alias* Farinelli (Riccardo's brother), made his spectacular London début. (When he presented himself at court, Princess Anne accompanied him at the harpsichord and naughtily made him sing two Handel arias at sight, which he did with some difficulty: we have the information from Burney). His attractive manners and courteous charm captivated everyone.

Handel countered with yet another revision of *Il pastor fido*, this time with a one-act opera ballet à la française for Sallé entitled *Terpsicore*. After a revival and a pasticcio, the new and powerful opera *Ariodante* (8 January 1735) followed, including ballet music: there were eleven performances and a revival in 1736. The king was, incidentally, not only a regular attender at Covent Garden but continued his patronage of Handel. Others were pleased at the composer's discomfiture:

> I don't pity Handell in the least, for I hope this mortification will make him a human creature; for I am sure before he was no better than a brute. [letter to Catherine Collingwood by an unknown friend, 27 December 1734; Deutsch, p. 378]

The worst was that Handel was now part of the battle between the king and the Prince of Wales. Lord Hervey's *Memoirs* elucidate the point:

> . . . Another judicious subject of his [the Prince of Wales'] enmity was her [the Princess Royal's] supporting Handel, a German musician and composer (who had been her singing master, and was now undertaker of one of the operas), against several of the nobility who had a pique to Handel, and had set up another person to ruin him; or, to speak more properly and exactly, the Prince, in the beginning of his enmity to his sister, set himself at the head of the other opera to irritate her, whose pride and passions were as strong as her brother's (though his understanding was so much weaker), and could brook contradiction, where she dared to resist it, as little as her father.
>
> What I had related may seem a trifle, but though the cause was indeed such, the effects of it were no trifles. The King and Queen were as much in earnest upon this subject as their son and daughter, though they had the prudence to disguise it, or to endeavour to disguise it, a little more. They were both Handelists, and sat freezing constantly at his empty Haymarket Opera, whilst the Prince with all the chief of the nobility went as constantly to that of Lincoln's Inn Fields. The affair grew as serious as that of the Greens and the Blues under Justinian at Constantinople. An anti-Handelist was looked upon as an anti-courtier, and voting against the Court in Parliament was hardly a less remissible or more venial sin than speaking against Handel, or going to Lincoln's Inn Fields Opera. The Princess Royal said she expected in a little while to see half the House of Lords playing in the orchestra in their robes and coronets; and the King (though he declared he took no other part in this affair than subscribing £1,000 a year to Handel) often added at the same time he did not think setting oneself at the head of a faction of fiddlers a very honourable occupation for people of quality; or the ruin of one poor fellow so generous or so good-natured a scheme as to do much honour to the undertakers, whether they succeeded or not; but the better they succeeded in it, the more he thought they would have reason to be ashamed of it. The Princess Royal quarelled with the Lord Chamberlain for affecting his usual neutrality on this occasion,

> and spoke of Lord Delaware, who was one of the chief managers against Handel, with as much spleen as if he had been at the head of the Dutch faction who opposed the making her husband Stadtholder.
>
> ... She had Handel and his opera so much at heart that even in these distressful moments [of her departure] she spoke as much upon his chapter as any other, and begged Lord Hervey to assist him with the utmost attention. [Deutsch, p. 380]

It has been sometimes considered that because of this rivalry between father and son, Frederick, Prince of Wales, did not appreciate Handel's music; but the evidence shows quite the contrary, and recently, new documents have come to light that show, in the words of the author[5] who analyses them, that not only was there no hostility on the part of the Prince of Wales towards Handel, but on the contrary the Prince was well disposed to the composer and often helped him.

As Lent 1735 approached, Handel's thought turned to his oratorios which had proved so successful. He had not only revived all three – *Esther, Deborah* and *Athalia* – but began to compose and play organ concertos in the intervals, recalling the tradition of his remarkable organ 'sonata' in the *Trionfo* of Roman days. The fickle London public almost seemed to be deserting the oratorios as well as the operas. In a curious newspaper entitled the *Old Whig: Or, The Conservative Protestant* of 20 March 1735, we read:

> *A Letter to a Friend in the Country.*
>
> ... The late Squabble at the Opera is pretty well adjusted. It had rose very high; Parties were formed, and Protests were just ready to be enter'd, to which many fair Hands had threaten'd to subscribe; when by accommodating Matters with *Senesino*, all the ruffled Passions were calmed, as it had been by the Melody of his Voice. *Farinello* surpasses every thing we have hitherto heard. Nor are we wanting in our Acknowledgments: For, besides the numerous Presents of considerable Sums made him by the Nobility, Foreign Ministers, and Others, (which amounted to some Thousand Pounds), he had an Audience at his Benefit larger than was ever seen in an *English* Theatre; and there was an Attention,

> that shew'd how much every one was charmed. – In the flourishing State of this Opera, 'tis no Wonder that the other Theatres decline. *Handel*, whose excellent Compositions have often pleased our Ears, and touched our Hearts, has this Winter sometimes performed to an almost empty Pitt. He has lately reviv'd his fine *Oratorio of Esther*, in which he has introduced two Concerto's on the Organ that are inimitable. But so strong is the Disgust taken against him, that even this has been far from bringing him crowded Audiences; tho' there were no other publick Entertainments on those Evenings. His Loss is computed for these two Seasons at a great Sum . . .

But Handel had no intention of relinquishing opera without a battle, and his final work of the season was one of his most magnificent: *Alcina*, with superb ballet music which has always been performed even when the opera itself was unjustly dormant on archive shelves. Charles Burney (1785, p. 24) tells us the amazing story of Carestini at first refusing to sing the Aria, 'Verdi prati', but being firmly overruled by the composer. 'Verdi prati' became an instantaneous best-seller and *Alcina* ran for eighteen performances. Sallé appeared as the model of a Greek statue in her bodice and under-petticoat covered by a transparent muslin robe. There was a scandal, but that did not prevent the whole royal family from attending by 14 May. Mrs Pendarves wrote to her mother, Mrs Mary Granville, after a rehearsal:

> Lower Brook Street, April 12, 1735.
>
> Yesterday morning my sister [Ann Granville] and I went with Mrs Donellan to Mr Handel's house to hear the first rehearsal of the new opera Alcina. I think it the best he ever made, but I *have thought so* of *so many*, that I will not say positively *'tis the finest*, but 'tis *so fine* I have not words to describe it. Strada has a whole scene of charming recitative – there are a thousand beauties. Whilst Mr Handel was playing his part, I could not help thinking him a necromancer in the midst of his own enchantments. [Deutsch, p. 385]

It was Marie Sallé's farewell appearance, and Handel's music for her is among his most enchanting creations. Apart from her *risqué* attire, she apparently created an uproar when she appeared in male disguise:

FROM PRÉVOST'S 'LE POUR ET CONTRE', PARIS, [June?] 1735 (Translated)

Mademoiselle Sallé, who had at first been as favourably received by the English as Farinelli (however, in due proportion to her talents), found herself afterwards bitterly attacked both in verse and in prose, without anyone knowing the reasons which might justify this change . . . The opera *Alcine* was given, the story of which is taken from *Ariosto*. Mlle Sallé had composed a ballet, in which she cast herself for the role of Cupid and took upon herself to dance it in male attire. This, it is said, suits her very ill and was apparently the cause of her disgrace. Her admirers in France will be less chagrined than herself over an incident which may hasten her return to the Parisian theatre, especially since the poor success of her *benefit*, which did not bring her even half as much as last year's. [Deutsch, pp. 390f.]

The composer was not bankrupt, but he was definitely out of pocket: his opera season had been a financial disaster, and opera as a whole was the talk of the town:

MRS PENDARVES TO SWIFT

May 16, 1735

Our Operas have given much cause of dissension; men and women have been deeply engaged; and no debate in the House of Commons has been urged with more warmth; the dispute of the merits of the composers and singers is carried to so great a height, that it is much feared, by all true lovers of music, that operas will be quite overturned. I own I think we make a very silly figure about it. [Deutsch, p. 390]

It was thought that Handel had lost £9,000 and the arrogant Nobility's Opera £10,000.

Handel retired to Kent to take the healing waters of Tunbridge Wells; he decided to give up opera (for the moment) and leave the field to his enemies. They too were now in a morass of financial chaos and even Farinelli's magic presence could not redeem Veracini's *Adriano in Siria*. On 25 November 1735 Lord Hervey went and wrote:

> I am this moment returned with the King from yawning four hours at the longest and dullest Opera that ever the enobled ignorance of our present musical Governors ever inflicted on the ignorance of an English audience; who, generally speaking, are equally skilful in the language of the drama and the music it is set to, a degree of knowledge or ignorance (call it which you please) that on this occasion is no great misfortune to them, the drama being composed by an anonymous fool, and the music by one Veracini, a madman, who to show his consummate skill in this Opera has, among half a dozen very bad parts, given Cuzzoni and Farinelli the two worst. The least bad part is Senesino's, who like Echo reversed, has lost all his voice, and retains nothing of his former self but his flesh . . . Handel sat in great eminence and great pride in the middle of the pit, and seemed in silent triumph to insult this poor dying Opera in its agonies, without finding out that he was a great a fool for refusing to compose, as Veracini had shown himself by composing, nobody feeling their own folly, though they never overlook other people's, and having the eyes of a mole for the one, with those of a lynx for the other . . . [Deutsch, pp. 395f.]

The end of the season caused the following summary of it to be printed in Prévost's 'Le Pour et Contre', Paris (translated):

> Signor Farinelli, who came to England with the highest expectations, has the satisfaction of seeing them fulfilled by generosity and favour as extraordinary as his own talents. The others were loved: this man is idolized, adored; it is a consuming passion. Indeed, it is impossible to sing better [than he does]. Mr Handel has not omitted to produce a new *Oratorio*, which is given on Wednesdays and Fridays, with chorus and orchestral accompaniments of great beauty. Everyone agrees that he is the Orpheus of his age and that this new work is a masterpiece. He plays the organ himself in it, with consummate skill. He is

> admired, but from a distance, for he is often alone; a spell draws the crowd to Farinelli's. Imagine all Senesino's and Carastino's art combined, with a voice more beautiful than those two taken together . . . [Deutsch, p. 390]

Being a stubborn man, Handel announced another opera season for 1736–7, but he was now seriously contemplating the composition of further English oratorios. On 19 February 1736 he produced *Alexander's Feast* after Dryden (word-book: Newburgh Hamilton), which was much applauded. The Earl of Egmont wrote in his Diary that it was 'very fine music' (Deutsch, p. 399) and an audience of 1,300 brought in £450. In fact oratorio was gradually beginning to overtake opera, to which Handel's principal contribution was *Atlanta*, part of the festivities in honour of the Prince of Wales's marriage with the Princess of Saxe Gotha. At their wedding ceremony, a new Anthem by Handel, 'Sing unto God', was 'wretchedly sung' but much admired by the royal couple, who loved Handel's music (despite fatherly protection . . .).

Otherwise, Handel's opera company was in serious, indeed terminal, difficulty (but then, so was the rival company too):

> BENJAMIN VICTOR TO MATTHEW DUBOURG, AT DUBLIN [London, *c.* 15th May 1736.]
>
> . . . The two opera houses are, neither of them, in a successful way; and it is the confirmed opinion that this winter will compleat your friend *Handel*'s destruction, as far as the loss of his memory can destroy him; I make no question but you have had a better description of his new singer than I can give you; I hear he supplies the loss of *Senesino* better than was expected, but it is principally in his action – his voice and manner being on the *new model* – in which *Farinelli* excels every one, and yet, the second winter, exhibited here to empty benches. We are not without hopes of *Senesino*'s return to England, and of once more seeing him in his most advantageous light, *singing Handel's composition*.
>
> On Tuesday last, we had a new opera of Handel's; and at the appearance of that great prince of harmony in the orchestra, there was so universal a clap from the audience that many were surprized, and some offended at it. As to the opera, the critics

> say, it is too like his former compositions, and wants variety – I heard his singer that night, and think him near equal in merit to the late *Carestini*, with this advantage, that he has acquired the happy knack of throwing out a sound, now and then, very like what we hear from a distressed young calf.
>
> . . . As to the Operas, they must tumble, for the King's presence could hardly hold them up, and even that prop is denied them, for his majesty will not admit his royal ears to be tickled this season. As to music, it flourishes in this place more than ever, in subscription concerts and private parties, which must prejudice all operas and public entertainments. [Deutsch, pp. 408f.]

The bright side of Handel's life was now the large number of oratorios which occupied almost half the composer's season from 15 February till 19 June at Lincoln's Inn Fields and Covent Garden: nine performances of *Alexander's Feast, Acis and Galatea* and *Esther* as against ten of *Ariodante* (revived from 1735) and *Atlanta*.

Marie Sallé had now left her prudish English audience and returned to France; Porpora had left the Opera of the Nobility. When Handel revived *Alcina* (6 November 1736) it was without the ravishingly lovely ballet music, which may perhaps explain its failure (only three performances). Even the presence of the Prince and Princess of Wales did not offset the public's indifference. 'Great fatigue and disappointment' were Handel's present rewards. He began to fail, in mind and in body.

NOTES

1 British Library R. M. 20. g. 9. Fleur-de-lis, lyre and letters 'LVG'.

2 A popular burlesque by a Manchester dancing master Samuel Johnson (1691–1773).

3 It is thought that the Countess of Burlington may have added the figure of Heidegger to the two by Marco Ricci [*recte*], who had died in Venice in 1729.

4 'Handel's Opera Finances in 1732–3' by Judith Milhous & Robert D. Hume, *Musical Times*, February 1984, pp. 86ff.

5 Carole Taylor: 'Handel and Frederick, Prince of Wales', *Musical Times*, February 1984, pp. 89ff.

VIII
The rise of Oratorio & the Queen's Funeral Anthem 1737

HANDEL'S SEASON FOR the winter of 1737 included no fewer than three new operas. The first was *Arminio*, which opened on 12 January. Mrs Pendarves was at a rehearsal and wrote to her sister, Ann Granville:

> Jan. 8, 1736–7.
>
> I was this morning regaled with Mr Handel's new opera called Arminius, it was rehearsed at Covent Garden; I think it as fine a one as any he has made, as I hope you will, 'tis to be acted next Wednesday [the 12th]. From the rehearsal I came home with my *neighbour Granville*![1] [Deutsch, p. 423]

But the public response was luke-warm and there were only six performances. Next followed a revival of *Partenope* on 29 January (four performances). The Prince and Princess of Wales, now the staunchest of Handelians, had attended the première of *Arminio* and two of the four evenings of *Partenope* were at their express command. (Curiously, the scores of these new operas sold rather well, for example *Armenio*, for which 143 copies were subscribed.)

Amidst growing indifference, Handel's next opera, *Giustino*, received its first performance on 16 February and could even register nine performances, but the composer was increasingly out of the public's favour:

MR. PENNINGTON TO MISS CATHERINE COLLINGWOOD, AT BATH

19th Feb. 1736–7.

> . . . Partys run high in musick, as when you shone among us. Mr Handel has not due honour done him, and I am excessively angry about it, which you know is of vast consequence. [Deutsch, p. 426]

Shortly thereafter Handel revived his royal Serenade, *Il Parnasso in Festa*, but the principal new oratorio was a curious revision of *Il trionfo* from Roman days, now refurbished and with considerable additions, under the title of *Il trionfo del Tempo e della Verità* (23 March, four performances). Here is the schedule of Handel's operas and oratorios at Covent Garden, every Wednesday and Friday (and later Passion Week):

> 25th February – *Giustino* (Friday)
> 2nd March – "
> 4th " – "
> 9th " – *Il Parnasso in Festa*
> 11th " – "
> 16th " – *Alexander's Feast*
> 18th " – "
> 23rd " – *Il Trionfo*
> 25th " – "
> 30th " – *Alexander's Feast*
> 1st April – *Il Trionfo* (Friday)
> 4th " – " (Monday)
> 5th " – *Alexander's Feast* (Tuesday)
> 6th " – *Esther* (Wednesday)
> 7th " – " (Thursday)
>
> For the last four performances, in Passion Week, Handel got special licence. [Deutsch, p. 427]

It will be seen that oratorios were gradually usurping operas. But operas were still Handel's grand passion, and at this juncture his failures were apparently so dejecting that he was seriously considering abandoning his profession:

MISS ANN GRANVILLE TO HER MOTHER, MRS. GRANVILLE

[London], 8th March 1737.

> Music is certainly a pleasure that may be reckoned intellectual, and we shall *never again* have it in the perfection it is this year, because Mr Handel will *not compose any more*! Oratorios begin next week, to my great joy, for they are the highest entertainment to me. [Deutsch, p. 428]

If Handel's operas were playing to empty houses, his oratorios were increasingly successful:

> FROM A LONDON NEWSPAPER, 17th March 1737
>
> Last Night Mr Dryden's Ode, call'd *Alexander's Feast*, was performed at the Theatre Royal in Covent-Garden, to a splendid Audience, where his Royal Highness the Prince and the Princess of Wales were present, and seem'd to be highly entertain'd, insomuch that his Royal Highness commanded Mr Handel's Concerto on the Organ to be repeated, and intends to Honour the same with his Presence once again, as likewise the new Oratorio call'd *Il Trionfo del Tempo e della Verità*, which is to be perform'd on Wednesday next [the 23rd]. [Deutsch, p. 429].

It was also the Prince and Princess of Wales who commanded the revival of *Il trionfo*.

On 13 April 1737, Handel planned to conduct a pasticcio entitled *Didone* (Metastasio, music mostly by Vinci). But that day he was struck down by a kind of stroke (or severe rheumatism) which paralysed his right arm. Here are three contemporary reports:

> . . . Though HANDEL had some good Singers, none of them could be compared to FARINELLI, who drew all the world to the Hay-market. And it soon appeared that the relish of the English for Music, was not strong enough to support two Operas at a time. There were but few persons of any other class, besides that of the Nobility, who had much knowledge of the Italian, any notion of such compositions, or consequently any real pleasure in hearing them. Those among the middling and lower orders, whom affectation or curiosity had drawn to the Theatre at his first setting out in conjunction with RICH, fell off by degrees. His expences in providing Singers, and in other preparations, had been very large;

and his profits were no way proportionate to such charges. At the end of three or four years, instead of having acquired such an addition to his fortune, as from his care, industry, and abilities, he had reason to expect, he was obliged to draw out of the funds almost all that he was worth, in order to answer the demands upon him. This upshot put an end for the present to all musical entertainments at Covent-garden, and almost put an end to the author of them. The violence of his passions made such a disaster operate the more terribly.

The observation that misfortunes rarely come single, was verified in HANDEL. His fortune was not more impaired, than his health and his understanding. His right-arm was become useless to him, from a stroke of the palsy; and how greatly his senses were disordered at intervals, for a long time, appeared from a hundred instances, which are better forgotten than recorded. The most violent deviations from reason, are usually seen when the strongest faculties happen to be thrown out of course.

[Mainwaring, pp. 119–22]

JAMES HARRIS TO THE EARL OF SHAFTESBURY

Sarum May 5 1737

Yr Lordp's information concerning Mr Handel's Disorder was ye first I received – I can assure Yr Lordp it gave me no Small Concern – when ye Fate of Harmony depends upon a Single Life, the Lovers of Harmony may be well allowed to be Sollicitous. I heartily regrett ye thought of losing any of ye executive part of his meritt, but this I can gladly compound for, when we are assured of the Inventive, for tis this which properly constitutes ye Artist, & Separates Him from ye Multitude. It is certainly an Evidence of great Strength of Constitution to be so Soon getting rid of So great a Shock. A weaker Body would perhaps have hardly born ye Violence of Medicines, wch operate So quickly.

. . . If Mr Handel gives off his Opera, it will be the only Pleasure I shall have left in ye musicall way, to look over his Scores, and recollect past Events – Here Strada used to shine – there Annibale – This was an Excellt Chorus, and that a Charming piece of Recitative – In that I shall amuse my Self much in the Same manner as Virgil tells of ye Trojans . . . the War yr Lordp

> knows was renewed with double Earnestness & Vigour. May my Pleasure find ye Same Fate, & be lost by ye Return of that Harmony wch I have given over, Supported & carried on by ye Same Spirit & Resolution. [Deutsch, p. 433]

From the Earl of Shaftesbury's Memoirs of Handel:

> . . . tho' he had several Capital Singers, and Exhibited such a Variety of Excellent New Opera's, vizt Arminius, Justin, Berenice, and the Il Trionpho del Tempo, he met with no Success. Great fatigue and disappointment, affected him so much, that he was this Spring (1737) struck with the Palsy, which took entirely away, the use of 4 fingers of his right hand; and totally disabled him from Playing: And when the heats of the Summer 1737 came on, the Disorder seemed at times to affect his Understanding . . . [Deutsch, p. 846]

In the midst of this disaster, the final Handel opera of the season, *Berenice*, was given on 18 May and was withdrawn after four performances. It was no particular consolation that the Opera of the Nobility failed prematurely on 11 June (due to Farinelli's becoming ill). Handel's physicians suggested that he take the cure at Aix-la-Chapelle (Aachen), famous for its sulphur baths:

> In this melancholic state, it was in vain for him to think of any fresh projects for retrieving his affairs. His first concern was how to repair his constitution. But tho' he had the best advice, and tho' the necessity of following it was urged to him in the most friendly manner, it was with the utmost difficulty that he was prevailed on to do what was proper, when it was any way disagreeable. For this reason it was thought best for him to have recourse to the vapor-baths of Aix la Chapelle, over which he sat near three times as long as hath ever been the practice. Whoever knows any thing of the nature of those baths, will, from this instance, form some idea of his surprising constitution. His sweats were profuse beyond what can well be imagined. His cure, from the manner as well as from the quickness, with which it was wrought, passed with the Nuns for a miracle. When, but a few hours from the

time of his quitting the bath, they heard him at the organ in the principal church as well as convent, playing in a manner so much beyond any they had ever been used to, such a conclusion in such persons was natural enough. Tho' his business was so soon dispatched, and his cure judged to be thoroughly effected, he thought it prudent to continue at Aix about six weeks, which is the shortest period usually allotted for bad cases. [Mainwaring, pp. 122f.]

These Baths had an amazing effect upon him, for in a few times using them, the use of his fingers was restor'd to him; his Spirits grew Calm, and he was able to perform upon the Harpsichord. His recovery was so compleat, that on his Return from thence to England, he was able to Play long Voluntaries upon the Organ. In one of the great Towns in Flanders, where he had asked Permission to Play, the Organist attended him, not knowing who he was; and seem'd Struck with Mr Handell's Playing when he began:

But when he heard Mr Handell lead off a Feuge, in Astonishment he ran up to him, & embracing him, said. 'You can be no other but the great Handell.' [the Earl of Shaftesbury's Memoirs of Handel; Deutsch, p. 847]

It was a modern miracle. After a further sojourn in the Baltic town of Elbing (where a selection of his operas was given as a pasticcio entitled *Hermann von Balcke* in October), Handel, cured in mind and body, set off for London, determined to continue his operatic career despite every setback. It may have been a misguided enthusiasm, yet it is rather touching.

But many people considered that Handel's career as a composer was finished. The following chilling report from the later Frederick the Great shows what intelligent Continental opinion thought of the Saxon master's future:

PRINCE FRIEDRICH OF PRUSSIA TO PRINCE WILLIAM OF ORANGE, 8th (19th) October 1737 (Translated)

Rheinsberg, October 19, 1737.

Pray convey every expression of my duty to your wife; she does me too much honour to be thinking of me in the matter of Hendel's

Handel. Caricature by F.L. Ghezzi. A drawing of the young composer. The scription reads 'The so-called Saxon, who arrived in Rome to stay with the rince of Massa on 21 October 1720 and is an excellent harpsichord player.' here is, however, no record of Handel being in Rome that year.

2 *Cardinal's Gallery. Oil by G.F. Panini. When Handel was in Rome, his patrons were the art-loving aristocrats and princes of the Church, who were connoisseurs and collectors, of painting and music. Handel's most important patrons were The Cardinals Grimani, Pamphili and Ottoboni.*

3 *Harpsichords:* LEFT *This particular instrument belonged to Cardinal Ottoboni and was decorated by his painter Francesco Trevisani: Handel may have played on the instrument.* RIGHT *This beautifully painted and decorated harpsichord was constructed in Rome about 1700.*

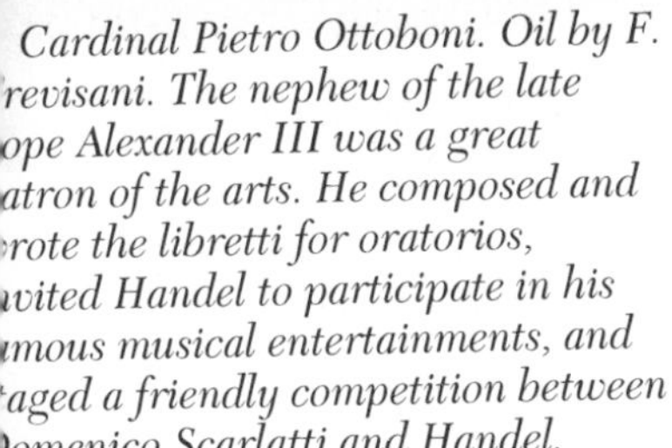

Cardinal Pietro Ottoboni. Oil by F. revisani. The nephew of the late ope Alexander III was a great atron of the arts. He composed and rote the libretti for oratorios, wited Handel to participate in his mous musical entertainments, and aged a friendly competition between omenico Scarlatti and Handel.

5 *Arcangelo Corelli. Portrait attributed to Hugh Howard. Corelli lived in the house of Cardinal Ottoboni and was the most famous musician in Rome. He was leader of the orchestra in the first performance of Handel's oratorio* La Resurezzione *in 1708.*

Palazzo della Cancelleria, Rome. Engraving by G. Rasi. Cardinal Pietro ttoboni lived in this palace until his death and gave many musical performances in the grand hall, which still stands.

7 ABOVE *Piazza del Populo, Rome. Anon. engraving of c.1700. Here, Handel's Roman Vespers for S. Maria di Monte Santo were first performed on 16 July 1707. The occasion was the Feast of Our Lady of Mount Carmel. Part of the original Vespers programme was recently sold at auction by Sotheby's.*

8 *Venice. Anon. engravings. In 1707, Handel travelled for the first time to the city, and had the good fortune to be introduced to the later King of England's brother, Prince Ernst August of Hanover, and also to the English Ambassador Charles, Earl of Manchester, who invited the composer to England. (a) Mass at S. Maria della*

alute. (b) Ceremony for he coronation of the Doge. c) The Piazetta at Carneval. (d) The Doge addresses the Council.

ABOVE *Domenico Scarlatti. Oil by D.A. de Velasco. Domenico, son of he famous composer Alessandro Scarlatti, played with Handel in a contest judged by Cardinal Ottoboni and was declared master of the harpsichord; Handel won the contest on he organ.* (see *Plate 2*)

0 ABOVE RIGHT *Henry Purcell. Oil by J. Closterman. Handel tudied Purcell's music ssiduously – particularly he anthems, but also the peras of the famous English composer.*

11 *George II, King of England. Oil from the studio of T. Hudson.*

12 *Nicola Porpora. Anon. portrait. Porpora was Handel's chief rival in London and a skilful composer. He taught Hasse and Haydn.*

13 *Adolf Hasse. Oil, unsigned. Hasse was invited to London in 1734 by the Opera of the Nobility, Handel's great rivals. He sent the score of* Artaserse *but declined to come in person. Faustina Bordoni, who Hasse later married, sang in Handel's* Alessandro *in 1726.*

14 *George III, when Prince of Wales. Oil by J. Reynolds. George III was a great admirer of the composer: he would doff his hat whenever Handel's Hallelujah was played.*

5 RIGHT *Westminster Abbey. ngraving by Walker. In the nave is epicted the canopy erected for eorge III and his consort during the landel memorial concert, in 1784.*

6 BELOW *The Foundling Hospital. non. engravings: (a) Handel helped aise funds for the hospital by erforming his oratorio* Messiah, *and eaving the hospital a manuscript of is work in his will. (b) The Chapel: ere Handel performed* Messiah *uring the last nine years of his life. he children's choir can be seen in the allery; the children sang every unday.*

17 *Handel. Oil by P. Mercier. This is the earliest authenticated portrait of the composer we have.*

> operas. I am infinitely obliged to her for her attentions, but I beg you will tell her that Hendel's great days are over, his inspiration is exhausted and his taste behind the fashion. Pray inform me if you have any singer and what kind of voice he has, and I will send you some airs by my composer, which I trust will be to the taste of your wife. [Deutsch, p. 441]

The prince had made a mistake, for Handel was about to be launched on a new and spectacular career, the fruits of which would include *Israel in Egypt, Saul, Messiah*, the Concerti Grossi Opus 6 and the *Musick for the Royal Fireworks*; and it can be said that *Messiah* would turn out to be possibly the most successful piece of music ever written. Frederick the Great had misjudged the future.

Handel returned from his cure at Aix-la-Chapelle at the end of October, full of his usual energy and optimism. By the middle of November, he had started on another opera, *Faramondo*, intended for Heidegger's forthcoming season at the King's Theatre, for which Handel had been engaged as composer-conductor at the substantial sum of £1,000 *per annum*. But five days after he had begun *Faramondo*, on 20 November 1737, Queen Caroline died, and the theatres were closed until the end of the year.

Handel probably met the Queen in Berlin, when they were both children; but from the time they had been together at Hanover, the Queen had supported him and when she moved to England she proved to be a faithful patron. There is every evidence that Handel genuinely admired and loved her, and certainly his grief was shared by the nation. George II mourned no less sincerely than his subjects. On her death-bed, Queen Caroline urged him to marry again. 'Non, non,' he is reported to have answered, 'j'aurai des maîtresses.' The Queen's exit line must be accounted one of the great ones of history: 'Mon Dieu, cela n'empêche pas.'

It was natural that Handel was called upon to write her Funeral anthem, 'The ways of Zion do mourn', which was performed in Westminster Abbey on 17 December, being preceded by a general rehearsal on the 14th at the Banqueting House, at which the royal family were present, though of course incognito. The Funeral anthem, although one of Handel's noblest and most beautiful compositions, is relatively seldom performed. As we shall see, Handel later attached it to *Saul*, then changed his mind and used it as a preface to *Israel in Egypt*, being loath to see such exceptional music disappear along with the bones of the Queen.

There are several remarkable features about the Funeral anthem, of which the most conspicuous is that it is entirely constructed of choruses. Jens Peter Larsen, whose analysis of the work is most penetrating (*Messiah*, op. cit. pp. 68ff.), writes,

> The use of the chorus . . . was determined by the special character of the work. Here, as in *Alexander's Feast*, the choir does not have to act as a collective body, in contrast to the soloist's expressions of the emotions of an individual. But whereas in *Alexander's Feast* the chorus was, from the point of view of expression, on a par with the aria, the situation in the Funeral Anthem is that the chorus alone has to create that variety which would normally be achieved by recitative, aria and chorus.

Handel does this by recourse to a surprising expedient: he takes the old chamber duet, of Steffani fame, and turns it into a chorus – there are three in the anthem: 'When the ear heard her', 'The righteous shall be had' and 'They shall receive a glorious kingdom'. This was the foundation of the famous 'chamber choruses' in *Messiah* ('For unto us', etc.). Apart from the chamber chorus, we also find choral recitative, regular fugue, a strict triple fugue and the most touching instance of all, a magnificent, *cantus firmus* setting for the very opening, 'The ways of Zion'. Professor Larsen was the first to identify precisely the old chorale on which the *cantus firmus* of another movement, 'She deliver'd the poor that cried' was based, and he quite rightly supposes that the choice of these ancient German chorales was a result of the recent trip to the country of Handel's birth, also of course the country of Queen Caroline's birth as well. Apart from using a famous and beautiful chorale melody for the opening, here is the later instance:

Du Friedensfürst, Herr Jesu Christ, wahr Mensch und wahrer Gott
Ein starker Nothelfer du bist, im Leben und im Tod.
Drum wir allein im Namen dein zu deinem Vater schreien.

Thus the much-loved Queen left Westminster Abbey to the melodies of venerable Lutheran lineage. And not only that: Handel made use of a *Sterbe-Motet* by Jacob Gallus (Handl), 'Ecce quomodo justus' as the basis for part of 'But their name liveth evermore', which 'Death Motet' was still in regular use in German funeral ceremonies. But, as Professor Larsen warns,

> this connexion with German church music traditions . . . must not be overemphasized . . . The Funeral anthem cannot be interpreted as a change of style towards the German cantata . . . In other respects the Funeral anthem seems linked rather strongly with English church-music (Purcell), but in the final analysis its strength lies above all in Handel's ability to synthesize highly varied material.' [Ibid., p. 70]

A few days after the Funeral anthem was performed at the Abbey, Handel finished *Faramondo* (it was the day before Christmas), and on Boxing Day (the Feast of St Stephen's) 1737 he began *Serse*. *Faramondo* was first performed on 3 January 1738; it was Handel's first appearance in a London theatre since his illness the year before, and the audience welcomed him back. The famous alto castrato, Caffarelli, made his début in London, and although the *cognoscenti* thought him the equal of, if not superior to, Farinelli, he was said to be in ill-health and was less of a success than had been hoped. Caffarelli's arrogance was also not such as to endear him to the British, who remembered Farinelli's courtesy and charm. If *Faramondo* was not much of a success, Handel, after having produced a pasticcio entitled *Alessandro Severo* on 25 February (also not a great success), achieved a huge personal triumph with a benefit concert on 28 April, entitled 'Oratorio'; various figures have been cited, all probably inaccurate, but of the evening's success there was no doubt. 'It is easy to understand,' writes Streatfeild,

> . . . how distasteful to a man of his independent spirit it must have been to accept a favour of this kind, but circumstances forbade him to stand upon his dignity. Del Pò [husband of the singer Anna Strada Del Pò], who was still one of his principal creditors,

was more insistent than ever, and even threatened the composer with a debtors' prison.[2] [p. 148]

But the Opera was still in serious trouble. People were bored with the endless cabals, scandals and rivalries, and *Serse*, when it was first performed on 15 April, was a resounding failure. Yet Handel's profound popularity with the British was illustrated in a dramatic way when, a few weeks after *Serse* had played to empty houses, Roubiliac's statue of the composer was unveiled in Vauxhall Gardens.[3]

NOTES

1 Bernard Granville was the sisters' brother and lived in Park Street, Grosvenor Square. [Deutsch, p. 423]

2 Streatfeild probably took the story of Del Po's threat from Burney 1785, p. 24.

3 It is now in the Victoria & Albert Museum, London.

IX
The Heroic Years 1737–1741

ONE OF THE subscribers to Handel's opera scores in 1725 had been Charles Jennens (1700–73), a rich, eccentric literary dilettante who lived at Gopsall in Leicestershire and collected Handel's music – not only operas but also oratorios and, for example, the *Water Musick* (the authentic copy of which, by the Smith scriptorium, is now in the Manchester Public Library). Handel was in all probability a frequent guest at Gopsall. In Nichols's *Literary Anecdotes*, a local parson wrote:

> I know not whether you are aware that there is a probability, I think almost an immediate proof, that Handel's oratorios took their rise in this county. The rich Mr Jennens of Gopsall was a man of great piety, beneficence and taste in the fine arts. He built a magnificent house, and in it a beautiful chapel, in which he read prayers to his family daily. Handel (who, as you know, loved good living) was often his guest, as also Dr Bentley of Nailston, his neighbour, nephew of the great Bentley.[1] I have heard that the idea of the oratorios was Mr Jennens's, and Dr Bentley furnished the words.

Jennens may not have been a great poet but he was an astute man-of-letters and gave us the word-books not only of *Saul* but probably of *Israel in Egypt* and certainly of L'*Allegro, il Penseroso ed il Moderato* and, of course and supremely, *Messiah*. He was very clever at adapting biblical stories and his libretto of *Saul* made a chaotic tale (First Book of Samuel) lively, dramatic and ideal for a man of Handel's temperament. It seems that theirs was a genuine case of collaboration, though Jennens (as might be expected) overrated his own part in the proceedings. It is thought that the letter Handel wrote on 28 July 1735 to Jennens, in which the composer states, 'What I could read of it in haste gave me a great deal of satisfaction' may refer to the new word-book for *Saul*. It is difficult to know to what extent the failing opera season of 1738 encouraged Handel to turn to oratorio, but the chronology involved suggests such an explanation.

Heidegger announced his subscription plan for the new opera season on 24 May 1738 but almost exactly two months later, on 25 July, the plan had to be dropped. On 23 July, Handel began *Saul*, finishing the first act on 1 August, and the second on 8 August. On 15 August the draft score was completed. At this point Handel intended to use, for the 'Elegy for Saul and Jonathan', large parts of the Funeral anthem; but he laid the new Oratorio aside and with his usual speed wrote an entire Opera between 9 and 20 September: *Imeneo*. Heidegger may have given up but not the stubborn Handel; in September he was visited by his librettist, who on the 19th wrote to Lord Guernsey as follows:

> Mr Handel's head is more full of maggots than ever. I found yesterday in his room a very queer instrument which he calls carillon (*Anglice*, a bell) and says some call it a Tubalcain. I suppose because it is both in the make and tone like a set of Hammers striking upon anvils. 'Tis played upon with keys like a Harpsichord and with this Cyclopean instrument he designs to make poor Saul stark mad. His second maggot is an organ of £500 price which (because he is overstocked with money) he has bespoke of one Moss of Barnet. This organ, he says, is so constructed that as he sits at it he has a better command of his performers than he used to have, and he is highly delighted to think with what exactness his Oratorio will be performed by the help of this organ; so that for the future instead of beating time at his oratorios, he is to sit at the organ all the time with his back to the Audience. His third maggot is a Hallelujah which he has trump'd up at the end of his oratorio since I went into the Country, because he thought the conclusion of the oratorio not Grand enough; tho' if that were the case 'twas his own fault, for the words would have bore as Grand Musick as he could have set 'em

> to: but this Hallelujah, Grand as it is, comes in very nonsensically, having no manner of relation to what goes before. And this is the more extraordinary, because he refused to set a Hallelujah at the end of the first Chorus in the Oratorio, where I had placed one and where it was to be introduced with the utmost propriety, upon a pretence that it would make the entertainment too long. I could tell you more of his maggots: but it grows late and I must defer the rest till I write next, by which time, I doubt not, more new ones will breed in his Brain.

Handel let himself be persuaded to move the 'Hallelujah' to the end of the choral sequence where, however, its tremendous force somewhat overpowers that section, making it sound as if the Oratorio were about to end there. Jennens's visit must have encouraged the composer to drop the idea of using the Funeral anthem and compose new music for the 'Elegy', which was completed on 27 September. The other revisions proved to be rather extensive, including the re-positioning of various numbers and the removal or adaptation of eight numbers; it is difficult to say at which point, chronologically, these revisions were made, but possibly it was during the course of the first performances early in 1739.

Four days after he completed *Saul* Handel embarked on his most ambitious oratorio project hitherto: *Israel in Egypt*. But at the beginning he seems to have envisaged a series of anthems, largely choral, along the lines of the Funeral anthem; and he called the new work 'Moses' Song, Exodus, chapter xv'. We do not know whether Handel himself compiled the text or whether, as is now thought likely, he received some help from Jennens. A month later the composer had finished this mighty epic, now enlarged and including a whole series of huge eight-part choruses. As Part One, he added the Funeral anthem. These two Oratorios were to be Handel's substitute for the ailing Italian opera (though, as we have seen, he had plans to revive that as well), and like everything else that he undertook, this new project was on a big scale. If the British public were going to be deprived of opera sets and famous castrati, Handel would see that they received other things instead, great and small.

Among the great things was the huge orchestra for *Saul*, which included three trombones as well as the usual oboes, bassoons, trumpets and kettledrums. In Jennens' letter we hear of the carillon, a keyed glockenspiel similar to the instrument Mozart later used in *The Magic Flute*. It is thought (Dean, *New Grove*, p. 49) that the new organ was a claviorganum, a combination of harpsichord and organ (several such instruments have survived and one is now in the Dublin Museum). And as for the percussion, Handel had conceived a bold plan. 'I hear,' wrote young Lord Wentworth to his father, 'that Mr Handell [*sic*] has borrow'd from the Duke of Argylle a pair of the largest kettle-drums in the Tower, so to be sure it will be most excessive noisy with a bad set off [*sic*] singers. I doubt it will not retrieve his former losses.'[2] These were double-bass kettledrums, tuned an octave below the usual pitch.

Saul's basic key is C major, and even the trumpets, usually pitched in D in Handel's England, are required to add a crook and play in C. That is also the key for the famous 'Dead March' which became one of the composer's most popular pieces. Handel's portrayal of Saul is a brilliant character study, certainly the most gripping aspect of this curiously neglected oratorio. The dark force of his jealousy is splendidly caught, perhaps most ominously in the chilling confrontation at Endor: in his tragedy is also a kind of grandeur, even as he confronts his own destruction. The chorus is, naturally, at the centre of Handel's calculations, for in it he represents the Israelites, horrified at the moral collapse of their king. The 'Envy' chorus, in its dark majesty, is justly celebrated, and the misplaced 'Hallelujah' chorus is every bit as magnificent as many of the choruses in *Messiah*. The orchestration, with its carillon, glitters in the opening scenes of the drama, but in the ghost scene, when Samuel's presence is called forth, the score sounds sinister, and the bassoons are used with special effect. There is also an elaborate solo organ part for Handel himself in the 'Symphony' that opens the section beginning 'Thy father is as cruel'. There is every reason why *Saul* should be a great popular favourite; but it is not, and if any one reason might be sought for its comparative neglect, it lies, perhaps, in the work's very diffuse qualities. Perhaps there are too many 'special effects', for there is a lack of that unity which makes *Messiah* so perfect and *Israel* so awe-inspiring.

Perhaps *Israel in Egypt* is the greatest piece of music Handel ever wrote, but it contains grave errors in calculation. The heavy borrowings have always bothered critics, but I do not think them a fit subject for endless discussion: when Handel takes Stradella's pretty *Serenata* and turns it into (a) 'He spake the word, And there came all manner of flies' and (b) the stupendous orchestral introduction to the 'Hailstone' Chorus, criticism must, quite simply, remain silent. If we knew nothing of the Stradella Serenade, we would think both choruses masterpieces; now that we know their origins, we cannot think them less masterly.[3] The defects of *Israel* are on quite another level. Fascinated – indeed hypnotized – as he now was with a work dominated by the chorus, Handel proceeded to give us his flawed choral masterpiece; for there are arias and duets, even a famous duet for two bass singers, 'The Lord is a man of war', but all are swamped in the mass of choral sound. The very magnitude of the choruses also makes the work fatiguing to the general listener; but having said that, one must admit that *Israel* is Handel's sublime masterpiece, where the inspiration is blazing and the effect electrifying. In a summary such as this we can but single out a few points: the extraordinary, repellent sound of 'he sent a thick darkness over the Land, even darkness which might be felt'. Here is the most perfect evidence of Handel's unique grasp of the bassoons' peculiar qualities, a knowledge he displays again and again (one thinks, too, of that incredible bassoon passage at the beginning of the Organ Concerto Op. 7, No. 4, originally a separate piece from *c.* 1738) but nowhere with more immediate force than here, where the gloom seems to penetrate our very souls – and how brilliant to end this number as a *recitative*, which trails away like the wisps of fog it so chillingly portrays. In the chorus 'But as for his people', we have a touching moment when the orchestra subsides to a 'pastoral pedal' as the altos sing 'He led them forth like sheep'. The eight-part choruses are staggering, often with the support of an orchestra almost the size of that in *Saul*. It might also be pointed out that Handel includes trombone parts in *Israel in Egypt* which bear interesting comparison with the trombone writing in *Saul*. And surely the greatest moment in all Handel's music is the final number 'Sing ye to the Lord for He hath triumphed gloriously' given out by soprano solo, totally unaccompanied, followed by the stunning force of the full orchestra and chorus singing 'The Lord shall reign for ever and ever'. The soprano solo, again frail in her solitary splendour, continues 'The horse and his rider hath He thrown into the sea', followed by (as it happens a repeat of) the choral 'For He hath triumphed gloriously'. One notes that Handel, always a master of the grand strategem, withholds his brass and timpani, only bringing them in after a dozen pages (in Arnold's full score) of silence to crash into the texture almost like the personification of the 'horse and his rider'. It is sublime music. Streatfeild has summed it up admirably:

> The subject is colossal, and its treatment no less so. The possibilities of choral music as a means of expression are practically exhausted in *Israel*. Nothing like it had been heard before its day, nor has been attempted since. *Israel* remains one of the most astonishing *tours de force* in the history of music. As a combination of massive grandeur of style and picturesque force, it stands alone. It is like a vast series of frescoes painted by a giant on the walls of some primeval temple. The colours may have faded, but the sublime conception and the grand strength of line survive to astonish later and more degenerate ages. [op. cit., p. 278]

In order to launch his new season, Handel made an arrangement with Heidegger, renting the King's Theatre for a dozen nights. *Saul* opened the season on 16 January 1739. The title role was sung by Gustavus Waltz, who was thought to have been Handel's cook, a notion exploded by William C. Smith in 1948.[4] 'La Francesina' alias Elisabeth Duparc and Cecilia Arne *née* Young were the leading ladies and John Beard was Jonathan. Other parts were given to actor-singers, and the cast as a whole was hardly distinguished; but the public liked the work and it was performed half a dozen times and revived in 1740, 1741, 1742, 1744, 1745, 1750 and 1754.

There were two revivals before *Israel* was given, *Alexander's Feast* and *Il trionfo del Tempo*, but finally, on 4 April, the great new work was given its first hearing. Even with Handel playing an organ concerto, the Oratorio was found bewildering, partly because many objected to hearing the Scriptures sung in a theatre, partly because of the work's novelty. But there were passionate adherents, and one gentleman published a long letter in the *London Daily Post*, from which we learn among other things that the Prince of Wales and his consort were there, 'sitting enchanted'; also that 'I have been told, the Words were selected out of the Sacred Writings by the Great Composer himself.' Perhaps after all, Handel's part in the word-book is greater than is now usually admitted. But Handel considered himself defeated and for the next performance *Israel* was 'shortened and Intermix'd with Songs', i.e., English songs and Italian arias. 'It must', writes Streatfeild (p. 152), 'have been a bitter pill to Handel to be compelled to mutilate his great work to suit the artistic depravity of London audiences.'

The autograph manuscript of Handel's next operation, *Jupiter in Argos (Giove in Argo)*, is dated 24 April 1739; it was a semi-staged pasticcio with some new arias and a final chorus, which was given, without notable acclaim, but with 'two Concerto's [*sic*] on the Organ' on 1 May and once repeated.

It was not Handel's best season but it was not a total failure, though the composer's expenditures on the huge forces necessary for *Saul* and *Israel* must have been high. And the country was about to go to war, and the theatre was not uppermost in people's thoughts. The 'Jenkins affair' or the 'War of Jenkins' Ear' turned into a full-fledged conflict with the old enemy, Spain. The Spanish rightly objected to British smuggling and the slave trade with the Spanish colonies, and when the Spanish boarded one of the British vessels, they found a master mariner named Jenkins whom they maltreated and whose ear they cut off, telling him to take it home to King George. In the House of Commons, they heard Jenkins say, 'In that supreme moment, I commended my soul to God and my cause to my country.' Walpole had given the British peace for thirty years; now, they no longer wanted it, and Walpole was forced to declare war, albeit very unwillingly.

Handel now transferred his venue to Rich's Theatre Royal in Lincoln's Inn Fields, and for the first concert of the 1739 season he opened on St Cecilia's Day (22 November) with two works, both dedicated to the patroness of music and the first newly composed, or rather newly stolen from Gottlieb Muffat's *Componimenti Musicali per il Cembalo*, which had appeared earlier that same year. This *Ode for St Cecilia's Day*, although not Handel at his very best (even as a great arranger), has always been popular. The opening, 'From Harmony, from heavenly Harmony' (the text is again by Dryden), starts as a rich accompanied recitative, and the words are then given to the chorus, which grows in beauty and power, 'Through all the compass of the notes it ran, The diapason closing full in Man'. But the climax of this piece, which is not unmindful of Purcellian and Clarkean predecessors, is the final number, for solo soprano with chorus, 'As from the power of sacred lays'. The use of the soprano, totally unaccompanied, followed by the chorus, is taken from the final chorus in *Israel*, mentioned above. When the text suggests, 'The trumpet shall be heard on high', it comes just after solemn music to describe 'So when the last and dreadful hour / This crumbling pageant shall devour.' And the trumpet's entry, followed by the kettledrums, is magnificent.

On 29 September 1739, Handel completed the autograph manuscript of a new concerto grosso, destined to become No. I of the famous Opus 6. He composed the others *en suite* and more or less in the order in which they were published (except a slight reversal of sequence for the last six). Whereas the previous Concerti Grossi Op. 3 had been largely put together from disparate sources, Op. 6 was conceived as an entity. Handel had composed a series of organ concertos, including the famous 'No. 13' – as it is usually numbered – with the fanciful title 'The Cuckoo and the Nightingale', completed two days before the first performance of *Israel* (4 April) and presumably the final one in the announcement from the *London Daily Post*: 'With several Concerto's on the Organ, and particular a new one'. But the beautiful organ concertos were always intended as virtuoso objects for their composer and written as separate entities, whereas Op. 6, which Handel completed by 30 October (i.e., requiring five weeks for the twelve works), was conceived as a grand cycle. On 29 October Handel himself and John Walsh, to whom Handel sold the rights, announced the subscription for 'Twelve Grand Concerto's, in Seven Parts, for four Violins, a Tenor, a Violoncello, with a Thorough-Bass for the Harpsichord. Compos'd by Mr Handel.' The price was to be two guineas to subscribers and the whole was to be delivered by next April (1740). To ensure against piracy, Walsh took out a second privilege of copyright (31 October 1739). It was to be the last work that Handel himself issued by subscription 'at his Home in Brook's-street, Hanover-square'.

Along with Bach's 'Brandenburg' Concertos of 1721, Handel's Concerti Grossi Op. 6 are the finest examples of Baroque orchestral music – even finer than the greatest products of Alessandro Scarlatti, Arcangelo Corelli or Antonio Vivaldi. The unique perfection of the Handelian opus lies firstly in its infinite variety, always one of its composer's particular attributes. The old division between *concertino* (two solo violins, solo cello and harpsichord) and the general *ripieno* is sometimes used to Corellian perfection, but often it is totally abandoned in favour of larger tutti groups or a chamber-music like movement. Handel added oboes to some of the works but decided not to include the parts when they were printed; and the works are usually performed without them. The French Overture, with its exaggerated dotted rhythm, is one of the elements that did not originally form part of the Corellian concerto grosso, but Handel embraces it gladly and in such a work as the Concerto No. 10 in D minor we find a fully fledged 'Ouverture' in the Lully fashion, whereby the dotted slow opening leads to a fugue. In its altered guise, as in No. 12 in B minor, the dotted slow introduction leads to a homophonic rather than a fugal continuation. Variety is the keystone of all these works. In Germany, the French Overture had been combined with the suite, ending with a series of dance movements, as in the celebrated Overtures for Orchestra Nos. 1–4 by J.S. Bach. Handel sometimes uses dance movements, even an English 'hornpipe' as in Concerto No. 7. One of his 'maggots' is the hypnotic usage of chain 'Lombard' rhythms (the opposite of dotted figures, or rather the dots reversed – ♬. rather than ♪.♬) in the 'Musette' of No. 6 in G minor. At times, as in No. 7, there is no *concertino* at all, and the Concerto is for orchestra without any real solo instruments. Languid sequences on Corellian 'walking basses' alternate with slow movements of life-enhancing beauty: in No. 12 is a famous Larghetto with variations on that which our grandfathers used to call 'one of Mr Handel's grand old tunes'. Handel has recourse to every style, every new device: the 'Siciliana' (No. 8) faces a 'Polonaise' in No. 3. Quirky, uneven-bar themes of eccentric design and uncommon intervals alternate with minuets (Nos. 5, 9) of French sophistication. Regularity is always balanced by irregularity. In short, these are masterpieces of design, of an endless melodic beauty and with a profound knowledge of the string family.

When Handel came to 'sandwich' his new concerti grossi into the intervals of his oratorios and other works, he found not only the indifference of the public – preoccupied with the war – galling but even worse the very elements seemed to conspire against him. Like the Egyptians with those plagues he had so magnificently set to music, Handel was beset by adversity: The river Thames froze over and birds dropped dead in flight. It was the coldest winter in living memory, and as early as 17 November, the newspapers were assuring Handel's recalcitrant subscribers to Lincoln's Inn Fields that 'Particular Preparations are making to keep the House warm; and the Passage from the Fields to the House will be cover'd for better Conveniency.' But worse than that, 'Particular care will be taken to have Guards plac'd to keep all the Passages clear from the Mob' (Deutsch, pp. 49Of.). From an advertisement in the *London Daily Post* of 13 December 1739, we learn that 'Two of the above Concerto's [Concerti Grossi Op. 6] will be perform'd this Evening' at a revival of *Acis and Galatea*. But as the freezing Christmas season arrived, people were not delighted at the theatrical and musical season. 'Plays we have none,' wrote Richard West to Horace Walpole on 13 December, 'or damned ones. Handel has had a concerto this winter. No opera, no nothing. All for war and Admiral Haddock.' (Commander of the Fleet in the Mediterranean; Deutsch, p. 492.) By 14 February of the next year, the newspapers were stating that 'Four of the above Concerto's [Op. 6] have been perform'd at the Theatre-Royal in Lincoln's-Inn Fields' (Deutsch, p. 495). A week later a new work by Handel was announced (27 February 1740): *L'Allegro, il Penseroso ed il Moderato*, a Pastoral Ode taken from Milton and put together by Charles Jennens, 'With two new *Concerto*'s for several Instruments [from Op. 6], and a new *Concerto* on the Organ.' The Organ Concerto Op. 7, No. I had been completed on 17 February; with its written-out pedal part it is unique among Handel's organ concertos and its massive first movement shows the composer at his greatest.[5]

Despite its Italian title, Handel's new *Pastoral Ode* is in English, and from the best source possible. He wrote it as usual with incredible speed – seventeen days. In its spirit it is an integral part of the whole series of English works derived from the English masque, which he had begun with *Acis and Galatea* many years earlier (1718). Jennens appears in his usual role as a very clever adaptor, and the third part (*Il Moderato*) is entirely his own. The cycle is a particularly beautiful and noble tribute to the land of his adoption on the part of its fabulously flexible composer. Jennens cleverly designed the word-book to display Handel's insights into humankind, from the depths of depression to the brightest of hedonistic joys. Critics have often pointed out how close the music is to the spirit of Purcell and the (still very much living) Thomas Arne; this is no doubt true, but Handel has nevertheless made the work very much his own. 'Melancholy' is a part from Milton which inspired Handel to compose music which is worthy of a 'Goddess sage and holy' – one more illustration of Handel's sensitivity to the female psyche. It is true, and profoundly moving; it is also a gracious tribute to a great country.

As the season drew to a close, Handel could be proud of his list of subscribers for the new Concerti Grossi: 100 subscribers for 122 copies, including the greatest names in the land – Cumberland, Orange (and three other Princesses), Earl Cowper, three Shaftesburys, innumerable music societies (two for the Academy of Musick in Dublin), two for Charles Jennens. Men were writing poems 'To Mr HANDEL, on hearing "Alexander's Feast", "L'Allegro, ed il Penseroso" etc.' (*Gentleman's Magazine* of May 1740). But Handel was restless and left for one of his regular trips to the Continent. The stage was set for the final operatic tragedy and for — *Messiah*.

NOTES

1 Richard Bentley.
2 *Wentworth Papers*, p. 543.
3 For a superimposition of Stradella on Handel, with music examples, see Sedley Taylor, *The Indebtedness of Handel to Works by Other Composers*, Cambridge 1906, pp. 68ff.
4 William C. Smith, *Concerning Handel*, London 1948, pp. 165ff.
5 The fact that Handel used a pedal in Opus 7, No. I shows that there must have been an organ with a pedal in the theatre at Lincoln's Inn Fields, a fact not hitherto noticed by experts. When Handel revised the Concerto for Organ, Opus 4, No. 3, he pencilled into the autograph some notes for a pedal part which the work did not have originally. Stanley Sadie (*Handel Concertos*, London 1972, pp. 26, 56) rightly surmises that the revision of Opus 4, No. 3 must have been for the Lincoln's Inn Fields organ and made for or during the 1740 season.

X
The Irish Interlude & Messiah *1741-1742*

IN SEPTEMBER 1738, Handel had drafted his penultimate opera, *Imeneo*, which became a grim failure when first performed as the opening Handelian work of the season 1740/1 at Lincoln's Inn Fields (St Cecilia's Day, 22 November 1740): after two evenings it was summarily removed. Handel's last opera, *Deidamia*, was another ignominious failure (10 January 1741, repeated twice): even Walsh, who announced publication of the score on 14 January, could not find enough subscribers to make such an operation worthwhile.

The history of Handel's operatic career, which extends from January 1705 in Hamburg to January 1741 in London, is a curious one. He had composed hours of brilliant, moving and original music; he had been the greatest and most successful opera composer of his age; but he had chosen London as the principal venue for his efforts, and that choice had proved fatal to his ultimate success. His operas soon disappeared from the repertoire, to be replaced by newer and more fashionable creations; so that, by the beginning of the twentieth century, Handelian opera was totally forgotten, although ironically almost all were by then available in editions by Friedrich Chrysander. Then, between the world wars, a mighty attempt to revive these works on the stage was made at the German university town of Göttingen and continued at another university town in Britain, Cambridge. After the Second World War, Handel's operatic cause was immeasurably aided by the advent of the long-playing record. Although many of these operas are now successfully staged, their revivals have not as yet placed Handel among the public's operatic favourites such as Mozart, Rossini, Verdi or Wagner; and it is indeed a moot question whether it will ever be possible for any eighteenth-century operas except Gluck's *Orfeo* and the Mozartian canon to hold the stage permanently. But Handel's operas are no longer forgotten, and it is highly unlikely that they ever will be again. In their revival and in an appreciation of their merits, the British scholar Winton Dean has been their scholarly, urbane and persuasive defender.

Handel's operatic career was now finished, and the great man bowed to the British public's indifference and even hostility. As an oratorio composer Handel was an undoubted success, but the London audiences were too sparse. A German baron summed up the music season in London three days before Handel conducted his last performance of *Deidamia*:

> . . . The eminent skill of the composers, the extraordinary quality of the voices, the rivalry in performance – all this made London then the centre of the musical world. But today it seems that Euterpe has abandoned the shores of Albion and we have nothing left but *Oratorio*, that is, a kind of sacred concert, which Mr Hendel [*sic*] occasionally puts on. [Deutsch, p. 511]

It was the end of the season, and Handel closed it with a performance at King's Theatre of *L'Allegro ed il Penseroso* 'With Concertos on the Organ, and several Instruments.'

> This being the last Time [8 April 1741] of performing, many Persons of Quality and others, are pleas'd to make great Demands for Box Tickets, which encourages me (and hope will give no Offense) to put the Pit and Boxes together, at Half a Guinea each . . .'. [Deutsch, pp. 517f.]

The rumour was that Handel intended to leave the country for good. The following letter showed that many people must have been appalled at the thought:

FROM THE *London Daily Post*, 4 April 1741

To the Author, &c..
Sir,
At a Time when Party runs so high, and Politicks seem to have

taken up not only all our publick Papers, but the Attention also of the Bulk of Mankind, it may seem strange to you to receive a Letter on the Subject of Musical Performances. . . .

I have been led into this Way of thinking [about the power of music] by one of Mr *Handel's* Bills for *Wednesday* next [the 8th], when we are to have his last Oratorio at *Lincoln's-inn-Fields*. He has charmed me from my Childhood to this Day, and as I have been so long his Debtor for one of the greatest joys our Nature is capable of, I thought it a Duty incumbent upon me at this Time, when it is become a Fashion to neglect him, (unknown as his Person is to me) to recommend him to the public Love and Gratitude of this great City, who have, with me, so long enjoyed the Harmony of his Composition. *Cotsoni, Faustina, Cenosini*, and *Farinelli*, have charmed our Ears: We ran mad after them, and entered into Parties for the one or the other with as much Vehemence as if the State had been at Stake. Their Voice indeed was grateful to the Ear; but it was *Handel* gave the Persuasion; it was his Composition that touched the Soul, and hurried us into the mad Extremes of Party-Rage for the particular Performers. His Influence prevailed, tho' his Power was invisible; and the Singer had the Praise and the Profit, whilst the Merit, unobserved, and almost unrewarded, was the poor, but the proud Lot of the forgotten Master.

Is there any Nation in the World, where the Power of Musick is known, in which *Handel* is not known? Are we not, throughout the Earth, distinguished by the envied Title of Encouragers of Arts and Sciences? and whilst they talk of the great Genius's which we have either produced or possessed, is *Handel* ever forgot amongst them? And shall we then, after so many Years Possession, upon a single Disgust, upon a *faux Pas* made, but not meant, so interely abandon him, as to let him Want in a Country he has so long served? in a Country of publick Spirit, where the polite Arts are in so high Esteem, and where Gratitude and Rewards have so remarkably accompanied the Merit of those who have excelled in them, that the great Genius's of other Countries have often even regretted that Part of their Fate, which gave them Birth in any other Place. It cannot be! if we are not careful for him, let us be for our own long-possessed Credit and Character in the polite World; and if old Age or Infirmity; if even a Pride so inseparable from great Men, a Pride which in *Horace* produced an *Exegi Monumentum*, in *Ovid* a *Jamque Opus Exegi*; a Pride which placed the Sphere and Cylinder on the Monument of *Archimedes*, and one of Corelli's Tunes as an Epitaph upon his Tomb-Stone; if even such a Pride has offended, let us take it as the natural Foible of the great Genius, and let us overlook them like Spots upon the Sun, which, Spots as they are, do not eclipse or obscure his great Talent.

You may, by this Time, Sir, easily see what I mean by this Letter; I wish I could urge this Apology to its full Efficacy, and persuade the Gentlemen who have taken Offence at any Part of this great Man's Conduct (for a great Man he must be in the Musical World, whatever his Misfortunes may now too late say to the contrary): I wish I could persuade them, I say, to take him back into Favour, and relieve him from the cruel Persecution of those little Vermin, who, taking Advantage of their Displeasure, pull down even his Bills as fast as he has them pasted up; and use a thousand other little Arts to injure and distress him. I am sure when they weigh the Thing without Prejudice, they will take him back into Favour; but in the mean time, let the Publick take Care that he wants not: That would be an unpardonable Ingratitude; and as this Oratorio of *Wednesday* next is his last for this Season, and if Report be true, probably his last for ever in this Country, let them, with a generous and friendly Benevolence, fill this his last House, and shew him on his Departure, that *London*, the greatest and richest City in the World, is great and rich in Virtue, as well as in Money, and can pardon and forget the Failings, or even the Faults of a great Genius. . . . [Deutsch, pp. 515f.]

The season ended, then, and Handel began composing a series of chamber duets, of which one, 'No, di voi non vuò fidarmi' (there are two versions, one of July 1741 and one of September 1742) was to become immortal as 'For unto us a child is born'.

Handel's fortunes were, however, about to undergo a sensational change for the better. He received, this summer of 1741, an invitation from the Lord Lieutenant of Ireland, William Cavendish, third Duke of Devonshire, to visit that country. In preparation for it, Handel composed two of his greatest oratorios, *Messiah* and *Samson*. He composed the first of them between 22 August and 14 September: the first part was completed on 28 August, the second on 6 September: the third on 12 September and the orchestration took precisely two days and was finished ('ausgefüllet den 14 dieses', wrote Handel, interestingly enough, in German) on the 14th. Even by Handelian standards, this was miraculous speed. *Samson* was completed on 29 October 1741; in the event, however, Handel did not perform it in Ireland but in London in February 1743; if *Messiah* made his fame in Ireland, *Samson* was to change his fortune in England.

It seems quite clear that from the outset Handel had destined *Messiah* in aid of certain charities in Dublin. The composer had always been receptive to charitable causes (as indeed his scores, with their boundless compassion, might have revealed to the perspicacious), and he probably knew from Cavendish even the names of the three Dublin charities destined to receive *Messiah*'s bounties – Mercer's Hospital, the Charitable Infirmary and the Charitable Music Society (for the relief of imprisoned debtors). It is characteristic of Handel that, in the midst of his sorrows and debts, he could dismiss both, as it were, with a wave of his pen and write his *magnum opus* for a charity far away. If Handel had been in Dublin, he could have read in *Faulkner's 'Dublin Journal'* for 14 March 1741 that the Charitable Music Society had released 188 'miserable persons of both sexes'. Two years later, 142 prisoners were liberated. 'The debts,' writes Herbert Weinstock (op. cit. p. 230), 'for which these 142 men and women had been incarcerated totalled not more than £1,225 17s., of which the Society paid the creditors £33. The debtors were usually little more pauperized than the creditors.'

Messiah's libretto, compiled with great sensitivity by Charles Jennens (whose book for *Saul* had been such a marked success), was sent to the composer in June 1741. On 10 July, Jennens wrote to his friend, Edward Holdsworth:[1]

> Handel says he will do nothing next Winter, but I hope I shall perswade him to set another Scripture Collection I have made for him, & perform it for his own Benefit in Passion week. I hope he will lay out his whole Genius & Skill upon it, that the Composition

> may excell all his former Compositions, as the Subject excells every other Subject. The Subject is Messiah. [Smithsonian, p. 5]

Handel did not tell Jennens that he had composed *Messiah*, nor did he tell him that he was about to leave for Ireland; Jennens writes to Holdsworth on 2 December 1741:

> I heard with great pleasure at my arrival in Town, that Handel had set the Oratorio of Messiah; but it was some mortification to me to hear that instead of performing it here he was gone into Ireland with it. However I hope we shall hear it when he comes back. [Smithsonian, p. 5]

Astonishing as it sounds, the pompous and arrogant Jennens did not approve of *Messiah*. To Holdsworth Jennens wrote on 14 January 1743:

> His Messiah has disappointed me, being set in great hast, tho' he said he would be a year about it, & make it the best of all his Compositions. I shall put no more Sacred Works into his hands, to be thus abus'd . . . [Smithsonian, p. 5]

And shortly afterwards, we learn in another letter (21 February 1743) to Holdsworth:

> As to the Messiah, 'tis still in his power by retouching the weak parts to make it fit for a publick performance; & I have said a great deal to him on the Subject; but he is so lazy and so obstinate, that I much doubt the Effect. [Smithsonian, p. 5]

To complete this extraordinary tale, we might append an extract from the following letter of Jennens to Holdsworth of 30 August 1754:

> I shall show you a collection I gave Handel, call'd Messiah, which I value highly, & he has made a fine Entertainment of it, tho' not near so good as he might & ought to have done. I have with

> great difficulty made him correct some of the grossest faults in the composition, but he retain'd his Overture obstinately, in which there are some passages far unworthy of Handel, but much more unworthy of the Messiah. [Smithsonian, p. 5]

Jennens probably formed the general plan of *Messiah* not by studying the Bible but by perusing the Prayer Book; for much of *Messiah*'s text comes from that source. The passages from Isaiah and the Gospels are in part from the Christmas service for the Church of England, while Part II uses the services for Holy Week, Easter, Ascensiontide and Whitsunday. Part III comes in large measure from the Burial Service. Geoffrey Cuming[2] considers that Handel himself may have added 'If God be for us' (Romans 8); the composer's profound knowledge of the Scriptures has been commented on, see above p. 127.

In his penetrating analysis of *Messiah* (from which book we have so often and so gladly quoted), J.P. Larsen (op. cit., p. 97) has summed up the revolutionary new content, so different from all previous oratorios (especially in basing the whole word-book on Scriptures):

I. The prophesy and realization of God's plan to redeem mankind by the coming of the Messiah;

II. The accomplishment of redemption by the sacrifice of Jesus, mankind's rejection of God's offer, and mankind's defeat when trying to oppose the power of the Almighty;

III. A Hymn of Thanksgiving for the final overthrow of Death.

Before he left London, Handel went to hear a new pasticcio, *Alessandro in Persia* (compiled by Baldassare Galuppi from works by Leonardo Leo, J.A. Hasse, Giuseppe Arena, G.B. Pescetti, G.B. Lampugnani and Giuseppe Scarlatti). As might have been expected, Handel loathed it, but it was precisely what the British public adored; and it ran for twenty-one nights after its première at the Haymarket Theatre on 31 October 1741. 'The audience was excessive,' wrote Horace Walpole to Horace Mann,[3] but one entire role had to be omitted. It was obviously high time for Handel to leave the world of Italian opera in London.

Handel travelled to Ireland via Parkgate (now a grassy plain but in 1741 a thriving harbour) but was delayed by contrary winds and forced to stay in the pretty cathedral town of Chester. For his stay there in early November we have first-hand evidence from Charles Burney, then a student:

> When Handel went through Chester, in his way to Ireland, this year 1741, I was at the Public-School in that city, and very well remember seeing him smoke a pipe over a dish of coffee at the Exchange Coffee-house; for, being extremely anxious to see so extraordinary a man, I watched him narrowly as long as he remained in Chester; which, on account of the wind being unfavourable for his embarking at Parkgate, was several days. During this time, he applied to Mr Baker,[4] the Organist, my first music-master, to know whether there were any choirmen in the cathedral who could sing *at sight;* as he wished to prove some books that had been hastily transcribed, by trying the choruses which he intended to perform in Ireland. Mr Baker mentioned some of the most likely singers then in Chester, and among the rest a printer of the name of Janson, who had a good base voice, and was one of the best musicians in the choir. At this time Harry Alcock, a good player, was the first violin at Chester, which was then a very musical place; for besides public performances, Mr Prebendary Prescot had a weekly concert, at which he was able to muster eighteen or twenty performers, gentlemen, and professors. A time was fixed for this private rehearsal at the *Golden Falcon*, where Handel was quartered; but, alas! on trial of the chorus in the Messiah, '*And with his stripes we are healed,*' – Poor Janson, after repeated attempts, failed so egregiously, that Handel let loose his great bear upon him; and after swearing in four or five languages, cried out in broken English, 'You shcauntrell tit you not dell me dat you could sing at soite?' – 'Yes, sir,' says the printer, 'and so I can, but not at *first sight*.' [Burney 1785, p. 26n.]

Handel's arrival and that of some of his musicians[5] was announced in *Faulkner's 'Dublin Journal'* for 21 November:

> Chester, Nov. 5. Yesterday arrived here, on his Way to Dublin, Mr Maclaine, who was invited to play on our Cathedral Organ this Day, on which he performed so well, to the entire Satisfaction of

the whole Congregation, that some of the best Judges in Musick said, They never heard that Organ truly plaid on before; and his Performance was allowed to be very masterly, and in the finest Taste.

[Dublin, Nov. 21.] And last Wednesday [the 18th] the celebrated Dr Handell arrived here in the Packet-boat from Holyhead, a Gentleman universally known by his excellent Compositions in all Kinds of Musick, and particularly for his *Te Deum, Jubilate, Anthems*, and other Compositions in Church Musick, (of which for some Years past have principally consisted the Entertainments in the Round Church, which have so greatly contributed to support the Charity of Mercer's-Hospital) to perform his Oratorio's, for which Purpose he hath engaged the above Mr Maclaine, his Wife, and several others of the best Performers in the Musical Way.

In the same newspaper it was further announced that a divine service 'After the Cathedral Manner' was to be performed on 10 December at St Andrew's Church, the sermon to be preached by the Rev. Dr Patrick Delany, who later married Handel's dear friend, Mrs Mary Pendarves, *neé* Granville. (In the event Dr Delany would be indisposed.) The music was by Handel, the *Te Deum, Jubilate* and 'two new Anthems' – all for the support of Mercer's Hospital, which institution borrowed the music from Handel's friend, the violinist Mathew Dubourg, conductor of the King's Band or Master of the State Music in Dublin. (The minutes of Mercer's Hospital show the Dubourg transaction, and their Archives own a word-book of this and other Handelian music dated 1741 and marked 'as they are performed by the Philharmonic Society in Dublin for the Improvement of Church Musick and the Further Support of Mercer's Hospital'. Dubourg became the leader of the Handelian orchestra in Dublin.)

The Hospital wanted the great composer's participation in their forthcoming concert:

FROM THE MINUTES OF MERCER'S HOSPITAL,
21 November 1741

At a Meeting of the Governors . . . Novr 21. 1741

Present: John Putland Esqr Dean Owen. Dr Wynne. Ld Bpp of Cork Order'd That Mr Putland Dean Owen, & Doc^{r} Wynne be & are hereby desir'd to wait on Mr Handel & ask the favour of him to play on the Organ att the Musical Performance at S[t] Andrew Church.

G.T. Maturin, Secretary.
[Deutsch, p. 526]

The Lord Lieutenant and Lady Devonshire were among those specially invited. On this same day

> Last Tuesday [the 21st] arrived in the Yatcht from Parkgate, Signiora Avolio, an excellent Singer, who is come to this Kingdom, to perform in Mr Handel's Musical Entertainments. [*Faulkner's 'Dublin Journal'*, 28 November 1741]

Handel's first public concert in Ireland was the benefit at St Andrew's (the Round Church), when John Owen, Dean of Clonmacnois and a prebendary of Christ Church Cathedral preached.

> FROM *Faulkner's 'Dublin Journal'*, 12 December 1741
> Last Thursday [the 10th] was performed at the Round Church, for the Benefit of Mercer's Hospital, Divine Service after the Cathedral Manner, with the *Te Deum, Jubilate*, and one of the Coronation Anthems compos'd by Mr Handel; after which there was a most excellent Sermon, suited to the Occasion, preached by the Revd. Dean Owens, and after Sermon an Elegant and Grand Anthem composed on the Occasion, by Mr Boyce,[6] Composer to his Majesty, at the Request of several well-wishers to the Charity; the Appearance was numerous, and it is hoped the Performance was so much to the Satisfaction of every Person who heard it, as to bespake the Favour of the Publick on the like Occasion.

In the same issue of *Faulkner's 'Dublin Journal'*, we learn where Handel lived and also of his subscription plans:

> On Monday next being the 14th of December (and every Day following) Attendance will be given at Mr Handel's House in Abby-street, near Lyffey-street, from 9 o'clock in the Morning till 2 in the Afternoon, in order to receive the Subscription Money for his Six Musical Entertainments in the New Musick-Hall in

Fishamble street, at which Time each Subscriber will have a Ticket delivered to him, which entitles him to three Tickets each Night, either for Ladies or Gentlemen. – *N.B.* Subscriptions are likewise taken in at the same Place.

And a few days later we hear of the first concert:

FROM *Faulkner's 'Dublin Journal'*, 19 December 1741

At the New Musick-hall in Fishamble-street, on Wednesday next, being the 23rd Day of December, Mr Handel's Musical Entertainment will be opened; in which will be performed, *L'Allegro, il Penseroso, & il Moderato*, with two Concertos for several Instruments, and a Concerto on the Organ. To begin at 7 o'clock. Tickets for that Night will be delivered to the Subscribers (by sending their Subscription Ticket) on Tuesday and Wednesday next, at the Place of Performance, from 9 o'clock in the Morning till 3 in the Afternoon. – And Attendance will be given this Day and on Monday next, at Mr Handel's House in Abbey-street, near Lyffey-street, from 9 o'clock in the Morning till 3 in the Afternoon, in order to receive the Subscription Money; at which Time each Subscriber will have a Ticket delivered to him, which entitles him to three Tickets each Night, either for Ladies or Gentlemen. – N.B. Subscriptions are likewise taken in at the same Place. Books will be sold at the said Place, Price a British Six-pence.

The 'New Musick-hall', also called 'Neal's Musick-hall', no longer exists. John and William Neal were music publishers in Dublin; William was treasurer of the Charitable Music Society.

Handel was already being lionized by the town:

FROM *Faulkner's 'Dublin Journal'*, 29 December 1741

Last Wednesday [the 23rd] Mr Handell had his first Oratorio, at Mr Neal's Musick Hall in Fishamble-Street, which was crowded with a more numerous and polite Audience than ever was seen upon the like Occasion. The Performance was superior to any Thing of the Kind in this Kingdom before; and our Nobility and Gentry to show their Taste for all Kinds of Genius, expressed their great Satisfaction, and have already given all imaginable Encouragement to this grand Musick.

On the day that splendid criticism was printed, Handel wrote a long and very interesting letter to his librettist, Charles Jennens:

Dublin Decem^br 29. 1741

S^r

it was with the greatest Pleasure I saw the Continuation of Your Kindness by the Lines You was pleased to send me, in Order to be prefix'd to Your Oratorio Messiah, which I set to Musick before I left England. I am emboldned, Sir, by the generous Concern You please to take in relation to my affairs, to give You an Account of the Success I have met here. The Nobility did me the Honour to make amongst themselves a Subscription for 6 Nights, which did fill a Room of 600 Persons, so that I needed not sell one single Ticket at the Door. and without Vanity the Performance was received with a general Approbation. Sig^ra Avolio, which I brought with me from London pleases extraordinary, I have form'd an other Tenor Voice which gives great Satisfaction, the Basses and Counter Tenors are very good, and the rest of the Chorus Singers (by my Direction) do exceeding well, as for the Instruments they are really excellent, Mr Dubourgh beeng at the Head of them, and the Musick sounds delightfully in this charming Room, which puts me in such Spirits (and my Health being so good) that I exert my self on my Organ with more than usual Success. I opened with the Allegro, Penseroso, & Moderato and I assure you that the Words of the Moderato are vastly admired. The Audience being composed (besides the Flower of Ladyes of Distinction and other People of the greatest Quality) of so many Bishops, Deans, Heads of the Colledge, the most eminents People in the Law as the Chancellor, Auditor General, &tc. all which are very much taken with the Poetry. So that I am desired to perform it again the next time. I cannot sufficiently express the kind treatment I receive here, but the Politeness of this generous Nation cannot be unknown to You, so I let You judge of the satisfaction I enjoy, passing my time with Honnour, profit, and pleasure. They propose already to have some more Performances, when the 6 Nights of

> the Subscription are over, and My Lord Duc the Lord Lieutenant (who is allways present with all His Family on those Nights) will easily obtain a longer Permission for me by His Majesty, so that I shall be obliged to make my stay here longer than I thought. One request I must make to You, which is that You would insinuate my most devoted Respects to My Lord and my Lady Shaftesbury, You know how much Their kind Protection is precious to me. Sir Windham Knatchbull will find here my respectfull Compliments. You will encrease my obligations if by occasion You will present my humble Service to some other Patrons and friends of mine. I expect with Impatience the Favour of Your News, concerning Your Health and wellfare, of which I take a real share, as for the News of Your Opera's, I need not trouble you for all this Town is full of their ill success, by a number of Letters from Your quarters to the People of Quality here, and I can't help saying but that it furnishes great Diversion and laughter. The first Opera I heard my Self before I left London, and it made me very merry all along my journey, and of the second Opera, call'd Penelope, a certain noble man writes very jocosly, il faut que je dise avec Harlequin, nôtre Penelôpe n'est qu'une Sallôpe. but I think I have trespassed too much on Your Patience. I beg You to be persuaded of the sincere Veneration and Esteem with which I have the Honnour to be
>
> S[r]
>
> Your
>
> most obliged and most humble Servant
>
> George Frideric Handel
>
> [Deutsch, pp. 530f.]

The lines which Jennens sent were those printed as 'mottos' on the title page of the first word-book of *Messiah*. The second opera was *Penelope* by Baldassare Galuppi in the newest Italian style.

Handel had, then, every reason to be in great good spirits. We have, again from Dr Burney (1785, p. 27n.), an amusing anecdote of these first Dublin concerts and Handel's leader, Mathew Dubourg:

> One night, while Handel was in Dublin, Dubourg having a solo part in a song, and a close to make, *ad libitum*, he wandered about in

different keys a great while, and seemed indeed a little bewildered, and uncertain of his original key . . . but, at length, coming to the shake, which was to terminate this long close, Handel, to the great delight of the audience, and augmentation of applause, cried out loud enough to be heard in the most remote parts of the theatre: 'You are welcome home, Mr Dubourg!' [Burney 1785, p. 27n.]

There were now plans to augment Handel's choir for the forthcoming oratorios:

FROM THE MINUTES OF MERCER'S HOSPITAL, 4 January 1742

Order'd That John Rockfort Ruthland, & Rich[d] Baldwin Esq[rs] be desir'd to apply in the name of the Governors of Mercer's Hospital to the Rev[d] the Dean & Chapter of S[t] Patricks Dublin for their leave that such of their Choir as shall be Willing may assist at the Phil-Harmonick Society Performances which are principally intended for the Benefit of the said Hospital and to notifie to them that the Dean & Chapter of Christ Church have been pleas'd to grant them the same request. [Deutsch, p. 534]

News of Handel's activities in the new year come to us from the newspaper reports and from the Minutes of Mercer's Hospital:

FROM *Faulkner's 'Dublin Journal'*, 9 January 1742

By their Graces the Duke and Duchess of Devonshire's special Command, at the New Musick-hall in Fishamble-street, on Wednesday next, the 13th Day of January (being the second Night of Mr Handel's Musical Entertainments by Subscription) will be performed, *L'Allegro, il Penseroso, & il Moderato*, with several Concertos on the Organ and other Instruments. . . . Printed Books are sold at the same Place, Price a British Six pence. To begin at 7 o'clock.

FROM *Faulkner's 'Dublin Journal'*, 16 January 1742

By their Graces the Duke and Duchess of Devonshire's special Command, at the New Musick-hall . . . on Wednesday next, being the 20th . . . will be performed, *Acis and Galatea*; to which will be added, an Ode for St Cecilia's Day, written by Mr Dryden, and newly set to Musick by Mr Handel, with several concertos on the Organ and other Instruments. . . . To begin at 7 o'clock. *N.B.* – Gentlemen and Ladies are desired to order their Coaches and Chairs to come down Fishamble-street, which will prevent a great deal of Inconvenience that happened the Night before; and as there is a good convenient Room hired as an Addition to a former Place for the Footmen, it is hoped the Ladies will order them to attend till called for. – Printed Books are sold at the same Place, Price a British Six pence.

FROM THE MINUTES OF MERCER'S HOSPITAL, 22 January 1742

Agreed That the R^{t} Honble the Lords Mountjoy & Tullamore be desired to wait upon their Excellences the Lord Justices and request the favour of their Company at the Musical performance in St Andrews Church on Tuesday at the 8th of February.

That the Honble Major Butler be desired to apply to the Government for a Captains Guard to attend at said Performance & dispose of the Guard to the best advantage.

The Governors of Mercer's Hospital give this publick Notice that there will be a Sermon preached at St Andrews Church, on Tuesday the 8th of February next when Divine Service will be performed as heretofore after the Cathedral manner with Te-Deum, Jubilate, & two new Anthems compos'd by Mr Handel – Tickets to be had at the said Hospital at half a Guinea each.

N.B. Benefit arising hereby is the Chief Support of the Hospital.

FROM THE *'Dublin News-Letter'*, 23 January 1742

On Wednesday Evening [the 20th] the Masque of Acis and Galatea, with one of Mr Dryden's Odes on St Cecelia's Day, were performed at the New Musick-Hall . . ., before a very splendid Audience, so as to give infinite Satisfaction: Being both set to Musick and conducted by that great Master Mr Handel, and accompanied all along on the Organ by his own inimitable Hand.

FROM *Faulkner's 'Dublin Journal'*, 23 January 1742

By their Graces the Duke and Duchess of Devonshire's special

Command, at the New Musick-hall . . . on Wednesday next [the 27th] will be performed, *Acis and Galatea*; to which will be added an Ode for St Cecilia's Day.

FROM THE MINUTES OF MERCER'S HOSPITAL,
23 January 1742

The Gentlemen deputed by this Board to the Chapter of St Patricks reported that they had applied to them according to the Order, Jan^ry 4 1741[-42], & receiv'd the following answer.

The Dean[7] & Chapter of St Patricks are ready to concur with the Dean & Chapter of Christ Church in permitting the Choir to assist at the Musical Performance of the Philharmonick Society, if the Dean & Chapter of Christ Church will concur with them in permitting the Choir to assist at Mr Handel's. They think that every argument in favour of the one, may be urged with equal strength at least in favour of the other, particularly that which with them is of greatest weight the advantage of Mercer's Hospital, Mr Handel having offer'd & being still ready in return for such a favour to give the Governors some of his choisest Musick, & to direct & assist at the Performance of it for the benefit of the Hospital, which will in one night raise a considerable Sum for their use, without lessning the Anual Contribution of the Philharmonick Society or any of their other funds. & in order to prevent the permission to be brought into a precedent which some time or other may be of Evil consequence the Dean & Chapter of St Patricks will concur with the Dean & Chapter of Christ Church in any proper rule to hinder their Voices or other members of the Choir from performing at any publick Musical Performance excepting in Churches without the joint permission of both Deans & Chapters first had & obtained.

The above answer being read and a motion being made that application be made to the Chapter of Christ Church in persuance to the desire of the Chapter of St Patricks – is passed in the negative. [Deutsch, pp. 534–36]

After initially allowing St Patrick's Cathedral choristers to participate in the forthcoming oratorios, Dean Swift now reversed his opinion – signs of his growing insanity, which later in the year would totally cloud his great mind. It was all a storm in a tea-cup but a sad footnote for all the fine plans of the Hospital and Handel:

DEAN SWIFT TO SUB-DEAN AND CHAPTER OF ST. PATRICK'S CATHEDRAL, 28 January 1742 [First Version]

. . . I do hereby require and request the Very Reverend Sub-Dean, not to permit any of the Vicar Chorals, choristers, or organists, to attende or assist at any public musical performances, without my consent, or his consent, with the consent of the Chapter first obtained.

And whereas it hath been reported, that I gave a licence to certain vicars to assist at a club of fiddlers in Fishamble Street, I do hereby declare that I remember no such licence to have been ever signed or sealed by me; and that if ever such pretended licence should be produced, I do hereby annul and vacate the said licence; intreating my said Sub-Dean and Chapter to punish such vicars as shall ever appear there, as songsters, fiddlers, pipers, trumpeters, drummers, drum-majors, or in any sonal quality, according to the flagitious aggravations of their respective disobedience, rebellion, perfidy, and ingratitude.

I require my said Sub-Dean to proceed to the extremity of expulsion, if the said vicars should be found ungovernable, impenitent, or self-sufficient, especially Taverner, Phipps, and Church, who, as I am informed, have, in violation of my Sub-Dean's and Chapter's order in December last, at the instance of some obscure persons unknown, presumed to sing and fiddle at the club above mentioned . . .

[Second Version]

Whereas several of the Vicar Chorals have disobeyed and transgressed some rules and orders made by my Sub-Dean and Chapter for regulating their behaviour and conduct and pretend and give out that they have my licence under my hand to act contrary to the said orders made by my Sub-Dean and Chapter: Now I do hereby declare, that to the best of my remembrance I never did sign any licence to any of the said vicars to perform at any musical society contrary to the said orders nor did I ever design it.

> And, if I have been so far imposed upon as to sign any deed or licence to the purposes aforesaid and it be produced to justify their behaviour, I do hereby annul and vacate the same . . . [Deutsch, pp. 536f.]

Handel's first Irish oratorio was to be *Esther*:

FROM *Faulkner's 'Dublin Journal'*, 30 January 1742

> By their Graces the Duke and Duchess of Devonshire's special Command, at the New Musick-hall . . . on Wednesday next [3rd February] will be performed, an Oratorio called ESTHER, with Additions, and several Concertos on the Organ and other Instruments . . . To begin at 7 o'clock. Printed Books are sold at the same Place, Price a British Six-pence. – N.B. It is humbly hoped that no Gentlemen or Ladies will take it ill, that none but Subscribers can be admitted, and that no Single Tickets will be delivered, or Money taken at the Door.

On 6 February, *Faulkner's 'Dublin Journal'* announced a new subscription:

> By the Desire of several Persons of Quality and Distinction there will be a new Subscription made for Mr Handel's Musical Entertainments, for Six Nights more, on the same Footing as the last. No more than 150 Subscriptions will be taken in, and no Single Tickets sold, or any Money taken at the Door. Subscriptions will be taken in at Mr Handel's House in Abby-street near Lyffee-street, on Monday next, being the 8th Day of February from 9 o'clock in the Morning till 3 in the Afternoon.
>
> N.B. The Tickets for the last Night of the First Subscription, will be delivered to the Subscribers on Tuesday and Wednesday next, at the New Musick hall in Fishamble-street from 10 o'clock in the Morning till 3 in the Afternoon; where Subscriptions are taken in likewise.

On the 8th was another Handel concert at St Andrew's Church for the benefit of Mercer's Hospital, which included the Utrecht *Te*

Deum, Jubilee and two Coronation anthems, 'My heart is inditing' and 'Zadok the Priest'.

More news of the subscription is found in *Faulkner's 'Dublin Journal'* for 9 February 1742:

> Whereas several of the Nobility and Gentry have been pleased to desire a second Subscription for Mr Handel's Musical Entertainments, on the same Terms as the first; Mr Handel being a Stranger, and not knowing where to wait on every Gentleman, who was a Subscriber to his first, to pay his Compliments, hopes that those who have a Mind to subscribe again, will be pleased to send in their Names this Day (being Tuesday the 9th of February) and To-morrow, at the Musick-hall in Fishamble-street, where Attendance will be given from 10 o'clock in the Morning till 3 in the Afternoon, and every following Day at his House in Abby street near Liffey-street.
>
> N.B. To-morrow being the last Night of Performance[8] of his first Subscription, the Tickets will be delivered to the Subscribers this Day and To-morrow at the Musick-hall . . . where new Subscriptions taken in likewise.

There turned out to be a special request to open the new subscription series on 17 February; but as matters turned out, the Duke and Duchess of Devonshire had to leave the country on the 16th for London. Handel had no need to worry: his place in the Irish esteem was now secure:

> FROM *Faulkner's 'Dublin Journal'*, 13 February 1742
>
> By their Graces the Duke and Duchess of Devonshire's special Command, at the New Musick-hall . . . on Wednesday next [17th February] will be performed, *Alexander's Feast*, with Additions and several Concertos on the Organ. Attendance will be given this Day at Mr Handel's House in Abby-street, and on Monday, Tuesday, and Wednesday at the Musick-hall . . ., in order to deliver to Subscribers their new Subscription Tickets (by sending their Subscription Money) in which Places Subscriptions are taken in likewise. None but Subscriber's Tickets can be admitted to the Publick Rehearsals. – N.B. For the conveniency of the ready

emptying of the House, no Chairs will be admitted in waiting but hazard Chairs, at the new Passage in Copper Alley.

Mercer's Hospital was meanwhile still trying to enlarge the choir for the forthcoming performance of *Messiah*:

FROM THE MINUTES OF MERCER'S HOSPITAL, 4 March 1742

Whereas Mr Putland reported from a Committee appointed to consider of a Performance design'd for the Benefit of this Hospital the Infirmary & the Prisoner of the Marshalseas That it was the desire of the Gentlemen of that Committee that a deputation from the Trustees for those several Charities shou'd attend the Deans & Chapters of Christ Church & St Patricks to desire their leave that the Choir of both Cathedrals may assist at the said Performance.

Order'd That the Trustees of this Hospital do concur with the Committee provided that the whole benefit of the said Performance & of all Rehearsals previous to it shall be intirely applied to the support of the said Charities, & that Tickets be given out for whatever Rehearsals shall be necessary. [Deutsch, p. 541]

Handel's *Imeneo* may have failed in London, but the composer, riding on the crest of Irish popularity, rightly considered that the Dublin public would appreciate this new 'Serenata' (as he cleverly re-titled it):

FROM *Faulkner's 'Dublin Journal'*, 6 March 1742

The new Serenata called HYMEN, that was to have been performed on Wednesday next [the 10th], at Mr Handel's Musical Entertainments at the New Musick-Hall in Fishamble-street, is by the sudden illness of Mrs Cibber, put off to the Wednesday following; and as many of Mr Handel's Subscribers are obliged to go out of Town soon, it is humbly hoped that they will accept of the *Allegro ed il Penseroso* for the next Night's Performance, which will be on Wednesday the 10th of March . . .

We may follow the concerts, or their postponement, as follows:

FROM *Faulkner's 'Dublin Journal'*, 9 March 1742

Several Gentlemen and Ladies Subscribers to Mr Handel's Musical Entertainments having desired that the Musical Performance should be put off till Wednesday se'night the 17th of March, Mrs Cibber being in a fair Way of Recovery. The new Serenata called Hymen, will be certainly performed on that Day.

FROM *Faulkner's 'Dublin Journal'*, 13 March 1742

At the new Musick-hall . . . on Wednesday next [the 17th] . . . will be performed a new Serenata called HYMEN. With Concertos on the Organ and other Instruments . . .

FROM *Faulkner's 'Dublin Journal'*, 16 March 1742

At the new Musick-hall . . . To-morrow . . . will be performed *L'Allegro ed il Penseroso*, with Concertos on the Organ; Mrs Cibber continuing so ill that the new Serenata called HYMEN cannot be performed on that Day . . .

FROM *Faulkner's 'Dublin Journal'*, 20 March 1742

At the new Musick-hall . . . on Wednesday next, being the 24th of March, will be performed . . . HYMEN . . .

The great moment was now approaching; on 27 March 1742, *Messiah* was announced in the *Faulkner's 'Dublin Journal'*:

For Relief of the Prisoners in the several Gaols, and for the Support of Mercer's Hospital in Stephen's Street, and of the Charitable Infirmary on the Inns Quay, on Monday the 12th of April, will be performed at the Musick Hall in Fishamble Street, Mr *Handel's new Grand Oratorio, call'd the* MESSIAH, in which the Gentlemen of the Choirs of both Cathedrals will assist, with some Concertoes on the Organ, by Mr Handell. Tickets to be had at the Musick Hall, and at Mr Neal's in Christ-Church-Yard, at half a Guinea each. N.B. No Person will be admitted to the Rehearsal without a Rehearsal Ticket, which will be given gratis with the Ticket for the Performance when pay'd for.

Further news of *Messiah* – in which we see that Mercer's Hospital's attempt to secure both Cathedral choirs was successful – and a repeat of *Esther* are announced in *Faulkner's 'Dublin Journal'* for 3 April:

> At the new Musick Hall . . . on Wednesday next, being the 7th of April, will be performed an Oratorio call'd ESTHER, with Concertos on the Organ, being the last Time of Mr Handel's Subscription Performance. The Tickets will be delivered to the Subscribers on Tuesday next at Mr Handel's House in Abby-street, from Ten o'clock in the Morning till Three in the Afternoon, and on Wednesday at the Musick Hall . . . from Ten o'clock in the Morning till the Time of the Performance.
>
> On Thursday next being the 8th Inst. at the Musick Hall . . . will be the Rehearsal of Mr Handel's new Grand Sacred Oratorio called *The* MESSIAH, in which the Gentlemen of both Choirs will assist: With some Concertos on the Organ by Mr Handel . . .

Messiah went into production – the dress rehearsal was, as we see, a day late – and from the extant newspapers one can, even at the interval of over two hundred years, sense the public excitement and the special position to which the connoisseurs rightly elevated it:

> FROM THE *'Dublin News-Letter'*, 10 April 1742
>
> Yesterday Morning, at the Musick Hall . . . there was a public Rehearsal of the Messiah, Mr Handel's new sacred Oratorio, which in the opinion of the best Judges, far surpasses anything of that Nature, which has been performed in this or any other Kingdom. The elegant Entertainment was conducted in the most regular Manner, and to the entire satisfaction of the most crowded and polite Assembly.
>
> To the benefit of three very important public Charities, there will be a grand Performance of this Oratorio on Tuesday next [the 13th] in the forenoon . . .

> FROM *Faulkner's 'Dublin Journal'*, 10 April 1742
>
> Yesterday Mr Handell's new Grand Sacred Oratorio, called, The MESSIAH, was rehearsed . . . to a most Grand, Polite and crouded Audience; and was performed so well, that it gave universal

Satisfaction to all present; and was allowed by the greatest Judges to be the finest Composition of Musick that ever was heard, and the sacred Words as properly adapted for the Occasion.

N.B. At the Desire of several Persons of Distinction, the above Performance is put off to Tuesday next [the 13th]. The Doors will be opened at Eleven, and the Performance begin at Twelve.

Many Ladies and Gentlemen who are well-wishers to this Noble and Grand Charity for which this Oratorio was composed, request it as a Favour, that the Ladies who honour this Performance with their Presence would be pleased to come without Hoops, as it will greatly encrease the Charity, by making Room for more company.

FROM *Faulkner's 'Dublin Journal'*, 13 April 1742

The Stewards of the Charitable Musical Society request the Favour of the Ladies not to come with Hoops this Day to the Musick-Hall in Fishamble-Street: The Gentlemen are desired to come without their Swords.

This Day will be performed Mr Handell's new Grand Sacred Oratorio, called The MESSIAH . . .

It is thought that for the first and/or subsequent performances, Signora Avoglio and Mrs Maclaine shared the soprano solo parts; Mrs Cibber, William Lamb(e) and Joseph Ward the contralto part; James Baileys and John Church the tenor; and John Hill and John Mason the bass. All the men except Mason (who was only in the service of Christ Church Cathedral) were members of both cathedrals.

Faulkner's 'Dublin Journal' (20 April) printed a poem[9] for the occasion:

On Mr *Handel's* Performance of his *Oratorio*, call'd the *Messiah*, for the Support of Hospitals, and other pious Uses, at the Musick-hall in Fishamble-street, on Tuesday, April 13th, 1742, before the Lords Justices, and a vast Assembly of the Nobility and Gentry of both Sexes.

By Mr *L. Whyte*.

What can we offer more in *Handel's* praise?
Since his *Messiah* gain'd him groves of Bays;

Groves that can never wither nor decay,
Whose *Vistas* his Ability display:
Here *Nature* smiles, when grac'd with *Handel*'s Art,
Transports the Ear, and ravishes the Heart;
To all the nobler *Passions* we are mov'd,
When various strains repeated and improv'd,
Express each different Circumstance and State,
As if each Sound became articulate.
None but the Great *Messiah* cou'd inflame,
And raise his Soul to so sublime a *Theme*,
Profound the Thoughts, the Subject all divine,
Now like the Tales of *Pindus* and the *Nine*:
Or Heathen Deities, those Sons of Fiction,
Sprung from old *Fables*, stuff'd with Contradiction;
But our *Messiah*, blessed be his Name!
Both Heaven and Earth his *Miracles* proclaim.
His Birth, his Passion, and his Resurrection,
With his Ascention, have a strong Connection;
What Prophets spoke, or Sybels could relate,
In him were all their Prophecies compleat,
The *Word* made Flesh, both God and Man became;
They let all Nations glorify his Name.
Let Hallelujah's round the Globe be sung,
To our *Messiah*, from a Virgin sprung.

[Deutsch, pp. 546f.]

Mrs Cibber's performance of 'He was despised' must have been magnificent (we must remember she was a great actress); it is reported that the Rev. Dr Delany was moved to shout, after hearing it, 'Woman, for this thy sins be forgiven thee!' It is perhaps apocryphal but has a nice touch of Handelian compassion about it.

The title-page of the first libretto contains Jennens's added mottos, and in one copy, discovered in 1891 and now in the British Library, a contemporary hand has added the names of the singers for the (first?) performance. Mrs Maclean, for example, sang 'I know that my Redeemer liveth', whereas Mrs Cibber and Signora Avoglio divided 'He shall feed His flock' (thus diverging from the autograph version for soprano alone).

The following criticism was printed in *Faulkner's 'Dublin Journal'* on 17 April and, without the final sentence, in the *Dublin Gazette* and *Dublin News-Letter* (*Pue's Occurences* printed its own, much briefer, report), which suggests that it was 'composed' by the Secretary of Mercer's Hospital. By reducing the ladies' hoops, and adding that 'Gentlemen are desired to come without their Swords', a hall designed for 600 accommodated 700.

> On Tuesday last [the 13th] Mr Handel's Sacred Grand Oratorio, the MESSIAH, was performed at the New Musick-Hall in Fishamble-street; the best Judges allowed it to be the most finished piece of Musick. Words are wanting to express the exquisite Delight it afforded to the admiring crouded Audience. The Sublime, the Grand, and the Tender, adapted to the most elevated, majestick and moving Words, conspired to transport and charm the ravished Heart and Ear. It is but Justice to Mr Handel, that the World should know, he generously gave the Money arising from this Grand Performance, to be equally shared by the Society for relieving Prisoners, the Charitable Infirmary, and Mercer's Hospital, for which they will ever gratefully remember his Name; and that the Gentlemen of the two Choirs, Mr Dubourg, Mrs Avolio, and Mrs Cibber, who all performed their Parts to Admiration, acted also on the same disinterested Principle, satisfied with the deserved Applause of the Publick, and the conscious Pleasure of promoting such useful, and extensive Charity. There were about 700 People in the Room, and the Sum collected for that Noble and Pious Charity amounted to about 400l. out of which 127l. goes to each of the three great and pious Charities.

After *Messiah*, Handel gave the Irish public his *Saul*, which was also a resounding success:

> FROM *Faulkner's 'Dublin Journal'*, 11 May 1742
>
> As several of the Nobility and Gentry have desired to hear Mr Handel's Grand Oratorio of Saul, it will be performed on the 25th Inst. at the New Musick-hall . . . with some Concertos on the Organ. Tickets will be delivered at Mr Handel's House in Abbey-street, and at Mr Neal's in Christ-church-yard, at Half a Guinea

each. A Ticket for the Rehearsal (which will be on Friday the 21st) will be given gratis with the Ticket for the Performance. Both the Rehearsal and the Performance will begin at 12 at Noon.

FROM *Faulkner's 'Dublin Journal'*, 22 May 1742

Yesterday there was a Rehearsal of the Oratorio of Saul at the Musick-Hall . . . at which there was a most grand, polite and numerous Audience, which gave such universal Satisfaction, that it was agreed by all the Judges present, to have been the finest Performance that hath been heard in this Kingdom.

[Performance on 25th May:] To begin at 7 o'clock. Books to be had at the Musick-hall, Price a British Sixpence.

Handel's final concert was a repeat of *Messiah*:

FROM *Faulkner's 'Dublin Journal'*, 29 May 1742

At the particular Desire of the Nobility and Gentry, on Thursday next, being the 3d Day of June, at the New Musick-Hall . . . will be performed, Mr Handel's new grand sacred Oratorio, called MESSIAH, with Concertos on the Organ. Tickets will be delivered at Mr Handel's House in Abby-street, and at Mr Neal's in Christ-church-yard, at half a Guinea each. A Rehearsal Ticket will be given gratis with the Ticket for the Performance. The Rehearsal will be on Tuesday the 1st of June at 12, and the Performance at 7 in the Evening. In order to keep the Room as cool as possible, a Pane of Glass will be removed from the Top of each of the Windows. – N.B. This will be the last Performance of Mr Handel's during his Stay in this Kingdom.

In view of the last sentence of the above newspaper notice, it seems unlikely that Handel actually participated as a performer (or conductor) in Mrs Cecilia Arne's and Mrs Cibber's joint concert on 21 July 1742. (Mrs Arne *née* Young was the wife of the composer, Thomas Augustine Arne, Mrs Cibber's brother: the Arnes had arrived in Dublin on 30 June.) It was a feast of Handel's music and interesting because it suggests the parts Mrs Cibber sang while in Dublin:

FROM *Faulkner's 'Dublin Journal'*, 13 July 1742

At the particular Desire of several Persons of Quality, for the

> Benefit of Mrs Arne, at the Theatre-royal in Aungier-street on Wednesday the 21st Inst. will be performed a Grand Entertainment of MUSICK, to be divided into three Interludes; wherein several favourite Songs and Duettos will be performed by Mrs Arne and Mrs Cibber. – In the first Interlude (after an Overture of Mr Handel's) . . . O beauteous Queen, from Mr Handel's Oratorio of Esther, by Mrs Cibber; . . . O fairest of ten thousand Fair, a Duetto, from Mr Handel's Oratorio of Saul, by Mrs Arne and Mrs Cibber. – In the second Interlude . . . Chi Scherza colle Rose, from Mr Handel's Opera of Hymen, by Mrs Cibber; . . . Vado e Vivo, a Duetto of Mr Handel's in Faramondo, by Mrs Arne and Mrs Cibber. – In the third Interlude . . . Un Guardo solo, from Mr Handel's Opera of Hymen, by Mrs Cibber; (by particular Desire) Sweet Bird, from Mr Handel's Allegro, by Mrs Arne; and Per le Porte del Tormento, a favourite Duetto from Mr Handel's in Sosarmes, by Mrs Arne and Mrs Cibber . . .

Ireland had been more than a personal triumph for Handel and his *Messiah*: it had restored his self-confidence and probably augmented his purse considerably. The visit was also a silent reproach to London, as Mainwaring clearly suggests:

> DUBLIN has always been famous for the gaiety and splendor of its court, the opulence and spirit of its principal inhabitants, the valour of its military, and the genius of its learned men. Where such things were held in esteem he rightly reckoned that he could not better pave the way to his success, than by setting out with a striking instance and public act of generosity and benevolence. The first step that he made, was to perform his MESSIAH for the benefit of the city-prison. Such a design drew together not only all the lovers of Music, but all the friends of humanity. There was a peculiar propriety in this design from the subject of the Oratorio itself; and there was a peculiar grace in it from the situation of HANDEL'S affairs. They were brought into a better posture by his journey to Dublin, where he staid between eight and nine months. The reception that he met with, at the same time that it shewed the strong sense which the Irish had of his extraordinary merit, conveyed a kind of tacit reproach on all those on the other side

of the water, who had enlisted in the opposition against him . . . [pp. 131–3]

Handel left the hospitable Irish on 13 August 1742:

FROM THE *Dublin News-Letter*, 14 August 1742

Yesterday the Right Hon. the Lady King, the celebrated Mr Handel, and several other Persons of Distinction, embarked on board one of the Chester Traders, in order to go to Parkgate.

The composer had wanted to visit Charles Jennens at Gopsal (near Atherstone, north of Coventry) between Parkgate and London:

HANDEL TO JENNENS, AT GOPSAL

London Sept.[r] 9th. 1742.

Dear S[r]

It was indeed Your humble Servant which intended You a visit in my way from Ireland to London, for I certainly could have given You a better account by word of mouth, as by writing, how well Your Messiah was received in that Country, yet as a Noble Lord, and no less then the Bishop of Elphim[10] (a Nobleman very learned in Musick) has given his Observation in writing of this Oratorio, I send you here annexed the Contents of it in his own words. – I shall send the printed Book of the Messiah to Mr Sted for You. As for my Success in General in that generous and polite Nation, I reserve the account of it till I have the Honour to see you in London. The report that the Direction of the Opera next winter is comitted to my Care, is groundless. The gentlemen who have undertaken to meddle with Harmony can not agree, and are quite in a Confusion. Whether I shall do some thing in the Oratorio way (as several of my friends desire) I can not determine as yet. Certain it is that this time 12 month I shall continue my Oratorio's in Ireland, where they are a going to make a large Subscription allready for that Purpose.

If I had know'n that My Lord Guernsey was so near when I pass'd Coventry, You may easily imagine, Sir, that I should not have neglected of paying my Respects to him, since You know the particular Esteem I have for His Lordship. I think it a very long time to the month of November next when I can have some hopes of seeing You here in Town. Pray let me hear meanwhile of Your Health and Wellfare, of which I take a real Share beeng with uncommon Sincerity and Respect

S[r]

Your most obliged humble Servant
George Frideric Handel.

To
Charles Jennens Esq.[r] Junior
at Gopsal near Atherstone
Coventry bag –

[Deutsch, pp. 554f.]

That 'polite and generous Nation' had been the host of the greatest single work Handel had hitherto composed, and although he never realized his intention of visiting Dublin again, the composer's recollection of the country and its inhabitants must have been especially warm.

NOTES

1 This interesting correspondence, owned by Mr Gerald Coke, was first published in the booklet accompanying the Smithsonian recording of *Messiah*, Washington 1981, written by Howard Serwer. Hereinafter abbreviated 'Smithsonian'.

2 'The text of "Messiah"', *Music & Letters* xxxi (1950), pp. 256ff.

3 Walpole *Letters*, London 1894, I, p. 84.

4 Edmund Baker.

5 Mrs Maclaine was a soprano. From London came the contralto, C(h)ristina Maria Avoglio and the great actress and contralto, Mrs Susanna Maria Cibber, *née* Arne. The Round Church was St Andrew's.

6 Note that instead of two Handel anthems, there was one, and another by William Boyce, who might be called Handel's most talented follower; he had been since 1736 composer to the Chapel Royal (London) and to the King. In the minutes of Mercer's Hospital, they thanked Boyce (not in attendance at the concert) and it was also 'Order'd . . . that Dr Wynne be desir'd to thank Mr Handel for his attendance' (Minutes, 12 December; Deutsch, 527).

7 Jonathan Swift was Dean of St Patrick's Cathedral, the Sub-Dean Dr John Wynne, one of the Governors of Mercer's Hospital and a member of the Charitable Music Society. The Dean of Christ Church was Dr Charles Cobbe, one of the Hospital's Trustees.

8 The performance was a repeat of *Esther*.

9 Deutsch (p. 547) suggests that this may have been a revised version of a lost poem.

10 Dr Edward Synge. Henege Finch, a cousin of Jennens, to whom the librettist wrote his famous 'Maggots' letter of 19 September 1738 (see above, p. 176), and who inherited Jennens's Handelian collection, now in the Central Library, Manchester. [H.C.R.L.]

XI
Messiah in London & the Foundling Hospital 1743

PERHAPS HANDEL WOULD have liked to put on *Messiah* in London at once after he had returned; but there seems to have been strong opposition to hearing the words of the New Testament in a theatre peopled by actors and actresses of loose morals and dubious sexual habits. If opera was largely supported by the aristocracy, oratorio was on the whole the province of the rapidly growing middle class, whose puritanism was in stark contrast to the generally profligate nobility. At any rate, Handel's calculations that the Old Testament *Samson* would not encounter these difficulties were – as we shall see in Chapter XII – quite correct. After its success, he dared to announce *Messiah*, not under its title but as a 'New Sacred Oratorio':

> BY SUBSCRIPTION.
> *The Ninth Night*.
>
> At the Theatre-Royal in Covent-Garden, on Wednesday next [the 23rd], will be perform'd A NEW SACRED ORATORIO. With a *Concerto* on the *Organ*. And a Solo on the Violin by Mr *Dubourg*.
>
> Tickets will be deliver'd to Subscribers on Tuesday next, at Mr Handel's House in Brooke-Street. . . . To begin at Six o'Clock.
>
> [*Daily Advertiser, London Daily Post*, 19 March, 1743, etc.]

That day, 19 March, some inkling of the opposition to be expected came in the following letter to the *Universal Spectator*:

> The following Letter may to many of my Readers, especially

those of a gay and polite Taste, seem too rigid a Censure on a Performance, which is so universally approv'd: However, I could not suppress it, as there is so well-intended a Design and pious Zeal runs through the whole, and nothing derogatory said of Mr *Handel's* Merit. Of what good Consequences it will produce, I can only say – *Valeat Quantum valere potest*.

To the AUTHOR of the *Universal Spectator*

SIR,

. . . My . . . Purpose . . . is to consider, and, if possible, induce others to consider, the Impropriety of *Oratorios*, as they are now perform'd.

Before I speak against them (that I may not be thought to do it out of Prejudice or Party) it may not be improper to declare, that I am a profess'd Lover of *Musick*, and in particular all Mr *Handel's Performances*, being *one* of the *few* who never deserted him. I am also a great Admirer of *Church Musick*, and think no other equal to it, nor any Person so capable to compose it, as Mr *Handel*. To return: An *Oratorio* either is an *Act* of *Religion*, or it is not; if it is, I ask if the *Playhouse* is a fit *Temple* to perform it in, or a Company of *Players* fit *Ministers* of *God's Word*, for in that Case such they are made.

Under the *Jewish Dispensation*, the *Levites only* might come near to do the Service of the *Tabernacle*, and no common Person might so much as touch the *Ark of God*: Is *God's Service* less holy now?

In the other Case, if it is not perform'd as an *Act of Religion*, but for *Diversion* and *Amusement* only (and indeed I believe few or none go to an *Oratorio* out of *Devotion*), what a *Prophanation* of *God*'s Name and Word is this, to make so light Use of them? I wish every one would consider, whether, at the same Time they are *diverting* themselves, they are not accessory to the breaking the *Third Commandment*. I am sure it is not following the Advice of the *Psalmist, Serve the Lord with Fear, and rejoice unto him with Reverence*: How must it offend a devout *Jew*, to hear the great *Jehovah*, the *proper* and most *sacred Name of God* (a Name a *Jew*, if not a *Priest*, hardly dare pronounce) sung, I won't say to a light Air (for as Mr *Handel* compos'd it, I dare say it is not) but by a Set of People very *unfit* to *perform* so *solemn a Service*. *David* said, *How can we sing the Lord's Song in a strange Land*; but sure he would have thought it much stranger to have heard it sung in a *Playhouse*.

But it seems the *Old Testament* is not to be prophan'd alone, nor *God* by the *Name of Jehovah* only, but the *New* must be join'd with it, and *God* by the most *sacred* the most *merciful Name of Messiah*; for I'm inform'd that an Oratorio call'd by that Name has already been perform'd in *Ireland*, and is soon to be perform'd *here*: What the Piece itself is, I know not, and therefore shall say nothing about it; but I must again ask, If the *Place* and *Performers* are fit? As to the Pretence that there are many Persons who will say their *Prayers* there who will not go to *Church*, I believe I may venture to say, that the Assertion is *false*, without *Exception*; for I can never believe that Persons who have so little regard for Religion, as to think it is not worth their while to go to *Church* for it, will have any *Devotion* on hearing a *religious* Performance in a *Playhouse*. On the contrary, I'm more apt to *fear* it gives great Opportunity to *prophane* Persons to ridicule Religion at least, if not to blaspheme it; and, indeed, every Degree of Ridicule on what is *sacred*, is a Degree of Blasphemy: But if the Assertion was true, are the most sacred Things, *Religion* and the *Holy Bible*, which is the *Word of God*, to be prostituted to the perverse Humour of a Set of obstinate People, on a Supposition that they may be forc'd thereby *once* in their Lives to attend to what is *serious*?

How will this appear to After-Ages, when it shall be read in History, that in such an Age the People of England were arriv'd to such a Height of *Impiety* and *Prophaneness*, that most *sacred Things* were suffer'd to be us'd as *publick Diversions*, and that in a *Place*, and by *Persons* appropriated to the Performance not only of *light* and *vain*, but too often *prophane* and *dissolute* Pieces? What would a *Mahometan* think of this, who with so much Care and Veneration keep their *Alcoran*? What must they think of us and our *Religion*? Will they not be *confirm'd* in their Errors? Will not they be apt to say, that surely *we ourselves* believe it no better than a *Fable*, by the Use we make of it; and may not the *Gospel*, by this Means (as well as by the wicked Lives of *Christians*) be hinder'd from spreading? A Thing of no small Consequence, and

> which ought to be consider'd by us who have the lively Oracles committed to us, and are bound by all the Ties of *Gratitude* and *Humanity*, as well as *Honour* and *Conscience*, to endeavour to enlarge that *Kingdom of Christ*, which we pray *should come*.
>
> PHILALETHES.

On 23 March 1743, the first London performance of *Messiah* probably included most of the soloists for *Samson, viz.* Signora Avoglio, Mrs Clive, Mrs Cibber, Miss Edwards, Beard, Lowe, Savage and Reinhold – and the same applied to the two repeat performances on the 26th and 29th. As in Dublin, there were at least two soloists for each of the SATB solo parts.

Listeners divided into camps, and someone felt obliged to write against the anonymous letter in the *Universal Spectator*:

Wrote extempore by a Gentleman, on reading the *Universal Spectator*.

> On Mr HANDEL's *new* ORATORIO,
> *perform'd at the Theatre Royal in Covent-Garden.*
>
> Cease, Zealots, cease to blame these Heav'nly Lays,
> For Seraphs fit to sing Messiah's Praise!
> Nor, for your trivial Argument, assign,
> 'The Theatre not fit for Praise Divine.' [etc.]
>
> [*Daily Advertiser*, 31 March 1743]

But the plain truth was, *Messiah* did not please. The Earl of Shaftesbury tells us in his *Memoirs*:

> In Lent 1743, at Covent Garden [Handel] performed his Oratorio of Sampson, and it was received with uncommon Applause. He afterwards performed The Messiah. But partly from the Scruples, some Persons had entertained, against carrying on such a Performance in a Play House, and partly for not entering into the genius of the Composition, this Capital Composition, was but indifferently relish'd. [Deutsch, p. 848]

(It must have been after *Messiah*'s failure in London that Handel suffered a relapse of his stroke or 'paralytic disorder' – see below.)

Two years later, in 1745, Messiah was revived at the King's Theatre (9 April, repeated two days later), billed as 'A' (or 'The') 'Sacred Oratorio'; but the work was still coldly received.

The old Bishop of London, Edmund Gibson, who had so bitterly opposed Handel's oratorios being given in costume in the theatre (that is to say as surrogate operas) was, in 1748, replaced by Thomas Sherlock, who seems to have been more moderate in his views on the subject. Accordingly, Handel now dared to produce *Messiah* under its real title at Covent Garden on 23 March 1749; but there was still only one performance.

The year 1750 saw a sudden breakthrough of the work – not the single performance ('Being the Last This Year') on 13 April at Covent Garden but a few days later, for the benefit of a charitable institution with which *Messiah* now became inseparably connected: the Foundling Hospital.

It had been founded in 1740 by Captain Thomas Coram as the 'Hospital for the Maintenance and Education of Exposed and Deserted Young Children' and since its beginning has counted among its patrons not only the wealthy but artists from Hogarth to Virginia Woolf. It still exists and is proud to show visitors its Handeliana and the furniture he used to know. Later on we shall see that the first concert Handel gave as a benefit for them included the *Fireworks Musick*, in 1749. A year later he decided to repeat the Dublin procedure and give *Messiah* as a benefit concert for them. Not only that, the composer caused a new organ to be built and installed in the Hospital Chapel at his expense:

From the Minutes of the General Committee of the Foundling Hospital, 18 April 1750

The Secretary acquainted the Committee that Mr Handel had agreed to the following Advertizement to be published for his intended Performance.

Hospital for the Maintenance and Education of Exposed and Deserted Young Children in Lamb's Conduit Fields, April 18th, 1750.

George Frederick Handel, Esq. having presented this Hospital with a very fine Organ for the Chapel thereof, and repeated his offer of assistance to promote this Charity; on Tuesday the First Day of May 1750 at Twelve o'Clock at noon Mr Handel will open the said Organ; and the sacred Oratorio called 'Messiah' will be performed under his direction.

Tickets . . . at half a Guinea each.

Ordered – That the said Advertizement be published [daily in the *Daily Advertiser*, twice a week in the *General Advertiser*, the *Gazetteer* and some evening papers]. [Deutsch, pp. 686f.]

Handel also offered them one of several portraits of himself painted by Thomas Hudson, but for some reason this plan failed to materialize:

FROM THE SAME

[The Treasurer reports] That Mr Hudson had offered to present the Hospital with Mr Handel's picture, and that Mr Handel had consented to sit for it. [Deutsch, p. 687]

The first Foundling Hospital *Messiah* took place on 1 May 1750, and was a huge success; the Oratorio suddenly took on a new dimension:

INVITATION TO THE *Messiah* PERFORMANCE IN THE FOUNDLING HOSPITAL, 1 May 1750

At the Hospital

For the Maintenance and Education of exposed and deserted Children in Lambs Conduit Fields,

On *Tuesday ye first day of May 1750 at 12* o'Clock *at Noon* there will be performed in the Chapel of the said Hospital, a Sacred Oratorio called 'The Messiah'

Composed by George Frederick Handel Esqr

The Gentlemen are desired to come without Swords, and the Ladies without Hoops.

NB. There will be no Collection. Tickets may be had of the Steward of the Hospital, at Arthur's Chocolate House in St James's Street, at Batson's Coffee House in Cornhill & at Tom's Coffee House in Devereux Court at half a Guinea each. [Deutsch, p. 688]

From a contemporary diary, we also learn that *Messiah* was used to celebrate the official opening of the Hospital's Chapel, for which the foundation-stone had been laid on the first of May three years earlier:

FROM DR WILLIAM STUKELEY'S DIARY

1 May, 1750. An infinite croud of coaches at our end of the town to hear Handel's music at the opening of the Chapel of the Foundlings. [Deutsch, p. 688]

To continue our documentary account:

FROM THE MINUTES OF THE GENERAL COMMITTEE OF THE FOUNDLING HOSPITAL, 2 May 1750

Resolved

That the Thanks of this Committee be given to George Frederick Handel Esq[r] for his Performance in the Chapel Yesterday, of the Oratorio called 'Messiah', to a very numerous Audience, who expressed the greatest Satisfaction at the Excellency thereof, and of his great Benevolence, in thus promoting this Charity; which the Chairman accordingly did.

Ordered

That a Copy of the said Minute be signed by the Secretary & given to Mr Handel.

Mr Handel attending and having generously offered another Performance of y[e] Oratorio called Messiah on Tuesday the 15th instant,

Resolved

That the Thanks of this Committee be given to Mr Handel for his said kind Offer, and the Committee do accept hereof.

Resolved

That the following Advertizement be published . . .[Deutsch, pp.688f.]

The overflowing audience caused chaos and a repeat performance was at once organized for those who had been turned away from the initial event:

FROM THE *General Advertiser*, 4 May 1750

Hospital . . . in Lamb's Conduit Fields, May 2, 1750

A Computation was made of what Number of Persons the Chapel of this Hospital would conveniently hold, and no greater Number of Tickets were delivered to hear the Performance there on the First Instant. But so many Persons of Distinction coming unprovided with Tickets and pressing to pay Tickets, caused a greater Number to be admitted than were expected; and some that had Tickets not finding Room going a way. To prevent any Disappointment to such Persons, and for the further Promotion of this Charity, this is to give Notice, that *George-Frederick* Handel, Esq; has generously offered, that the Sacred Oratorio called MESSIAH, shall be performed again under his Direction, in the Chapel of this Hospital on Tuesday the 15th Instant, at Twelve of the Clock at Noon, and the Tickets delivered out, and not brought in on the 1st Inst. will be then received . . .

HARMAN VERELST, Se.

[Deutsch, p.689]

Later in the year we have an enthusiastic letter from one of Handel's many admirers on the subject of the Oratorio:

MRS DEWES TO HER BROTHER, BERNARD GRANVILLE, AT LONDON

Welsbourne, 3rd Dec[r] 1750.

I hope you find Mr Handel well. I beg my compliments to him: he has not a more real admirer of his great work than myself; his wonderful Messiah will never be out of my head; and I may say *my heart* was raised almost to heaven by it. It is only those people who have not felt the leisure of devotion that can make any objection to that performance, which is calculated to raise our devotion, and make us truly sensible of the power of the divine words he has chose beyond any human work that ever yet appeared, and I am sure I may venture to say ever will. If anything can give us an idea of the Last Day it must be that part – 'The trumpet shall sound, the dead shall be raised'. It is [to] few people I can say so much as this, for they would call me an enthusiast; but when I wish to raise my thoughts above this world and all its trifling concerns, I look over what oratorios I have, and even

> my poor way of fumbling gives me pleasing recollections, but I have nothing of the Messiah, but *He was despised*, &c. Does Mr Handel do anything new against next Lent? surely Theodora will have justice at last, if it was to be again performed, but the generality of the world have ears and *hear not*. [Deutsch, p.695]

Mrs Dewes was Mrs Delany's and Bernard Granville's sister.

And so, every year, *Messiah* was performed as a benefit for the Foundling Hospital in London – in Handel's lifetime from 1750 to and including 1759 (the last performance conducted by Smith Jr., as the composer was dying).
In 1750, they made £728 3s. 6d. from the performance of 1 May alone. The records of these performances are in the Minutes of the Hospital and are invaluable among other things because they provide authentic evidence of the precise size of Handel's forces, first in the year 1754:

From the Minutes of the General Committee of the Foundling Hospital, 29 May 1754

> The Treasurer reported, that the Net Money arising from the Performance of the Oratorio of the Messiah in the Chapel of his Hospital the 15th instant, amounted to the sum of £607.17.6. . . .

To wit . . .	£	s.	d.
For 1219 Tickets, and by Cash received	666.	15.	0
Paid for Musicians, Constables, etc., as by the following Account	58.	17.	6
	£607.	17.	6

		£	s.		£	s.	d.
	Messrs. Brown	£1.	1.–		£	s.	d.
	Collet		15.–	Brt. forwd.	19.	8.	6
	Freek		15.–				
Violins	Claudio		10.–	Christo. Smith			
Violins	Scarpettini		10.–	Org.			
Violins	Wood		10.–				
	Wood Jnr.		10.–	Beard	[blank]		
	Jackson		10.–	Frasi	6.	6.	–

	Abbington	10.–
	Dunn	10.-
	Stockton	10.–
	Nicholson	10.–
	Neal	8.–
	Davis	8.–
	Rash	8.–
Tenors	Smith	8.–
	Warner	8.–
	Warner Jnr.	8.–
	Rawlins	8.–
	Ebelin	8.–
Violin–celli	Gillier	10.6
	Haron	10.6
	Hebden	10.6
Contra Bassi	Dietrich	15.–
	Thompson	15.-
Bassons	Baumgarden	10.–
	Jarvis	8.–
	Goodman	8.–
	Dyke	8.–
Hautboys	Eyford	10.–
	Teede	10.–
	Vincent	10.–
	Simpson	8.–
	Adcock	10.6
	Willis	8.–
	Fr.Smith	10.6
	Trova	10.6
	Miller	10.6

	Name	£	s.	d.
Singers	Galli	4.	14.	6
	Passerini	4.	14.	6
	Wass	1.	11.	6
	Boys	3.	3.	-
	Baildon		10.	6
	Barrow		10.	6
	Cheriton		10.	6
	Ladd		10.	6
	Baildon Junr.		10.	6
	Vandenon		10.	6
	Champness		10.	6
	Courtney		10.	6
	Wilder		10.	6
	Dupee		10.	6
	Walz		10.	6
	Cox		10.	6
	Legg		10.	6
Servts	Le Blanc	1.	1.	–
	Gundal		10.	6
	Prince		10.	6
	Lee		10.	6
	Shepherd		10.	6
	Musick Porters	1.	1.	–
		£50.	18.	6
	Presented Mr. Ch. Smith	5.	5.	-
		£56.	3.	6
	To the Constables	2.	2.	–
	Organ Blowers 4/– Porterage of Tickets 8/–		12.	–

Carried up, £19. 8.6 £58. 17. 6
[Deutsch, 75of.]

It was a considerable orchestra and choir. The five anonymous players listed after the 'Hautboys' were in fact two horn players, two trumpeters and one kettledrummer. We know this because of a second list which has been preserved, that of 1758:

ORCHESTRA BILL FOR THE *Messiah* PERFORMANCE AT THE FOUNDLING HOSPITAL, COMPILED *c* 1 May 1758
A List of the Performers and [. . .]
Messiah on Thursday April the 27th 1758.–

Violins	Messrs Brown	£1 1 –
	Collet	″– 15 –
	Freeks	″– 15 –
	Frowd	″– 15 –
	Claudio	″– 10 –
	Wood	″– 10 –
	Wood Junr	″– 10 –
	Denner	″– 10 –
	Abbington	″– 10 –
	Grossman	″– 10 –
	Jackson	″– 10 –
	Nicholson	″– 10 –
Tenners	Rash	″– 8 –
	Warner	″– 8 –
	Stockton	″– 8 –
Hautbois	Eyferd	″– 10 6
	Teede	″– 10 6
	Vincent	″– 10 –
	Weichsel	″– 8 –
Bassoons	Miller	″– 10 6
	Baumgarden	″– 10 6

Violoncellos	Gillier	£– 10 6
	Haron	″– 10 6
	Hebden	″– 10 6
Double Basses	Dietrich	″– 15 –
	Sworms	″– 10 –
Horns, Drums	Adcock	″– 10 6
	Willis	″– 10 6
Trumpets, & Kettle	Trowa	″– 10 6
	Miller	″– 10 6
	Fr:Smith	″– 10 6
		£ 5 9 –
	brought over	12 6 –
	in all	£17 15 –

Goodman	″– 8 –
Owen	″– 8 –
	£12 6 –

As it happens, we have a reliable eye-witness for the performance of 1754 which was, as usual, conducted by the composer – Mrs Delany, on a visit to London from Ireland:

Mrs Delany to Mrs Dewes

Suffolk Street, 16th May, 1754.

D.D. [the Rev. Patrick Delany] gave Miss Mulso a ticket for the 'Messiah', and I took her with me – my brother [Bernard Granville] called for us both; the music was *too fine*, I never heard it so well performed. The chapel is fine, and the sight of so many poor children brought up (I hope to good purpose), was a pleasant sight. [Deutsch, pp.750]

But the score of Messiah contains no parts for horns, nor does the extant orchestral material in Foundling Hospital (which was from a score left to them in Handel's will and may thus be dated *c.* 1760). It seems that they simply doubled the trumpets throughout (except perhaps for the trumpets' *da lontano* participation in 'Glory to God'). The bassoons – also not specifically required in *Messiah's* score – doubled the bass line as was then the practice.

General Bill for the *Messiah* Performance on 27th April, Dated 2 May 1758

Singers at the Performances of the Oratorio at the Foundling Hospital

		Servants	
Sigra Frasi	£6 6 –		
Miss Frederick	″4 4 –	John Duburgh Mr Handels Man	£1 1 –
Miss Young [Mrs.Scott]	″3 3 –		
Mr Beard	″– – –	Evens	″– 10 6
Mr Champness	″1 11 6	Condel	″– 10 6
Mr Wass	″1 1 –	Green	″– 10 6
6 Boy's	″4 14 6	Mason	″– 10 6

Bailden	″1 1 –
Barrow	″1 1 –
Champness	″– 10 6
Bailden Jun[r]	″– 10 6
Ladd	″– 10 6
Cox	″– 10 6
Munck	″– 10 6
Reinhold	″– 10 6
Walz	″– 10 6
Courtney	″– 10 6
Kurz	″– 10 6
	£27 16 6

Musick porters	″1 11 6
	£4 14 6
Singers	″27 16 6
Orchestra	″17 15 –
	£50 6 –
M[r] Smith	″5 5 6
May 2 1758	£55 11 6

Received of Lan' Wilkinson, the sum of Fifty Five Pounds Eleven Shillings for the Performance of the Oratorio 27 April 1758 in full of all Demands

by me
Christopher Smith

£55 11 0

For the Constable for their Attendance 3 3 –

£58 14 – [Deutsch, pp.800f.]

We may sum up this extraordinary history of Handel and the Foundling Hospital in Mainwaring's words:

> . . . his MESSIAH which had before been received with so much indifference, became from this time the favourite Oratorio. As in the year 1741, it was applied to the relief of persons exposed to all the miseries of perpetual confinement; it was afterwards consecrated to the service of the most innocent, most helpless, and most distressed part of the human species. The Foundling Hospital originally rested on the slender foundation of private benefactions. At a time when this institution was yet in its infancy; when all men seemed to be convinced of its utility;

when nothing was at all problematical but the possibility of supporting it; – HANDEL formed the noble resolution to lend his assistance, and perform his MESSIAH annually for its benefit. The sums raised by each performance were very considerable, and certainly of great consequence in such a crisis of affairs. But what was of much greater, was the magic of his name, and the universal character of his sacred Drama. By these vast numbers of the nobility and gentry were drawn to the hospital; and many, who, at the first, had been contented with barely approving the design, were afterwards warmly engaged in promoting it. In consequence of this resort, the attention of the nation was also drawn more forcibly to what was indeed the natural object of it. So that it may truly be affirmed, that one of the noblest and most extensive charities that ever was planned by the wisdom, or projected by the piety of men, in some degree owes its continuance, as well as prosperity, to the patronage of HANDEL.

The very successful application of this wonderful production of his genius to so beneficent a purpose, reflected equal honour on the Artist and the Art. [pp.135–7]

One contemporary and one near-contemporary report may sum up this documentary report of *Messiah*. The first is included because it must reflect the loving opinion of thousands who then (and now) were (and are) moved by this visionary music; and the second records the origin of our tradition of standing through the 'Halleluja Chorus' – in those days they stood through the 'Dead March' in *Saul* as well – and preserves a characteristic statement of Handel's regarding the work's essence.

MISS CATHARINE TALBOT TO MRS ELIZABETH CARTER

St Paul's, April 13, 1756

The only public place I have been to this winter, was last Friday [the 9th], to hear the Messiah, nor can there be a nobler entertainment. I think it is impossible for the most trifling not to be the better for it. I was wishing all the Jews, Heathens, and Infidels in the world (a pretty full house you'll say) to be present.

The Morocco Ambassador was there, and if his interpreter could do justice to the divine words (the music any one that has a heart must feel) how must he be affected, when in the grand choruses the whole audience solemnly rose up in joint acknowledgment that He who for our sakes *had been despised and rejected of men*, was *their Creator, Redeemer, King of kings, Lord of lords*! To be sure the playhouse is an unfit place for such a solemn performance, but I fear I shall be in Oxfordshire before it is to be heard at the Foundling Hospital, where the benevolent design and the attendance of the little boys and girls adds a peculiar beauty even unto this noblest composition. But Handel who could suit such music to such words deserves to be maintained, and these two nights [7th and 9th March], I am told, have made amends for the solitude of his other oratorios. How long even this may be fashionable I know not, for next winter there will be (if the French come) two operas; and the opera and oratorio taste are, I believe, totally incompatible. Well they may! [Deutsch, p.773]

James Beattie to the Rev. Dr Laing

Aberdeen, 25th May 1780.

I lately heard two anecdotes, which deserve to be put in writing and which you will be glad to hear. When Handel's 'Messiah' was first performed, the audience was exceedingly struck and affected by the music in general; but when that chorus struck up, 'For the Lord God Omnipotent reigneth', they were so transported, that they all, together with the king (who happened to be present), started up, and remained standing till the chorus ended: and hence it became the fashion in England for the audience to stand while that part of the music is performing. Some days after the first exhibition of the same divine oratorio, Mr Handel came to pay his respect to lord Kinnoull, with whom he was particularly acquainted. His lordship, as was natural, paid him some compliments on the noble entertainment which he had lately given the town. 'My lord,' said Handel, 'I should be sorry if I only entertained them, I wish to make them better.' These two anecdotes I had from lord Kinnoull himself. You will agree with me, that the first does great honour to Handel, to music, and

> to the English nation: the second tends to confirm my theory, and sir John Hawkins testimony, that Handel, in spite of all that has been said to the contrary, must have been a pious man. [Deutsch, pp. 854f.]

What is it that sets *Messiah* apart from all the other works of this great composer? For one thing, it is the work's perfect proportions – there is none of the lop-sided grandeur of *Israel in Egypt*. And this exquisite sense of proportion extends to all the details: the change – from the Overture's stormy and restless E minor to the heavenly peace of E major and the words of the Prophet Isaiah which every schoolboy learns (or used to learn) in Advent tide – is typical of this matchless sense of timing and proportion. The scoring is equally fastidious: not for *Messiah* the double bassoons, trombones and carillons of *Saul*. Trumpets appear for the first time in the Chorus 'Glory to God' towards the end of Part One, and kettledrums for the first time in the 'Halleluja Chorus' at the end of Part Two. The oboes and bassoons are used only for colour and at first were hardly considered in the autograph: their function is to add delicate and pastel shades to the basic string orchestra (with harpsichord and organ continuo). The trumpets and kettledrums are used sparingly and with telling effect: the only *obbligato* solo part is the trumpet in 'The trumpet shall sound'.

Handel's feeling for the proper voice at the right occasion is never more aptly illustrated than here: the air 'He was despised' is given to the alto (Mrs Cibber) and we cannot imagine it sung by a male voice. By contrast, 'Comfort ye' (which might have been given to one of the ladies) is magnificent in its high male tessitura. 'Why do the nations' is not only a perfect vehicle for the bass but the coloratura passages are peculiarly suited to the lower male voice (for example those massive triplets). 'I know that my Redeemer liveth' is not only ideally suited for soprano voice but – and this is characteristic of the whole work, with its impeccable sense of timing – perfectly placed, after the 'Halleluja Chorus' and after the interval that followed. Its quiet sense of rapture could only make its full mark after the audience has settled and has, for a time, heard no other music. It does not matter if an organ concerto were played 'between the acts' – on the contrary, it would lengthen the space between the orchestral explosion in D and the inner calm of E major (in which key the Air is written). It also does not matter if 'He was despised' was specially composed with Mrs Cibber in mind: it has been specially written for every great contralto voice ever since: *an* occasion becomes *the* occasion.

Handel used all his experience in setting this text. Jennens was too limited to realize that it would have made no difference whether Handel took twenty-four days or one year. On the other hand, Handel surely meant it quite literally when he told Jennens that he intended to 'make it the best of all his Compositions'. Nowadays critics sometimes like to denigrate *Messiah* at the expense of *Semele* or *Hercules*, but it is difficult for many of us to agree: *vox populi, vox Dei*, and it is most unlikely that *Messiah* will suddenly yield its place to another Handelian work, or indeed to any other work at all. It has, of course, become a cult. Handel turned to dramatic recitative and operatic aria, to church anthem and the mighty choruses of the Coronation anthems, to German Passion, British masque, Italian chamber duet, and music of the Abruzzi shepherds (*Pifa*) – they all have their role in *Messiah*. The sophisticated chamber chorus, such as 'For unto us a child is born' (which as we have seen is taken from an Italian chamber duet, 'No, di voi non vuò fidarmi') is characteristic of the delicate and small scale of many such choruses. (The fact that it sounds beautiful even if inflated by a choir of three hundred only shows how indestructible the basic fabric remains.) Larsen, in a deft sentence, writes (op. cit. p. 121): 'There is a grace and freshness about this chorus, a spontaneous, poised strength reminiscent of the harmony of an antique masterpiece: this is music stamped by noble simplicity of expression and perfect mastery of form.'

From darkness to light: the 'people that walked in darkness' see the light in 'For unto us'. Just before all this, Handel has given us, in the hauntingly beautiful Arioso 'For behold, darkness shall cover the earth' (Isaiah 40:2), another magnificent transition to light, illuminating 'but the Lord shall arise upon thee' with the bass voice (again the perfect choice of register) rising majestically to D and modulating in the process from dark B minor to bright D major, the key in which the work is basically written from the end of Part Two.

One of the features about the celebrated 'Halleluja Chorus' needs to be reiterated. Part of its peculiar force is that, despite a fugal entry in the middle, the music hardly strays from the tonic before that slow moving phrase, 'King of Kings, and Lord of Lords', rising upwards a fourth and supported by the trumpet:

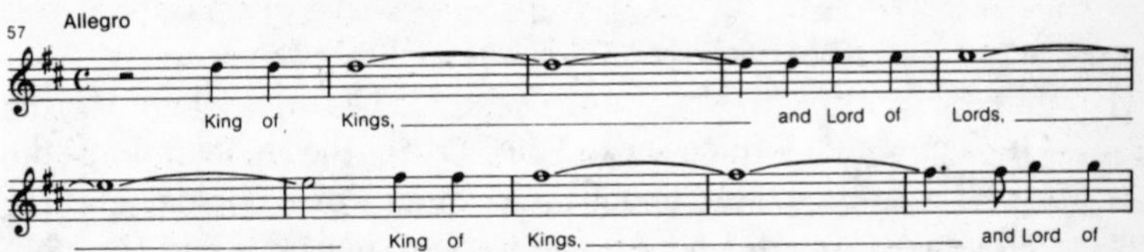

This is the first instance of large-scale tension and the first (albeit brief) excursion away from D major; but brief though it is, it provides the diversion necessary for the tonic insistence of all the remaining music. (There is another interesting example of this adherence to the tonic, and that is in Mozart's shining Overture to *Les petits riens*, composed in Paris in 1778.)

In the monumental final 'Amen Chorus', notice again the supreme skill with which Handel prepares the first entry of the whole orchestra combining trumpets and drums. The massive choral fugue stops just when we are led to expect the first big tutti: instead, we have the first two entries of the fugal theme given only to the two violins, whereupon the third (bass) entry coincides with the first real tutti. Even it is carefully disturbed by two more bars of the violins' dialogue before we are plunged into the dominant for yet another bass entry with trumpets and drums. All this is a fascinating combination of fugal grandeur and structural surprise.

As *Messiah* became ever more popular, different singers filled the solo parts and Handel made many small changes in their parts. These changes have been the subject of endless comment, but are perhaps *ultimately* less important than scholars believe; one may study them in excellent books – apart from Larsen's also in W. Shaw (1963) and J. Tobin (1969). The question of ornamentation, vocal and instrumental, or the lack of it, has been hotly debated. Historically, there is one letter on the subject by a dear friend of Handel's that requires quotation. After Handel left Ireland, *Messiah* continued to have a life of its own there, since the composer had been generous enough to leave behind him a score. His friend Mrs Delany gives us evidence that not all performances of Corelli's Christmas Concerto (for that is what Mrs Delany means by 'the eighth') were played with the copious ornaments – on the violin or harpsichord – which are now thought to be necessary towards the end of the final *siciliano*. Mrs Delany cannot have been alone in hating them:

MRS DELANY TO MRS DEWES

Delville, 10 Dec. 1750.

On Tuesday morning next [the 11th], the rehearsal of the Messiah is to be for the benefit of debtors – on Thursday evening it will be performed. I hope to go to both; our new, and *therefore* favourite performer Morella[1] is to play the first fiddle, and conduct the whole. I am afraid *his French taste* will prevail; I shall *not be able to endure* his introducing *froth and nonsense* in that sublime and awful piece of music. What makes me fear this will be the case, is, that in the closing of the eighth concerto of Corelli, instead of playing it *clear and distinct*, he filled it up with *frippery and graces which quite destroyed the effect* of the sweet notes, and solemn pauses that conclude it. [Deutsch, p. 695]

The last word on this kind of ornamentation, and on the latest fad for superimposing cadences over the vocal parts in recitatives,[2] has in my opinion not been spoken.

And if there is no such thing as a definitive edition of *Messiah*, that fact has never prevented the work from being the favourite of the public, especially in Anglo-Saxon countries. I for one do not propose to argue against that definitive choice. But let a contemporary have the last word on this indefatigable masterpiece, which survives every mutilation, re-orchestration and other indignities without number:

BENJAMIN VICTOR TO THE REV. WILLIAM ROTHERY, IN CHELSEA

[Dublin,] December 27, 1752.

. . . You must be a lover of music – If *Handel's Messiah* should be performed in London, as it undoubtedly will in the lent season, I beg it as a favour to me, that you will go early, and take your wife with you, your time and money cannot be so well employed; take care to get a book of the oratorio some days before, that you may well digest the subject, there you will hear *glad tidings* and truly divine rejoicings at the birth of *Christ*, and feel real sorrows for his sufferings – but, oh! when those sufferings are over, what a transporting full chorus! where all the instruments, and three sets of voices are employed to express the following passage, which I must quote –

'Lift up your heads, O ye gates! and be ye lift up ye
Everlasting doors, and the king of glory shall come in.
Who is the king of glory? The Lord strong and mighty,
He is the king of glory!
And he shall reign for ever, King of Kings, Lord of Lords.'

How truly poetical is the diction of the Oriental writers.

Mr Handel, when he was here, composed this excellent oratorio, and gave it to a charitable musical society; by whom it is annually performed, for the relief of poor debtors, and very well, as we have good cathedral singers, to whom this music is chiefly adapted – the performance is just over, and you will conclude I am never absent. As much as I detest fatigue and inconvenience, I would ride forty miles in the wind and rain to be present at a performance of the Messiah in London, under the conduct of Handel – I remember it there – He had an hundred instruments, and fifty voices! O how magnificent the full chorusses. [Deutsch, p. 729]

NOTES

1 G.B. Marella [*recte*], who published six violin sonatas in Dublin in 1753. [H.C.R.L.]

2 Haydn was a pupil of Porpora who, as we have seen, appeared in London in Handel's time; and in 1768 Haydn specifically instructs his singers *not* to engage in this superimposition but to allow the vocal parts to end first, *even if the notation is to the contrary*.

XII
The Age of Samson 1743–1748

IN PREPARATION FOR the première of *Samson* (18 February 1743), Handel completed a new organ concerto, later known as Opus 7 No. 2 (in A), the fugue and other material taken from music by Gottlieb Muffat (now identified by Dr Susan Wollenberg, Oxford). The composer offered his usual subscription for six Lenten concerts at Covent Garden. 'And if Mr Handel should have any more Performances after the six first Nights, each Subscriber may continue on the same Conditions' (*Daily Advertiser*, 12 February 1743). *Samson*'s word-book was fashioned by a clever man-of-letters, Newburgh Hamilton, who dedicated it to Frederick, Prince of Wales. The title role was sung by Beard and Mrs Cibber was Micah.

Perhaps the public wanted to make amends; certainly they were moved by the grand and tragic tale, so magnificently told, of the Old Testament hero. Whatever the reason, Handel found himself suddenly back in fashion.

> At his return to London in 1741–2, the minds of most men were much more disposed in his favour. He immediately recommenced his Oratorios at Convent-Garden. SAMPSON was the first he performed. And now (to use the expressive phrase of TACITUS) *blandiebatur cœptis fortuna*; Fortune seemed rather to court and caress, than to countenance and support him. This return was the era of his prosperity. Indeed, in the year 1743, he had some return of his paralytic disorder; and the year after fell under the heavy displeasure of a certain fashionable lady [unidentified]. She exerted all her influence to spirit up a new opposition against him. But the world could not long be made to believe that her card-assemblies

> were such proper entertainments for Lent, as his Oratorios. It is needless to enlarge upon particulars which are easily remembered, or to give a minute account of things generally known. It is sufficient just to touch on the most remarkable. . . . [Mainwaring, pp. 134f.]

A few days after the performance of *Samson*, one of Handel's friends wrote a letter to Dublin which found its way into *Faulkner's 'Dublin Journal* of 15 March; it explains why the composer's fortunes had altered so dramatically:

> Extract of a private Letter from London, March 8.
>
> Our friend Mr Handell is very well, and Things have taken a quite different Turn here from what they did some Time past; for the Publick will be no longer imposed on by Italian Singers, and some wrong Headed Undertakers of bad Opera's, but find out the Merit of Mr Handell's Composition and English Performances: That Gentleman is more esteemed now than ever. The new Oratorio (called SAMSON) which he composed since he left Ireland, has been performed four Times to more crouded Audiences than ever were seen; more People being turned away for Want of Room each Night than hath been at the Italian Opera. Mr Dubourg (lately arrived from Dublin) performed at the last, and played a Solo between the Acts, and met with universal and uncommon Applause from the Royal Family and the whole Audience.

Horace Walpole (no friend of Handel's) wrote on 24 February to Horace Mann:

> . . . Handel has set up an Oratorio against the Operas, and succeeds. He has hired all the goddesses from [the] farces [Cibber and Clive] and the singers of *Roast Beef* from between the acts at both theatres, with a man with one note in his voice [Beard] and a girl without eve[n] an one [Cibber?]; and so they sing, and make brave hallelujas; and the good company encore the recitative. . . . [Deutsch, p. 560]

But the public was of another opinion:

Miss Catherine Talbot to Mrs Elizabeth Carter

Cuddesdon, 27 December 1743.

. . . I will own having been highly delighted with several songs in Sampson, and especially with the choruses. I heard that oratorio performed this winter in one of the College Halls, and I believe to the full as finely as it ever was in town: and having never heard any oratorio before, I was extremely struck with such a kind of harmony as seems the only language adapted to devotion. I really cannot help thinking this kind of entertainment must necessarily have some effect in correcting or moderating at least the levity of the age; and let an audience be ever so thoughtless, they can scarcely come away, I should think, without being the better for an evening so spent. I heartily wish you had been with me when I heard it. [Deutsch, p. 577]

Handel, finding his subscription such a success, announced another six concerts on 12 March. But the strain of *Messiah*'s failure, discussed in the previous chapter, caused another paralytic breakdown, and on 4 May Horace Walpole writes to Mann, 'Handel has had a palsy, and can't compose' (Deutsch, p. 569). A month later we hear in another letter that 'The Opera is bankrupt. The Directors have run out £1,600 . . .'

In the summer, Handel composed a new 'Oratorio' but it was in fact a disguised opera which was entitled 'The Story of Semele' (after William Congreve). Jennens, who was offended at *Messiah* (see above, p. 191) and also at the composer's present choice of Hamilton as (successful) librettist, thought it 'a bawdy opera'. It contains brilliant music of astonishing power and finely delineated characters. Meanwhile the desperate Opera, encouraged by the Prince of Wales, was offering Handel 1,000 guineas for two new operas, but the composer had learned his lesson. The Opera's second offer, 100 guineas to revive and adjust each old opera, fell on more welcome ears, and Handel allowed *Alessandro* of 1726 to re-appear on 15 November 1743 as *Rossane* with Giulia Frasi as Tassile; she would later be one of Handel's leading sopranos for the Foundling Hospital's annual performances of *Messiah*.

Mrs Delany thought 'Alexander' (as she called it) '. . . infinitely better than any Italian opera, but it vexed me to hear some favourite songs mangled' (Deutsch, p.574). Meanwhile stirring events on the Continent dictated Handel's new composition.

On 27 November there occurred a grand *Te Deum* at St James's Chapel to celebrate the victory at Dettingen on the river Main in Germany: there George II had won a great victory over the French army in a crucial battle in the War of the Austrian Succession. That struggle was concerned with Empress Maria Theresa's right to wear the Austrian crown, disputed of course by the French. The king returned to England in November. On the 10th Mrs Delany heard a rehearsal of the new Dettingen *Te Deum* which her favourite composer had written to celebrate the event; she thought it 'excessively fine, I was all rapture and so was [her husband, Dr Delany] as you may imagine; everybody says it is the finest of all his compositions; I am not well enough acquainted with it to pronounce that of it, but it is heavenly. (Deutsch, p.573). After one rehearsal on the 18th there was a review of the new *Te Deum* together with the new anthem, 'The king shall rejoice' (Psalms XX and XXI) in the *Daily Advertiser*, in which the two works

> are said by the best Judges to be so truly masterly and sublime, as well as new in their kind, that they prove this great Genius not only inexhaustible, but likewise still rising to a higher Degree of Perfection. . . . [Deutsch, p.574]

Nowadays the *Te Deum*, which borrows heavily from music by Urio, is less favoured than many other of the composer's 'public' pieces; but for years it was greatly loved and admired.

The composer's new subscription series for the Lenten season of 1744 was announced on 9 January: there were to be twelve concerts, with 'two New Performances (and some of his former Oratorios, if Time will permit).' The first work was *Semele* and Mrs Delany thought at the rehearsal 'It is a delightful piece of music, quite new and different from anything he has done . . .' (Deutsch, p.579). The first performance was on 10 February with Beard as Jupiter, Signora Avoglio as Iris and Signora Francesina (Elizabeth Duparc) as Semele. The 'house was full, though not crowded', wrote Mrs Delany, who ten days later added an interesting comment:

MRS DELANY TO MRS. DEWES

Clarges Street, 21 Feb. 1744.

Semele is charming; the more I hear it the better I like it, and as I am a subscriber I shall not fail one night. But it being a profane story D.D. does not think it proper for him to go; but when Joseph or Samson is performed I shall persuade him to go – you know *how much* he delights in music. They say Samson is to be next Friday, for Semele has a strong party against it, viz. the fine ladies, petit maîtres, and *ignoramus*'s. All the opera people are enraged at Handel, but Lady Cobham, Lady Westmoreland, and Lady Chesterfield never fail it. [Deutsch, p.584]

'It is unfortunate', writes Herbert Weinstock

> that the single term 'oratorio' must, by force of custom, be used to indicate works so various in nature as, on one side, *Messiah* and *Israel in Egypt*, and, on the other, *Samson*, some of the earlier works, and all the subsequent ones. *Israel in Egypt*, particularly, and *Messiah* almost as much, are epics on a vast, non-human, universal scale. *Samson* and the others are dramas of a less vast, more human sort. For *Semele*, Handel himself used the phrase 'English opera', indicating not only that it was sung in English, but that it was done without the stage action essential to Italian opera. It is a better description of *Semele* than 'oratorio'. But time has not allowed the phrase to endure despite its useful purpose. [op. cit. p.247]

A new, and hitherto unstated, observation is simply that the wrong title of 'oratorio' may have been in the end *Semele*'s undoing: opera houses do not stage it because it is an 'oratorio' and oratorio societies do not perform it because they sense in it, and rightly, a pagan love story, a 'bawdy opera'. The more's the pity, for it is a work of unsurpassed beauty and power.

Our news about *Samson*'s revival and the catastrophic rehearsals of the second new work, *Joseph and his Brethren*, comes from another letter by Mrs Delany:

MRS DELANY TO MRS. DEWES

Clarges Street, Feby 25th, 1743–4.

I was last night to hear Samson. Francesina sings most of Mrs Cibber's part and some of Mrs Clive's: upon the whole it went off very well, but not better than last year. Joseph, I believe, will be next Friday, but Handel is mightily out of humour about it, for Sullivan, who is to sing Joseph, *is a block* with a very fine voice, and Beard has *no voice at all*. The part which Francesina is to have (of Joseph's wife) will not admit of much variety; but I hope it will be well received; the houses have not been crowded, but pretty full every night. [Deutsch, p.585]

James Miller's word-book for *Joseph* was dedicated to John, Duke of Montague, and the first performance was on 2 March with Signora Francesina, Beard and the usual other singers, all British except for Signora Galli (Phanor) from the rival Haymarket Theatre. The Earl of Egmont thought it 'an inimitable composition' and on 10 March Mrs Delany could report:

The oratorios fill very well, not withstanding the spite of the opera party: nine of the twelve are over. Joseph is to be performed (I hope) once more, then Saul and the Messiah finishes; as they have taken very well, I fancy Handel will have a second subscription [he did not] . . . [Deutsch, p. 587]

But Handel was still chary of *Messiah*, and Mrs Delany had to write, on 22 March, 'Last night, alas! was the last night of the oratorio: it concluded with Saul: I was in hopes of the Messiah . . .' (Deutsch, p.588). On 3 April Mrs Delany was to 'have a treat that I shall most ardently wish you and my mother could share of Handel, my brother, and Donnellan *dine here*, and we are to be entertained with *Handel's playing over Joseph to us* . . .' (Deutsch, p. 589).

Meanwhile relations with Jennens had improved to the point where the composer was about to set a new word-book, *Belshazzar*:

HANDEL TO JENNENS

London Jun 9th 1744

Dear Sir,

It gave me great Pleasure to hear Your safe arrival in the Country, and that Your Health was much improved. I hope it is by this time firmly establichd, and I wish You with all my Heart the Continuation of it, and all the Prosperity.

As You do me the Honour to encourage my Musicall Undertakings, and even to promote them with a particular Kindness, I take the Liberty to trouble You with an account of what Engagement I have hitherto concluded. I have taken the Opera House in the Haymarketh, engaged, as Singers, Sigra Francesina, Miss Robinson, Beard, Reinhold, Mr Gates with his Boyes's and several of the best Chorus Singers from the Choirs, and I have some hopes that Mrs Cibber will sing for me. She sent me word from Bath (where she is now) that she would perform for me next winter with great pleasure if it did not interfere with her playing, but I think I can obtain Mr Riches's permission (with whom she is engaged to play in Covent Garden House) since so obligingly he gave Leave to Mr Beard and Mr Reinhold.

Now should I be extremely glad to receive the first Act, or what is ready of the new Oratorio with which you intend to favour me, that I might employ all my attention and time, in order to answer in some measure the great obligation I lay under. This new favour will greatly increase my Obligations. I remain with all possible Gratitude and Respect

Sr
Your
most obliged and most humble
Servant
George Frideric Handel
[Deutsch, pp. 590f.]

The correspondence is valuable for the insights it gives us into Handel's approach to such a task:

HANDEL TO JENNENS

Dear Sr

Your most excellent Oratorio has given me great Delight in setting it to Musick and still engages me warmly. It is indeed a Noble Piece, very grand and uncommon; it has furnished me with Expressions, and has given me Opportunity to some very particular

Ideas, besides so many great Chorus's. I intreat you heartily to favour me Soon with the last Act, which I expect with anxiety, that I may regulate my Self the better as to the Length of it. I profess my Self highly obliged to You, for so generous a Present, and desire You to believe me to be with great Esteem and Respect

S^r^
Your
Most obliged and most humble
Servant
George Frideric Handel

London
Sept^br^13.
1744

To
Charles Jennens (Junior) Esqr
at Gopsal near Atherstone
Leicestershire

HANDEL TO JENNENS

Dear S^r^

I received the 3^d^ Act, with a great deal of pleasure, as you can imagine, and you may believe that I think it a very fine and sublime Oratorio, only it is realy too long, if I should extend the Musick, it would last 4 Hours and more.

I retrench'd already a great deal of the Musick, that I might preserve the Poetry as much as I could, yet still it may be shortned. The Anthems come in very proprely but would not the Words (tell it out among the Heathen that the Lord is King) Sufficient for one Chorus? The Anthem (I will magnify thee O God my King, and I will praise thy name for ever and ever, vers). the Lord preserveth all of them that love him, but scattreth abroad all the ungodly. (vers and chorus) my mouth shall speak the Praise of the Lord and let all flesh give thanks unto His holy name for ever and ever Amen.) concludes well the Oratorio. I hope you will make a visit to London next Winter. I have a good Set of Singers. S. Francesina performs Nitocris, Miss Robinson Cyrus, Mrs Cibber Daniel, Mr Beard (who is recovered) Belshazzar, Mr Reinhold Gobrias, and a good Number of Choir Singers for the Chorus's. I propose 24 Nights to perform this Season, on Saturdays, but in Lent on Wednesday's or Fryday's. I shall open on 3^d^ of Novemb^r^ next with [?] Deborah. I wish You heartily the Continuation of Your health, and professing my [?] grateful acknowledgments for your generous favours, and am with great Esteem and Respect

London Sr
Octo[br] 2 Your
1744. most obliged and most humble Servant
George Frideric Handel

To Charles Jennens Esqr.
Gopsall
Leicestershire.

[Deutsch, pp. 595f.]

Emboldened by the success of his previous season, Handel now proposed to give an entire winter's season beginning in the autumn of 1744:

FROM THE *Daily Advertiser*, 20 October 1744
By particular Desire.

Mr HANDEL proposes to perform by Subscription, Twenty-Four Times, during the Winter Season, at the King's Theatre in the Hay-Market, and engages to exhibit two new Performances, and several of his former Oratorios. The first Performance will be on Saturday the 3d of November, and continue every Saturday till Lent, and then on Wednesdays and Fridays. Each Subscriber is to pay Eight Guineas at the Time he subscribes, which entitles him to one Box Ticket for each Performance.

Subscriptions are taken in at Mr Handel's House in Brooke-Street, near Hanover-Square; at Mr Walsh's, in Katherine-Street in the Strand; and at White's Chocolate-House in St James's Street.

Those Gentlemen and Ladies who have already favoured Mr Handel in the Subscription, are desired to send for their Tickets at his House in Brooke-street [etc.].

The first new work of the 1744/5 season at King's Theatre, Haymarket, was 'Hercules, A new Musical Drama' with Mrs Cibber (who was indisposed on the first night) and Beard as well as Signora Francesina on 5 January 1745. This noble drama – another opera *manqué* – with words from Sophocles' *Trachiniae*, adapted by Thomas Broughton, suffered grievously in the making. Mrs Cibber's participation was only assured after the score had been largely completed, and Handel expanded her role greatly (originally Lichas was destined to be a minor tenor part), adding six airs for her. Her illness meant that her music had to be re-distributed or cut. Some numbers (for example the Chorus 'Wanton god') never made the performance at all and were later used elsewhere. The resultant confusion led to one of the composer's monumental failures, from which *Hercules* has yet to recover (it has never become popular). He was forced to admit defeat yet again in the following open letter:

FROM THE *Daily Advertiser*, 17 January 1745

Sir.

Having for a Series of Years received the greatest Obligations from the Nobility and Gentry of this Nation, I have always retained a deep Impression of their Goodness. As I perceived, that joining good Sense and significant Words to Musick, was the best Method of recommending *this* to an English Audience; I have directed my Studies that way, and endeavour'd to shew, that the English Language, which is so expressive of the sublimest Sentiments is the best adapted of any to the full and solemn Kind of Musick. I have the Mortification now to find, that my Labours to please are become ineffectual, when my Expences are considerably greater. To what Cause I must impute the loss of the publick Favour I am ignorant, but the Loss itself I shall always lament. In the mean time, I am assur'd that a Nation, whose Characteristick is Good Nature, would be affected with the Ruin of any Man, which was owing to his Endeavours to entertain them. I am likewise persuaded, that I shall have the Forgiveness of those noble Persons, who have honour'd me with their Patronage, and their Subscription this Winter, if I beg their Permission to stop short, before my Losses are too great to support, if I proceed no farther in my Undertaking; and if I intreat them to withdraw three Fourths of their Subscription, one Fourth Part only of my Proposal having been perform'd.

I am, sir,
Your very humble Servant,
G.F. Handel.

Attendance will be given at Mr Handel's House in Brook's Street, near Hanover-Square, from Nine in the Morning till Two in the Afternoon, on Monday, Tuesday, and Wednesday next, in Order to pay back the Subscription Money, on returning the Subscription Ticket.

Some of the subscribers were embarrassed and offered to help:

FROM THE *Daily Advertiser*, 18 January 1745

To the Author,

Sir,

Upon Reading Mr Handel's Letter in your Paper this Morning I was sensibly touch'd with that great Master's Misfortunes, failing in his Endeavours to entertain the Publick; whose Neglect in not attending his admirable Performances can no otherwise be made up with Justice to the Character of the Nation, and the Merit of the Man, than by the Subscribers generously declining to withdraw the Remainder of their Subscriptions.

I would lament the Loss of the Publick in Mr Handel, in Strains equal to his if I was able, but our Concern will be best express'd by our Generosity.

We are, Sir,
Your obedient Servants,
Subscribers.

St James's,
Jan. 17, 1744–5

But as Shaftesbury records (Deutsch, p. 848) 'this proved a very bad Season and he performed with considerable loss.' The composer answered his subscribers' letter as follows:

FROM THE *Daily Advertiser*, 25 January 1745

Sir,

The new Proofs which I have receiv'd of the Generosity of my Subscribers, in refusing upon their own Motives, to withdraw their Subscriptions call upon me for the earliest Return, and the warmest Expressions of my Gratitude; but natural as it is to feel, proper as it is to have, I find this extremely difficult to express. Indeed, I ought not to content myself with bare expressions of it; therefore, though I am not able to fulfil the whole of my Engagement, I shall think it my Duty to perform what Part of it I can, and shall in some Time proceed with the Oratorios, let the *Risque* which I may run be what it will.

I am, Sir,
Your very humble Servant,
G.F. Handel.

One of Handel's grandest efforts, *Belshazzar* (Jennens), opened on 27 March. Mrs Cibber was again ill and had to cancel, so that the final cast included Beard in the title role, Miss Robinson, Mr Reinhold and Signora Francesina, with all their parts totally reshuffled and transposed. The result is graphically shown by the following letter:

MRS. ELIZABETH CARTER TO MISS CATHERINE TALBOT

London, 2 March [or rather, April] 1745

Handel, once so crowded, plays to empty walls in that opera house, where there used to be a constant *audience* as long as there were any dancers to be *seen*. Unfashionable that I am, I was I own highly delighted the other night at his last oratorio. 'Tis called Belshazzar, the story the taking of Babylon by Cyrus; and the music, in spite of all that very bad performers could do to spoil it, equal to any thing I ever heard. There is a chorus of Babylonians deriding Cyrus from their walls that has the best expression of scornful laughter imaginable. Another of the Jews, where the name, Jehovah, is introduced first with a moment's silence, and then with a full swell of music to solemn, that I think it is the most striking lesson against common genteel swearing I ever met with. [Deutsch, pp. 610f.]

The mighty *Belshazzar* has, in more recent times, fared better than *Hercules* and is now gradually gaining its rightful place in the Handelian canon.

Here is what Shaftesbury says of the forthcoming season:

> The Lent following (1745/6) he perform'd only a very few times, his Occasional Oratorio at Covent Garden. It was then new . . . [Deutsch, p. 848]

It was not all that new, for it included parts of *Israel, Athalia* and other earlier works such as the much-quoted Coronation anthems. Handel had, perhaps, two purposes in putting together this pasticcio (which did, however, also contain some new music). The first was to satisfy his subscribers of the previous season (as he himself said in the *General Advertiser* on 31 January), and the second was to capitalize on the defeat of Charles Stuart, the Pretender, who had landed in July 1745 in Scotland and pushed southwards.

Handel's health was again causing him great difficulties: the Earl of Shaftesbury wrote to his cousin, James Harris, on 24 October 1745 from London (Deutsch, p. 624) that 'Poor Handel looks something better. I hope he will entirely recover in due time, though he has been a good deal disordered in his head.'

Gluck now arrived to compose for the London Opera, his first offering being *La caduta de' giganti*. Handel, reported Burney (1785, p. 33), said about Gluck, 'he knows no more of contrapunto as mein cook, Waltz', which was supposed to mean Gustav Waltz (who was never in fact Handel's cook). Gluck's second opera was *Artamene* (4 March 1746). Horace Walpole writes on 28 March:

> The operas flourish more than in any latter years; the composer is Gluck, a German: he is to have a benefit, at which he is to play on a set of drinking-glasses, which he modulates with water . . . (Deutsch, p. 632)

– in other words the predecessor of the 'glass harmonica'. The concert took place at the New Theatre on 23 April, in which Gluck played on '26 drinking glasses tuned with spring water, accompanied with the whole band, being a new instrument of his own invention' (Deutsch, p. 632).

The Occasional Oratorio was on the whole quite successful, perhaps because of its topical allusion: the Rev. William Harris wrote:

> The words . . . are scriptural, but taken from various parts, and are expressive of the rebel's flight and our pursuit of them. Had not the Duke [of Cumberland] carried his point triumphantly, this Oratorio could not have been brought on . . . [Deutsch, pp. 629f.]

Finally, on 16 April 1746, the Duke of Cumberland defeated the Pretender at Culloden: it was the end of Stuart hopes and a total consolidation of Hanoverian power. Handel was not a man to let such an occurrence pass without some grand musical comment, and he turned to Thomas Morell for assistance; Morell has left entertaining recollections of their collaboration:

FROM A LETTER OF THOMAS MORELL TO . . . (*c.* 1764)

> . . . And now as to Oratorio's: – 'There was a time (says Mr Addison), when it was laid down as a maxim, that nothing was capable of being well set to musick, that was not nonsense.' And this I think, though it might be wrote before Oratorio's were in fashion, supplies an Oratorio-writer (if he may be called a writer) with some sort of apology; especially if it be considered, what alterations he must submit to, if the Composer be of an haughty disposition, and has but an imperfect acquaintance with the English language. As to myself, great a lover as I am of music, I should never have thought of such an undertaking (in which for the reasons above, little or no credit is to be gained), had not Mr Handell applied to me, when at Kew, in 1746, and added to his request the honour of a recommendation from Prince Frederic. Upon this I thought I could do as well as some that had gone before me, and within 2 or 3 days carried him the first Act of *Judas Maccabaeus*, which he approved of. 'Well,' says he, 'and how are you to go on?' 'Why, we are to suppose an engagement, and that the Israelites have conquered, and so begin with a chorus as
>
> Fallen is the Foe
>
> or, something like it.' 'No, I will have this,' and began working it, as it is, upon the Harpsichord. 'Well, go on', 'I will bring you more tomorrow.' 'No, something now,'

'So fall thy Foes, O Lord'

'that will do,' and immediately carried on the composition as we have it in that most admirable chorus.

That incomparable Air, *Wise men flattering, may deceive us* (which was the last he composed, as *Sion now his head shall raise*, was his last chorus) was designed for *Belshazzar* but that not being perform'd he happily flung it into *Judas Maccabaeus*. N.B. The plan of *Judas Maccabaeus* was designed as a compliment to the Duke of Cumberland, upon his returning victorious from Scotland. I had introduced several incidents more apropos, but it was thought they would make it too long and were therefore omitted. The Duke however made me a handsome present by the hands of Mr Poyntz. The success of this Oratorio was very great. And I have often wished, that at first I had ask'd in jest, for the benefit of the 30th Night instead of a 3d. I am sure he would have given it me: on which night the[re] was above 400*l*. in the House. He left me a legacy however of 200*l*. [Deutsch, p. 851]

We also have a candid and interesting 'snapshot' of Handel by Charles Burney, who was then nineteen:

Handel at this time 'did bestride our musical world like a Colossus.' He had done with operas; and after his return from Ireland, applied himself wholly to the composition of sacred Music. In 1745, I performed in his band, sometimes on the violin, and sometimes on the tenor [viola], and by attending the rehearsals, generally at his own house in Lower Brook-street, and sometimes at Carlton-house, at the desire of his constant patron the late prince of Wales, father to his present Majesty [George III], I gratified my eager curiosity in seeing and examining the person and manners of so extraordinary a man, as well as in hearing him perform on the organ. He was a blunt and peremptory disciplinarian on these occasions, but had a humour and wit in delivering his instructions, and even in chiding and finding fault, that was peculiar to himself, and extremely diverting to all but those on whom his lash was laid. [A *General History of the Science and Practice of Music*, London 1789, vol. IV, pp. 666f.]

It appears as if opposition to Handel was dwindling to nothing. In January 1747, the Earl of Shaftesbury's son said the composer was 'now in perfect health and I really think grown young again . . .' Handel was also gleefully spiteful of 'a most absurd and ridiculous opera going forward at present . . .'[1]

Judas Maccabaeus was an instant success at its first performance on 1 April 1747 at Covent Garden: it was repeated five times in the 1747 season and enjoyed six performances in 1748; it was repeated year after year, in the course of which Handel revised it frequently, adding 'See, the conquering hero comes' from *Joshua* (1748). Present-day critics are slightly supercilious about the work, but for years 'Sound an alarm' used to rival *Messiah*'s individual numbers in the concert hall; and there is no doubt that it not only reversed Handel's fortunes permanently but it also became the most popular oratorio during his lifetime. (It goes without saying that Walsh issued scores, mostly by subscription, of the majority of these oratorios, and usually soon after their first performances.) The original singers included Beard in the heroic title role, Reinhold and two Italian ladies, Signore Gambarini and Galli, from the Haymarket Theatre – a sign that relations between the Opera and Handel's Oratorio were on the mend. In fact the composer probably allowed the Haymarket team to stage a Handelian pasticcio entitled *Lucio Vero* (14 November 1747) which turned out to be a great success.

For the 1748 Lenten season, Handel composed *Alexander Balus* and *Joshua* during the summer of 1746: in the event, the two were given in the reverse order of their composition, *Joshua* (librettist unknown) on 9 March 1748 with Messrs. Lowe and Reinhold and Signore Galli and Casarini, both the latter again borrowed from the Haymarket Opera. This was followed by *Alexander Balus*, Morell's continuation of *Judas Maccabaeus*. We have Morell's lively description of their collaboration:

> The next year he desired another and I gave him *Alexander Balus*, which follows the history of the foregoing in the *Maccabees*. In the first part there is a very pleasing Air, accompanied with the harp, *Hark, Hark he strikes the Golden Lyre*. In the 2d, two charming duets, *O what pleasure past expressing*, and *Hail, wedded Love, mysterious Law*. The 3d begins with an incomparable Air, in the

affettuoso style, intermixed with the chorus Recitative that follows it. And as to the last Air, I cannot help telling you, that, when Mr Handell first read it, he cried out '*D – n* your Iambics'. 'Dont put yourself in a passion, they are easily Trochees.' '*Trochees, what are Trochees?*' 'Why, the very reverse of Iambics, by leaving out a syllable in every line, as instead of

Convey me to some peaceful shore,
Lead me to some peaceful shore.'

'That is what I want.' 'I will step into the parlour, and alter them immediately.' I went down and returned with them altered in about 3 minutes; when he would have them as they were, and set them most delightfully accompanied with only a quaver, and a rest of 3 quavers. [Deutsch, p. 852]

In each of these new oratorios, Handel played a new organ concerto: the composer was revered and applauded. Some of the connoisseurs reminded themselves that those who now loudly extolled the master's praise had not always done so. 'Our friend,' wrote Lady Luxborough to William Shenstone in April of 1748, 'speaks with such ecstasy of the music [*Judas Maccabaeus*] . . . But I suppose he sets his judgment to that of the multitude . . .' (Deutsch, p. 651).

By early in 1749, with two new oratorios (*Susanna* and *Solomon*, written in reverse order) ready to be performed, Shaftesbury's son[2] thought 'the old Buck is excessively healthy and full of spirits.'

NOTES

1. Dean, *New Grove*, p. 63.
2. Idem.

XIII
The Fireworks Musick 1749–1750

S*USANNA* – WITH THREE Italian ladies (Giulia Frasi in the title role, also Sibilla and Galli), Lowe and Reinhold – was the first offering of the 1749 season, at Covent Garden, on 10 February. The Countess of Shaftesbury wrote the next day to James Harris (Shaftesbury's cousin):

> [London] February 11, 1749
>
> My sister went with me last night to hear the Oratorio, where we wished much for the agreeable company of our Salisbury friends.
>
> I cannot pretend to give my poor judgment of it from one hearing, but believe it will not insinuate itself so much into my approbation as most of Handel's performances do, as it is in the light *operatic* style; but you will receive an opinion of it from much better judges than myself, as I saw both my cousins Harris peeping out of a little box, and very attentive to the music. I think I never saw a fuller house. Rich told me that he believed he would receive near 400*l*. [Deutsch, p. 657]

The Countess's prophecy has, alas, been fulfilled, and *Susanna*, for all its many beauties, is hardly ever performed.

After revivals of *Hercules* and *Samson*, Handel gave London its second new oratorio of the season, *Solomon* ('With a Concerto') for 17 March 1749. Curiously, we have never learned who wrote the word-books for either of the new oratorios this season. The cast of *Solomon* again included three Italian ladies, Signora Galli (title role), Giulia Frasi and Signora Sibilla. Lowe was Zadok and Reinhold 'A Levite'. It was only moderately successful (three performances) and was not revived for ten years.

Once again, as was the case with the victory at Dettingen, public events were responsible for another interesting commission. To celebrate the Peace of Aix-la-Chapelle in October 1748 – a treaty signed by the Republic of Genoa, the Duchy of Modena, the Kingdom of Sardinia, Spain, England, France, Bohemia, Hungary and Holland to guarantee the Austrian succession, that is, the crown of Maria Theresa – England decided to put on a huge celebration, culminating in a gigantic display of fireworks on a 'machine' of wood in the Doric temple-style designed by Jean-Nicholas Servan (known as 'Le Chevalier Servandoni', from the Paris Opéra) and erected in Hyde Park. 'When it was finished on April 26, 1749,' writes Herbert Weinstock, 'it stood 410 feet long and 114 feet high.

> It consisted of an intricately elaborate central structure bearing the arms of the Duke of Montague (in charge of the celebrations as well, probably, as of paying for most of it), figures of appropriate Greek gods, a bas-relief of George II, and a pole bearing aloft – to perhaps a height of two hundred feet above the turf – a huge conventional representation of the Sun. The building had steps, pillars, and passageways. In two directions from it there were extended walks laid above arched colonnades and ending in small pedimented structures.' [op. cit., p. 279]

Handel was asked to write the music, which he at first entitled 'Concerto' (on the autograph) but which later came to be known as *Musick for the Royal Fireworks* (or, in short form, *Fireworks Musick*). The composer would have liked to use strings and winds, but the king insisted on the use of martial instruments only which, in the event, consisted of twenty-four hautboys, a dozen bassoons, one double-bassoon, nine horns, nine trumpets, three pairs of kettledrums and a serpent. (A story goes that Handel, seeing the serpent for the first time, asked, 'What the Devil be that?' 'It is a new instruments called the serpent.' 'Oh! The serpent', said Handel, 'Aye, but it not be the serpent what seduced Eve'; Streatfeild, p. 202.)

The Duke of Montague wrote to Charles (later Sir Charles) Frederick, 'Comptroller of his Majesty's Fireworks as well as for War as for Triumph' and later Surveyor-General of the Ordnance, on 28 March 1749:

I don't see any kind of objection to the rehersal of the [fireworks] musick at Voxhall being advertised, and when that is done, if any questions are asked how it comes to be there, the true reason must be given.

I think Hendel now proposes to have but 12 trumpets and 12 French horns; at first there was to have been sixteen of each, and I remember I told the King so, who, at that time, objected to their being any musick; but, when I told him the quantity and nomber of martial musick there was to be, he was better satisfied, and said he hoped there would be no fidles. Now Hendel proposes to lessen the nomber of trumpets, &c. and to have violeens. I dont at all doubt but when the King hears it he will be very much displeased. If the thing war to be in such a manner as certainly to please the King, it ought to consist of no kind of instrument but martial instruments. Any other I am sure will put him out of humour, therefore I am shure it behoves Hendel to have as many trumpets, and other martial instruments, as possible, tho he dont retrench the violins, which I think he shoud, tho I beleeve he will never be persuaded to do it. I mention this as I have very lately been told, from very good authority, that the King has, within this fortnight, expressed himself to this purpose. [Deutsch, p. 661]

Ten days later, in another letter by Montague, we learn that the composer was proving very difficult and threatening to withdraw his 'Overture' (that is, the whole piece):

THE DUKE OF MONTAGUE TO MR. FREDERICK, 9 April 1749

I think it would be proper if you would write an other letter to Hendel, as from yourself, to know his absolute determination, and if he wont let us have his overture we must get an other, and I think it would be proper to inclose my letter to you in your letter to him, that he may know my centiments; but don't say I bid you send it to him.

THE DUKE OF MONTAGUE TO MR. FREDERICK

Sunday, 9 April, 1749.

Sir, – In answer to Mr Hendel's letter to you (which by the stile

> of it I am shure is impossible to be of his inditing) I can say no more but this, that this morning at court the King did me the honor to talke to me conserning the fireworks, and in the course of the conversation his Majesty was pleased to aske me when Mr Hendel's overture was to be rehersed; I told his Majesty I really coud not say anything conserning it from the difficulty Mr Hendel made about it, for that the master of Voxhall, having offered to lend us all his lanterns, lamps, &c. to the value of seven hundred pounds, whereby we woud save just so much money to the office of Ordnance, besides thirty of his servants to assist in the illuminations, upon condition that Mr Hendel's overture shoud be rehearsed at Voxhall, Mr Hendel has hitherto refused to let it be at Foxhall, which his Majesty seemed to think he was in the wrong of; and I am shure I think him extreamly so, and extreamly indifferent whether we have his overture or not, for it may very easily be suplyed by another, and I shall have the satisfaction that his Majesty will know the reason why we have it not; therefore, as Mr Hendel knows the reason, and the great benefit and saving it will be to the publick to have the rehersal at Voxhall, if he continues to express his zeal for his Majesty's service by doing what is so contrary to it, in not letting the rehersal be there, I shall intirely give over any further thoughts of his overture and shall take care to have an other.
>
> I am, S[r]
> Your most humble servant,
> Montague.
>
> [Deutsch, pp. 662f.]

The rehearsal was postponed from the proposed date of 17 April while the matter was being considered. On that day, the Duke wrote once again to Frederick:

> The Duke [of Cumberland], as I told you, intends to hear the rehersal of Hendel's musick. You was saying you thought Munday woud be a good day for it. Munday is a drawing-room day and therefore, may be, woud not be agreeable to the Duke. Would Saturday be a good day? Tuesday would be too near the firework day, I believe. But I think it woud be quite right and well taken to

> know of the Duke what day he would lyke best, and ill taken if you do not; and I wish you coud contrive to see C. Napier to-morrow morning and talke to him about it, and get him to know of the Duke what day he woud lyke to have it. If there is but a day or two's notice in the news there will be people enough there; but it shoud certainly not be advertised tyll you know what day the Duke woud lyke it on. [Deutsch, p. 665]

A day later the newspapers began announcing Handel's public rehearsal at half-a-crown per ticket for the great event, which then had to be shifted once again for the Duke of Cumberland:

> FROM THE *General Advertiser*, 19 April 1749
>
> By *Special Desire, the Rehearsal* (in the Spring Garden, VAUXHALL) of Mr HANDEL's *Musick* for the Royal-Fireworks, which was advertis'd for Monday the 24th Instant, is now appointed for Friday next the 21st, and to begin at 11 o'Clock in the Morning. . . . N.B. Any Persons who have already taken out Tickets for the abovesaid Rehearsal, and cannot conveniently come to it on Friday next, may have their Money return'd, any Time before that Day, at the several Places where they purchased their Tickets.

The actual event, and the rehearsal, gave Handel the biggest single audience of his lifetime (12,000 at the general rehearsal). After the music, there was a Royal Salute of 101 brass ordnance: seventy-one six-pounders, twenty twelve-pounders and ten twenty-four pounders.

Now we come to a curious and interesting point: the newspapers tell us that the orchestra consisted of a hundred players. The wind-band figures (cited above) from Handel's own autograph, however, come to fifty-nine players. The autograph shows that, at least for the actual Foundling Hospital performance (for which see below), the composer added string parts. But did Handel, after all, have strings for the general rehearsal? And not for the actual performance? Or did he suddenly augment the wind band? In the autograph, the string parts for the movements after the Overture were cancelled. It seems unlikely that the figure of one hundred is a journalistic invention.

FROM THE *General Advertiser*, 22 April 1749

Yesterday there was the brightest and most numerous Assembly ever known at the Spring Garden, Vauxhall; on Occasion of the Rehearsal of Mr Handel's Music, for the Royal Fire Works.

Several Footmen who attended their Masters, &c. thither, behaved very sausily, and were justly corrected by the Gentlemen for their Insolence.

FROM *A View of the Public Fire-Works, etc.*, April 1749

. . . The Steps, which go up to a grand Area before the Middle Arch, where a Band of a hundred Musicians are to play before the Fire-Works[1] begin; the Musick for which is to be composed by Mr Handel. . . .

FROM *A Description of the Machine for the Fireworks . . . exhibited in St James's Park, Thursday, April 27, 1749, on account of the General Peace, Signed at Aix La Chapelle, October 7, 1748*

After a grand Overture of Warlike Instruments, composed by Mr *Handel*, a Signal is given for the Commencement of the Firework, which opens by a Royal Salute of 101 Brass Ordnance.

JOHN BYROM TO HIS WIFE, 27 April 1749

Green Park, 7 o'clock, Thursday night,
before Squib Castle.

Walking about here to see sights I have retired to a stump of a tree to write a line to thee lest anything should happen to prevent me by and by . . . they are all mad with thanksgivings, Venetian jubilees, Italian fireworks, and German pageantry. I have before my eyes such a concourse of people as to be sure I never have or shall see again, except we should have a Peace without a vowel. The building erected on this occasion is indeed extremely neat and pretty and grand to look at, and a world of fireworks placed in an order that promises a most amazing scene when it is to be in full display. His Majesty and other great folks have been walking to see the machinery before the Queen's Library; it is all railed about there, where the lords, ladies, commons, &c. are sat under scaffolding, and seem to be under confinement in comparison of us mobility, who enjoy the free air and walks here.

It has been a very hot day, but there is a dark overcast of cloudiness which may possibly turn to rain, which occasions some of better habits to think of retiring; and while I am now writing it spits a little and grows into a menacing appearance of rain, which, if it pass not over, will disappoint expectations. My intention, if it be fair, is to gain a post under one of the trees in St James's Park, where the fireworks are in front, and where the tail of a rocket, if it should fall, cannot but be hindered by the branches from doing any mischief to them who are sheltered under them, so I shall now draw away to be ready for near shelter from either watery or fiery rain.

11 o'clock: all over, and somewhat in a hurry, by an accidental fire at one of the ends of the building, which, whether it be extinguished I know not, for I left it in an ambiguous condition that I might finish my letter, which otherwise I could not have done. I saw every fine show in front, and I believe no mischief was done by the rockets, though some pieces of above one pound and a half fell here and there – some the next tree to my station, and being on the watch I perceived one fall, and after a tug with four or five competitors I carried it off.

My dear, I shall be too late if I don't conclude; I am all of a sweat with a hasty walk for time to write; and now I'll take some refreshment and drink all your healths.

FROM THE *Daily Advertiser*, 29 April 1749

His Majesty and the Duke of Cumberland, attended by the Dukes of Montague, Richmond, and Bedford, and several others of the Nobility, were at the Library to see the Fireworks, from whence they walk'd about 7 o'clock into the Machine, after visiting which his Majesty made a present of a Purse to the Officers employ'd in the different Branches. The whole Band of Musick (which began to play soon after 6 o'Clock) perform'd at his Majesty's coming and going, and during his Stay in the Machine.

FROM THE *Gentleman's Magazine*, April 1749

FRIDAY, 21

Was performed, at *Vauxhall Gardens* the rehearsal of the music for the fireworks, by a band of 100 musicians, to an audience of above 12,000 persons (tickets 2s. 6d.). So great a resort occasioned such a stoppage on *London Bridge*, that no carriage could pass for 3 hours. – The footmen were so numerous as to obstruct the passage, so that a scuffle happen'd, in which some gentlemen were wounded.

[About the performance.]

Tickets were delivered for places erected by the government for seeing the fireworks; each member of the privy council had 12, every peer 4, every commoner 2, and a number was dispersed to the lord mayor, aldermen, and directors of the trading companies.

While the pavilion was on fire, the Chevalier *Servandoni*, who designed the building, drawing his sword and affronting *Charles Frederick*, Esq; Comptroller of the Ordnance and Fireworks, he was disarmed and taken into custody, but discharg'd the next day on asking pardon before the D. of *Cumberland*. [Deutsch, pp. 666–69]

Handel now decided to offer his already famous *Fireworks Musick* to the Foundling Hospital and (after postponement) he conducted it on 27 May 1749. The relevant documents are as follows:

FROM THE MINUTES OF THE GENERAL COMMITTEE OF THE FOUNDLING HOSPITAL AT THE HOSPITAL, May 7, 1749

Mr Handel being present and having generously and charitably offered a performance of vocal and instrumental musick to be held at this Hospital, and that the money arising therefrom should be applied to the finishing the chapel of the Hospital.

Resolved – That the thanks of this Committee be returned to Mr Handel for this his generous and charitable offer.

Ordered – That the said performance be in the said Chapel on Wednesday, the 24th inst., at eleven in the forenoon.

Resolved – That the gentlemen present and the rest of the members of the General Committee, or any two of them be a Committee to carry into execution this intention with the advice and direction of Mr Handel.

Resolved – That George Frederick Handel Esq. in regard to this his generous proposal be recommended to the next General Court to be then elected a Governor of this Hospital. [Deutsch, p. 669]

FROM THE SAME, 10 May 1749

The Minutes of the last Meeting were Read and Approved. The Secretary acquainted the Committee That Mr Handell called upon him last Saturday [the 6th] and returned his Thanks to the Committee for the Honour intended him of being a Governor of this Hospital; But he desired to be excused therefrom, for that he should Serve the Charity with more Pleasure in his Way, than being a Member of the Corporation.[2]

The Treasurer acquainted the Committee That the 24th instant being Prince George's Birth Day, Mr Handel desires his intended Performance may be on Tuesday the 23rd instant, and that thereupon he had Stopped the Printing of the Tickets and the Advertisement.

ORDERED

That 1,300 Tickets be printed off for the said Performance on Tuesday the 23rd instant, and that the Advertizement ordered, the last Meeting be publishing for the first time in the Daily Advertizer tomorrow.

FROM THE *General Advertiser*, 19 May 1749

Hospital for the Maintenance and Education of Exposed and Deserted Young Children, May 10, 1749.

GEORGE-FREDERICK HANDELL,

Esq; having generously offered his Assistance to promote this Charity, on Thursday the 25th Day of this Instant May, at Twelve o'Clock at Noon, there will be a Grand Performance of Vocal and Instrumental MUSICK. Under his Direction, consisting of several Pieces[3] composed by him.

First. The Musick for the late *Royal Fireworks* and the *Anthem* on the *Peace*.

Second. Select Pieces from the Oratorio of *Solomon*, relating to the *Dedication of the Temple*.

Third. Several Pieces composed for the Occasion, the Words taken from Scripture, and applicable to this Charity and its Benefactors.

The Performance will be in the Chapel, which will be sash'd, and made commodious for the Purpose . . . printed Tickets . . . are . . . delivered at Half a Guinea each, at the Hospital.

N.B. There will be no Collection; and Mr *Tonson* having printed the Words of the Performance, for the Benefit of this Charity, Books may be had . . . at One Shilling each.

By Order of the General Court,

HARMAN VERELST, Sec.

FROM THE *General Advertiser*, 23 May 1749

Hospital for the Maintenance . . . of . . . Young Children, in Lamb's Conduit Fields, May 19, 1749.

Notice is hereby given that Alterations being necessary to be made for the Reception of some Persons of High Distinction, the MUSICK, which was advertised for *Thursday* the 25th, to be performed in the Chapel, is deferred till *Saturday* the 27th, at Twelve at Noon, and the Tickets for the 25th will be then received.

FROM THE *General Advertiser*, 26 May 1749

We are assured, that their Royal Highnesses the Prince and Princess of Wales, and the young Princes and Princesses will Honour the Foundling Hospital with their Presence To morrow, at the Grand Performance of Musick, composed by Mr Handel, for the Benefit of that Charity; and that above One Hundred Voices and Performers have engaged to assist upon that Laudable and Charitable Occasion. [Deutsch, pp. 669–72]

The *London Evening Post* (30 May) reported that there were present 'in the new Chapel' – which was not yet completed – 'their Royal Highnesses the Prince and Princess of Wales, some others of the Royal Family, and a prodigious Concourse of the Nobility and Gentry' (Deutsch, p. 672), and in another paper the performance was judged to be 'most complete and solemn.' This concert marked the first in a long series Handel conducted there to raise money for the institution.

Handel's *Fireworks Musick* is now often played in its supposed original version for wind band.[4] It is a blazingly effective and thrilling piece of music which is justly one of his most popular works. There are five sections:

1. Overture
2. Bourrée
3. La Paix
4. La Réjouissance
5. Minuets I & II

The Overture exists in different and possibly slightly *later* versions (usually they are said to be earlier, but the autographs' watermarks do not suggest an earlier date). One of these[5] is in F and uses four horns with oboes, bassoons and strings (the second movement is different from that of the *Fireworks Musick*), but the grandest and most interesting is a version in D which is a kind of organ concerto in which the solo part is not written out. This version is scored for two oboes, bassoons, four horns, two trumpets and kettledrums, with the customary strings. By simply omitting the 'ad libitum' organ improvisation, one can make of the Concerto a superb two-movement work. The second movement is a brilliant fugue whose octave jumps in the theme and its continuation lie perfectly for *clarino* (high trumpet) and natural horn technique. This work used to be very popular between the world wars in a rather lush orchestration by Sir Hamilton Harty (Universal Edition, Vienna) and is now available in a modern critical score based on the autograph (University College Press, Cardiff). It should become one of Handel's most popular orchestral pieces.

There are three so-called 'Double' Concertos for (in fact) *three* choirs, two of winds and one of strings. Nos. 1 and 2 might be called 'potpourri' concertos and were probably first performed during *Joshua* and *Alexander Balus*.

No. 1 in B flat. Scoring: 2 choirs each of oboes, bassoon and horns, third choir of strings. Uses material from *Alexander Balus, Messiah, Belshazzar, Ottone, Semele* and *Lotario*. Probably for *Joshua*.

No. 2 in F. Scoring: 2 choirs each of oboes, bassoon and horns, third choir of strings. Uses material from *Esther, Messiah* and *Occasional Oratorio*. Probably for *Alexander Balus*.

No. 3 in F. Scoring: 2 choirs each of oboes, bassoon and horns, third choir of strings. One movement from *Partenope*, one part uses material from the 'Fitzwilliam Overture' for two clarinets and horns (first edited by J.M. Coopersmith and Jan LaRue); but otherwise this attractive piece appears to be an original composition. On all accounts No. 3 is the most original and successful of the trio, Handel at his most jubilant and winning.

An old friend died on 5 September 1749; the next day the *General Advertiser* reports:

> Yesterday Morning, and not before, died at his House at Richmond, aged 85, John-James Heidegger, Esq; whose well known Character wants no Encomium; of him, it may be truly said, what one Hand received from the Rich, the other gave to the Poor.

In the autumn Handel drew up plans for a new organ to adorn the Jennens estate at Gopsall; the letter shows the composer's expert knowledge of organ building, a talent he shared with J.S. Bach:

HANDEL TO JENNENS, 30 September 1749

Sir

Yesterday I received Your Letter, in answer to which I hereunder specify my Opinion of an Organ which I think will answer the Ends You propose, being every thing that is necessary for a good and grand Organ, without Reed Stops, which I have omitted, because they are continually wanting to be tuned, which in the Country is very inconvenient, and should it remain useless on that Account, it would still be very expensive althou' that may not be Your Consideration. I very well approve of Mr Bridge[6] who without any Objection is a very good Organ Builder, and I shall willingly (when He has finished it) give You my Opinion of it. I have referr'd You to the Flute Stop in Mr Freemans Organ being excellent in its kind, but as I do not referr you in that Organ, The System of the Organ I advise is, Vizt

The Compass to be up to D and down to Gamut,

full Octave, Church Work

One Row of Keys, whole Stops and none in halves.

Stops

An Open Diapason – of Metal throughout to be in Front.

A Stopt Diapason – the Treble Metal and the Bass Wood.

A Principal – of Metal throughout.
A Twelfth – of Metal throughout.
A Fifteenth – of Metal throughout.
A Great Tierce – of Metal throughout.
A Flute Stop – such a one is in Freemans Organ.

I am glad of the Opportunity to show you my attention, wishing you all Health and Happiness,

I remain with great Sincerity and Respect

Sir

Your

London, Sept. 30. 1749.

most obedient and most humble Servant

Georg Frideric Handel.

[Deutsch, pp. 675f.]

Early in 1750 we have an interesting letter about the composer:

THE EARL OF SHAFTESBURY TO HIS COUSIN, JAMES HARRIS, IN SALISBURY

London, February 13, 1750.

I have seen Handel several times since I came hither, and think I never saw him so cool and well. He is quite easy in his behaviour, and has been pleasing himself in the purchase of several fine pictures, particularly a large Rembrandt,[7] which is indeed excellent. We have scarce talked at all about musical subjects, though enough to find his performances will go off incomparably.[Deutsch, p. 680]

For his coming season, the composer needed the double-bass timpani for *Saul* and *Judas Maccabaeus*:

HANDEL TO THE KEEPER OF THE ORDNANCE OFFICE, 24th February 1750

S[r]

I having received the Permission of the Artillery Kettle Drums for my use in the Oratorio's in this Season;

> I beg you would conseign them to the Bearer of this Mr Frideric Smith
>
> I am
>
> Saturday Your very humble Servant
> Febr: 24 G.F. Handel
> 1750. [Deutsch, p. 681]

Handel had in the summer of 1749 completed a new oratorio entitled *Theodora*, for which Morell wrote the word-book; once again he has left us amusing notes about his collaboration with the composer:

> The next I wrote was *Theodora* (in 1749), which Mr Handell himself valued more than any Performance of the kind; and when I once ask'd him, whether he did not look upon the Grand Chorus in the Messiah as his Master Piece? '*No*', says he, '*I think the Chorus at the end of the 2d part in Theodora far beyond it*. He saw the lovely youth &c.'
>
> The 2d night of *Theodora* was very thin indeed, tho' the Princess Amelia was there. I guessed it a losing night, so did not go to Mr Handell as usual; but seeing him smile, I ventured, when, 'Will you be there next Friday night,' says he, 'and I will play it to you?' I told him I had just seen Sir T. Hankey, 'and he desired me to tell you, that if you would have it again, he would engage for all the Boxes.' '*He is a fool; the Jews will not come to it (as to Judas) because it is a Christian story; and the Ladies will not come, because it [is] a virtuous one*.' [Deutsch, p. 852]

The first performance included a new alto castrato, Gaetano Guardagni, who was to become a regular contributor to the oratorios of Handel's old age and still later, in 1762, would create the title role in Gluck's *Orfeo* in Vienna.

London was in the midst of an earthquake scare – a rare event – and perhaps it was this that contributed to a notable lack of enthusiasm about *Theodora*, which ran only three nights and was later revived only once (1755). Burney (1785, p. 29n.) records that:

> In 1749 [sc.: 1750] *Theodora* was so very unfortunately abandoned, that he was glad if any professors, who did not

perform, would accept of tickets or orders for admission. Two gentlemen of that description, now living, having applied to Handel, after the disgrace of *Theodora*, for an order to hear the *Messiah*, he cried out, 'Oh your sarvant, Mien-herren! you are tamnaple tainty! you would not co to *Teodora* – der was room enough to tance dere, when dat was perform.'

Sometimes, however, I have heard him, as pleasantly as philosphically, console hi[s] friends, when, previous to the curtain being drawn up, they have lamented that the house was so empty, by saying, 'Never moind; di moosic vil sound de petter.'

We have a vivid portrait of Handel in his oratorio concerts from a French lady; the new organ concerto of the season was in G minor (later Opus 7, No. 5), which had been completed on 31 January:

MADAME ANNE-MARIE FIQUET DU BOCAGE TO HER SISTER, MADAME DU PERRON

London, April 15, 1750.

The Oratorio, or pious concert, pleases us highly, *English* words are sung by *Italian* performers, and accompanied by a variety of instruments. HANDEL is the soul of it: when he makes his appearance, two wax lights are carried before him, which are laid upon his organ. Amidst a loud clapping of hands he seats himself, and the whole band of music strikes up exactly at the same moment. At the interludes he plays concertos of his own composition, either alone or accompanied by the orchestra. These are equally admirable for the harmony and the execution. The *Italian* opera, in three acts, gives us much less pleasure . . . [Deutsch, p. 686]

Handel may have been 'cool and well'; he was certainly at the summit of his wealth and popularity; but nevertheless he now decided to draw up his will, which in the interests of continuity we shall reproduce here with all its four codicils. A few weeks later, on 17 (28) July 1750, J.S. Bach died at Leipzig; and although there seems to have been some communication between them, the two greatest composers of their age never met.

HANDEL'S WILL, 1 June 1750

In the Name of God Amen.

I George Frideric Handel considering the Uncertainty of human Life doe make this my Will in manner following

Viz.

I give and bequeath unto my Servant Peter le Blond, my Clothes and Linnen, and three hundred Pounds sterl: and to my other Servants a year Wages.

I give and bequeath to Mr Christopher Smith my large Harpiscord, my little House Organ, my Musick Books, and five hundred Pounds sterl:

Item I give and bequeath to Mr James Hunter five hundred Pounds sterl:

I give and bequeath to my Cousin Christian Gottlieb Handel of Coppenhagen one hundred Pounds sterl:

Item I give and bequeath to my Cousin Magister Christian August Rotth of Halle in Saxony one hundred Pounds sterl:

Item I give and bequeath to my Cousin the Widow of George Taust, Pastor of Giebichenstein near Halle in Saxony three hundred Pounds sterl: and to Her six Children each two hundred Pounds sterl:

All the next and residue of my Estate in Bank Annuity's or of what soever kind of Nature,

I give and bequeath unto my Dear Niece Johanna Friderica Flöerken of Gotha in Saxony (born Michäelsen in Halle) whom I make my Sole Exec^{trix} of this my last Will.

In witness Whereof I have hitherto set my hand this I day of June 1750.

George Frideric Handel

[Deutsch, p. 691]

NOTES

Christopher Smith = J.C. Smith, Handel's principal copyist.

Hunter = a 'scarlet-dyer at Old Ford' who was also a copyist in the Smith scriptorium.

Christian Gottlieb Händel = a grandson of Handel's brother Karl, born 1714.
Georg Taus = Handel's uncle.
Johanna Friederika Flörke *née* Michaelsen = second child of Handel's sister, Dorothea Sophia, married to M.D. Michaelsen.
Handel's large harpsichord, by Johannes Ruckers (1612), is now owned by the Crown.
Handel's small Harpsichord, by Andreas Ruckers (1651), is now in the Victoria & Albert Museum, London.

The First Codicil to Handel's Will, 6 August 1756

I George Frideric Handel make this Codicil to my Will.

I give unto my Servant Peter le Blond Two Hundred Pounds additional to the Legacy already given him in my Will.

I give to M[r] Christopher Smith Fifteen Hundred Pounds additional to the Legacy already given him in my Will.

I give to my Cousin Christian Gottlieb Handel of Coppenhagen Two Hundred Pounds additional to the Legacy given him in my Will.

My Cousin Magister Christian August Rotth being dead I give to his Widow Two Hundred Pounds and if she shall die before me I give the said Two Hundred Pounds to her Children.

The Widow of George Taust and one of her Children being dead I give to her Five remaining children Three Hundred Pounds apiece instead of the Legacy given to them by my Will.

I give to Doctor Morell of Turnham Green Two Hundred Pounds.

I give to M[r] Newburgh Hamilton of Old Bond Street who has assisted me in adjusting words for some of my Compositions One Hundred Pounds.

I make George Amyand Esquire of Lawrence Pountney Hill London Merchant Coexecutor with my Niece mention'd in my Will, and I give him Two Hundred Pounds which I desire him to accept for the Care and Trouble he shall take in my Affairs. In Witness whereof I Have hereunto set my hand this Sixth day of August One Thousand and Seven Hundred and Fifty Six. George Frideric Handel.

On the day and year above written this Codicil was read over to the said George Frideric Handel and was by him Sign'd and Publish'd in our Presence.

Tho: Harris.
John Hetherington.
[Deutsch, p. 776]

NOTES

Magister Rotth died in 1752.
Morell = Handel's librettist.
George Amyand = a Hamburg merchant who emigrated to England and was created a baronet in 1764.
Thomas Harris = one of Salisbury's three brothers.
John Hetherington = belonged to the Middle Temple, Inns of Court, London.

The Second Codicil to Handel's Will, 22nd March 1757

I George Frideric Handel do make this farther Codicil to my Will.

My old Servant Peter Le Blond being lately dead I give to his Nephew John Duburk the sum of Five Hundred Pounds.

I give to my Servant Thomas Bramwell the Sum of Thirty Pounds in case He shall be living with me at the time of my Death and not otherways.

In Witness whereof I have hereunto set my hand this Twenty Second day of March one thousand Seven hundred and Fifty Seven.

George Frideric Handel.

On the day and year above written this Codicil was read over to the said George Frideric Handel and was by him Sign'd and Publish'd in our Presence.

Tho: Harris.
John Hetherington.
[Deutsch, p. 784]

NOTE

John Duburk (Du Bourke) = he succeeded his uncle in Handel's service.

THE THIRD CODICIL TO HANDEL'S WILL.

I George Frideric Handel do make this farther Codicil to my Will.

My Cousin Christian Gottlieb Handel being dead, I give to his Sister Christiana Susanna Handelin[8] at Goslar Three hundred pounds, and to his Sister living at Pless near Teschen in Silesia Three hundred pounds.

I give to John Rich Esquire my Great Organ that stands at the Theatre Royal in Covent Garden.

I give to Charles Jennens Esquire two pictures the Old Man's head and the Old Woman's head done by Denner.

I give to——Granville Esquire of Holles Street the Landskip, a view of the Rhine, done by Rembrand, & another Landskip said to be done by the same hand, which he made me a Present of some time ago.

I give a fair copy of the Score and all Parts of my Oratorio called The Messiah to the Foundling Hospital.

In witness whereof I have hereunto Set my hand this fourth day of August One thousand seven hund^{d} & fifty seven.

George Frideric Handel.

On the day & year above written this Codicil was read over to the said George Frideric Handel and was by him signed and published in our presence.

Tho: Harris.

John Maxwell.

[Deutsch, pp. 788f.]

NOTES

Christian Gottlieb Händel = his younger sister at Pless was Rahel Sophia.

John Rich = manager of Covent Garden Theatre. The organ was destroyed by fire in 1808.

Balthasar Denner = apart from his celebrated *genre* pictures (old men, old women), he painted Handel's portrait twice: one is in the National Gallery, London, and one was formerly owned by Lord Sackville at Sevenoaks.

Granville = Handel could not remember his Christian name, Bernard.

Messiah = It is said that the Trustees (Governors) of the Hospital, learning of Handel's intention to give them a score of *Messiah* after his death, tried to gain exclusive rights to the work before then, to which end they even proposed to petition Parliament. Handel was justifiably annoyed at this operation and is reported to have exclaimed: 'The Devil! For what shall the Foundlings put mine oratorio in the Parliament? The Devil! Mine Music shall not go to Parliament.' It did not.

The Fourth, and Last, Codicil to Handel's Will, 11th April 1759

I George Frideric Handel make this farther Codicil.

I Give to the Governors or Trustees of the Society for the Support of decayed Musicians and their Families one Thousand pounds to be disposed of in the most beneficiall manner for the objects of that Charity.

I Give to George Amyand Esquire one of my Executors Two Hundred pounds additional to what I have before given him.

I Give to Thomas Harris Esquire of Lincolns Inn Fields Three Hundred Pounds.

I Give to M[r] John Hetherington of the First Fruits Office in the Middle Temple One Hundred pounds.

I Give to M[r] Mathew Dubourg Musician One Hundred Pounds.

I Give to my Servant Thomas Bremwell Seventy Pounds aditional to what I have before given him.

I Give to Benjamin Martyn Esquire of New Bond Street Fifty Guineas.

I Give to M[r] John Belchar of Sun Court Threadneedle Street Surgeon Fifty Guineas.

I Give all my wearing apparel to my servant John Le Bourk.

I Give to M[r] John Cowland of New Bond Street Apothecary Fifty Pounds.

I hope to have the permission of the Dean and Chapter of Westminster to be buried in Westminster Abbey in a private manner at the discretion of my Executor, M[r] Amyand and I desire that my said Executor may have leave to erect a monument for me there and that any sum not Exceeding Six Hundred Pounds be expended for that purpose at the discretion of my said Executor.

I Give to M[rs] Palmer of Chelsea widow of M[r] Palmer formerly of Chappel Street One Hundred Pounds.

I Give to my Maid Servants each one years wages over and above what shall be due to them at the time of my death.

I Give to Mrs Mayne of Kensington Widow Sister of the late Mr Batt Fifty Guineas.

I Give to Mrs Donnalan of Charles Street Berkley Square Fifty Guineas.

I Give to Mr Reiche Secretary for the affairs of Hanover Two Hundred Pounds.

In Witness whereof I have hereunto set my hand and Seal this Eleventh day of April 1759.

G.F. Handel.

This Codicil was read over to the said George Friderick Handel and by him Signed and Sealed in the Presence, on the day and year above written, of us

A.J. Rudd

J. Christopher Smith.

[Deutsch, pp. 814f.]

NOTES

Society = Royal Society of Musicians of Great Britain; Handel had been a founder member in 1739.
Thomas Harris = Master in Chancery.
James Smyth = perfumer in London.
Mathew Dubourg = the violinist and frequently the leader of Handel's band.
Thomas Bramwell = Handel's servant.
Benjamin Martin = the would-be biographer of the third Lord Shaftesbury.
Miss Don(n)ellan = Mrs Delany's friend.
Reich = possibly Christian Reich who lived in London.

Among the disappointments of 1750 was the collapse of Tobias Smollett's tragedy *Alceste*, with music by Handel, both text and music commissioned by Rich for Covent Garden, the decorations to have been by 'Chevalier Servandoni' of *Fireworks Musick* fame. Handel salvaged some of the beautiful music and used it in *The Choice of Hercules*, 'a musical interlude' which the composer wrote in the summer of 1750, shortly before he left for the Continent.

This journey to Germany is shrouded in darkness: we know that he suffered a serious coach accident in Holland and that, as he was leaving The Hague, a letter from the composer Georg Philipp Telemann was delivered. Handel was fond of his very old compatriot and sent him a crate of flowers 'which experts assure me are very choice and of admirable rarity' (Handel was writing in French, the language he preferred when corresponding even with Germans).

His friends thought 'his late journey has help'd his constitution vastly' (Earl of Shaftesbury on 16 February 1751.)[9] They were too sanguine.

NOTES

1 The fireworks were designed by two Italians, Giuseppe Sarti of Bologna and Gaetano Ruggieri. Italians, and especially Neapolitans, were the great experts in the eighteenth century for fireworks, in the organization of which they had become real artists. [H.C.R.L.]

2 Musicians hate serving on committees, but Handel could not avoid it and they elected him a Governor on 9 May 1750. Prince George is of course the later George III, a staunch Handelian. [H.C.R.L.]

3 A word-book has survived, dated 25 May (King's College, Cambridge), but the performance took place two days later. The contents of this word-book are:

I. The Musick as composed for the Royal Fire-Works.

The Anthem composed on the Occasion of the Peace.

[This was the so-called *Anthem on the Peace*, 'How beautiful are the feet', using the Chapel Royal setting of 'I will magnify' as well as Occasional Oratorio and *Messiah*]

II. Symphony Chorus (Your Harps). Air, etc. [all from *Solomon*]

III. A Concerto. The Anthem composed on this Occasion. Chorus ('Blessed are they') and Verse.

[The Anthem, 'Blessed are they that considereth the poor', is partly original (the airs and duet) but mostly from the Funeral anthem, *Susanna* and the Halleluja chorus from *Messiah*.] [H.C.R.L.]

4 It was recorded in the huge original orchestration by Sir Charles Mackerras.

5 The *Fireworks Musick* and two other versions of the Overture, one in F and one in D, are all bound together in the British Library, Royal Music, R. M. 20. g. 7.

6 Richard Bridge, who had in 1730 constructed the largest organ in England, Christ Church, Spitalfields. [H.C.R.L.]

7 Deutsch (p. 680) thought that movements in Handel's bank account might suggest that he paid £8,000 for it and other canvases. The large Rembrandt was a view of the Rhine, but is now lost or unidentified: possibly it and another Rembrandt now go under the name of Philips Koninck, Rembrandt's pupil. Handel also owned two pictures by Balthasar Denner, which he left to Jennens. He left the Rembrandts to Bernard Granville. See above, p. 272.

8 'in' in German denotes female gender, i.e. 'Handelin' = Miss Handel.

9 Dean, *New Grove*, p. 66.

XIV
Jephta & the Final Harvest 1751–1759

A NEWSPAPER REPORT on Handel's accident (*General Advertiser*, 21 August 1750) says that 'he was terribly hurt, [but] is now out of Danger'. Possibly he sustained more injuries than was at first apparent, for on 21 January 1751 he began *Jephtha*, his last oratorio, but three weeks later his eyesight suddenly began to fail; he had reached the second part of the oratorio, the word-book of which is by Morell. In the autograph we can see his sight literally failing at this point, the cross-beams stopping, leaving only the naked notes without even the stems. On this page of the autograph, from the Royal Music Library, we find this pathetic note wherein Handel suddenly reverts to his native language: 'biss hierher kom̄en den 13 Febr. ☿ 1751 verhindert worden wegen relaxation des gesichts meines linken auges' [got this far on 13 Feb. 1751, couldn't go on because the sight of my left eye gave way]. Ten days later, he could start again, and the score notes 'den 23 ♄ dieses etwas besser worden wird angegangen' [the 23rd inst. a little better, started work again]. It was Handel's birthday: he had just turned sixty-six.

The season went on, and the first new work presented was *The Choice of Hercules* (1 March 1751), the music mostly from the discarded *Alceste* and the text arranged from Robert Lowth's *The Judgement of Hercules* of 1723.

'Noble Handel hath lost an eye,' wrote Sir Edward Turner to Sanderson Miller (Deutsch, p. 703) on 14 March, 'but I have the Rapture to say that St Cecilia makes no complaint of any Defect in his Fingers.' For this season Handel composed what is probably his last instrumental work, the Organ Concerto in B flat (later Opus 7, No. 3), completed between 1–4 January 1751 just before his blindness began.

The composer's season closed prematurely, after a revival of *Judas Maccabaeus* on 20 March, because on that day the Prince of Wales died and the theatres and other places of amusement were at once shut down. After the annual *Messiah* for the Foundling Hospital, at which there were '500 coaches besides chairs, & c. and the tickets amounted to above 700 guineas' (*Gentleman's Magazine* for May 1751), Handel took his failing body to the spa at Cheltenham. Upon his return he was treated for his eye troubles by Samuel Sharp, surgeon at Guy's Hospital, who diagnosed incipient *gutta serena* or cataracts. In the future, the old and sick composer was to be treated by two other doctors, William Bramfield (surgeon to the Princess of Wales) and a curious half-fraud, John Taylor, who was also to mismanage an operation to restore J.S. Bach's eyesight early in 1750.

Handel was well enough to complete *Jephtha* on 30 August 1751, the autograph of which registers that its composer was then '*aetatis 66*'. His next season, 1752, saw *Jephtha*'s première at Covent Garden on 26 February with Beard in the title role, Signore Galli and Frasi, and other, English singers: it had a very modest run of three performances and was revived in 1753 (two performances), 1756 (one) and 1758 (one). Hardly anyone could doubt that the tremendous inner tension of the chorus 'How dark, O Lord, are thy decrees' – during which Handel had started to go blind – was a harrowing personal record. He seems to have been suffering from more than failing sight, for on 17 August 1752 the *General Advertiser* wrote 'We hear that George-Frederick Handel Esq.; the celebrated Composer of Musick was seized a few Days ago with a Paralytick Disorder in his Head, which has deprived him of Sight' (Deutsch, p. 726). After regaining the use of his eyes for a short period, we read in a London newspaper of 27 January 1753, 'Mr Handel has at length, unhappily, quite lost his sight.

> Upon his being couch'd some time since, he saw so well, that his friends flattered themselves his sight was restored for a continuance; but a few days have entirely put an end to their hope.' [Deutsch, p. 731]

As if to mark some kind of conclusion, on 8 February 1753 Walsh advertised Handel's twenty-two oratorios in score, bound in twelve volumes (Deutsch, p. 735).

Nevertheless the indomitable old master went ahead with an oratorio season of revivals at Covent Garden, beginning with *Alexander's Feast* on 9 March 'With an Interlude, call'd the CHOICE OF HERCULES' (*Public Advertiser*, 9 March). Later there were *Jephtha, Judas Maccabaeus, Samson* and a single performance of *Messiah*. We have a moving account of this, Handel's first 'blind' season, from Lady Shaftesbury:

COUNTESS OF SHAFTESBURY TO JAMES HARRIS, AT SALISBURY

[London,] March 13, [1753?]

My constancy to poor Handel got the better of . . . my indolence, and I went last Friday [the 9th] to 'Alexander's Feast'; but it was such a melancholy pleasure, as drew tears of sorrow to see the great though unhappy Handel, dejected, wan, and dark, sitting by, not playing on the harpsichord, and to think how his light had been spent by *being overplied in music's cause*. I was sorry to find the audience so insipid and tasteless (I may add unkind) not to give the poor man the comfort of applause; but affectation and conceit cannot discern or attend to merit. [Deutsch, p. 703; misdated 1751]

In March 1753 he was just able to add autograph corrections to a quintet inserted in *Jephtha* (performed on the 16th); but he could and did play organ concertos and improvise on the organ. On 3 April Shaftesbury wrote that his organ performance was 'beyond what even He ever did' (Dean, *New Grove*, p. 69); while Hawkins (v, p. 413) tells us that these late concertos were introduced by a grand improvised prelude,

a voluntary movement on the diapasons, which stole on the ear in a slow and solemn progression; the harmony close wrought, and as full as could possibly be expressed; the passages concatenated with stupendous art, the whole at the same time being perfectly intelligible, and carrying the appearance of great simplicity. This kind of prelude was succeeded by the concerto itself.

And Charles Burney, an eye-witness of these tragic years, remembered:

> To see him . . . led to the organ . . . and then conducted towards the audience to make his accustomed obeisance, was a sight so truly afflicting and deplorable to persons of sensibility, as greatly diminished their pleasure, in hearing him perform.
>
> During the Oratorio season, I have been told, that he practised almost incessantly; and, indeed, that must have been the case, or his memory uncommonly retentive; for, after his blindness, he played several of his *old* organ-concertos, which must have been previously impressed on his memory by practice. At last, however, he rather chose to trust to his inventive powers, than those of reminiscence: for, giving the band only the skeleton, or ritornels of each movement, he played all the solo parts extempore, while the other instruments left him, *ad libitum*; waiting for the signal of a shake, before they played such fragments of symphony [i.e. ritornello] as they found in their books. [Burney 1785, pp. 29f.]

The afore-mentioned Concerto in D for organ and large orchestra fashioned partly from the Overture to the *Fireworks Musick* (see above, p. 264), with its *ad libitum* organ part, must have been such a work as those referred to at the conclusion of Burney's report. The organ at Covent Garden, incidentally, was very like the one Handel suggested to Jennens, except that instead of Covent Garden's Trumpet (8') the composer suggested a Flute (8'): Handel's organs were all basically chamber instruments, elegant but with an 'open' and bright sound.

When *Samson* was performed during this or a subsequent season, William Coxe (*Anecdotes of G.F. Handel and J.C. Smith*, 1799, p. 63) wrote that when

> Beard sang, with great feeling,
> Total eclipse – no sun, no moon,
> All dark, amid the blaze of noon,

> the recollection that Handel had set this air to Music, with the view of the blind Composer then sitting by the Organ, affected the audience so forcibly, that many present were moved even to tears.

A curious event was the revival, at the King's Theatre, Haymarket, on

12 March 1754 (the rival Opera, in other words), of Handel's *Admeto*, for which the composer presumably lent his score. It proved to be the last revival of any Handel opera during the master's lifetime, and ironically it was quite a success (five performances). Handel himself was still organizing his oratorio series and, of course, his yearly *Messiah* performances for Foundling Hospital; but his audiences were fickle as always, and during the 1755 season Mrs Delany wrote on 3 March

> . . . The oratorio was miserably thin; the Italian opera is in high vogue, and always full, though one song of the least worthy of Mr Handel's music is worth all their frothy compositions. [Deutsch, p.761]

We must, however, realize that Handel's music was now beginning to sound decidedly old-fashioned: Johann Stamitz and Franz Xaver Richter had been composing popular symphonies in the new 'Mannheim style' which were already being published with signal success in Paris, and, soon, Haydn's first quartets and symphonies would be conquering Europe; nearer home, William Shenstone was writing to Lady Luxborough on 30 March 1755, lamenting that 'the Town at Present is much fonder of Arne than Handel . . .' (Deutsch, p.762). That was only natural, and it is astonishing that Handel's staying-powers kept his conservative style alive in London all during the rest of the century – a simple explanation, too, for England's isolated musical conservatism amid the whirlpool of stylistic upheaval in Vienna and Paris (Italy had long departed from Handelian paths, leaving *il Sassone* congealed in a style already obsolete in Italy for nearly half a century).

By 1757 the old giant had yet again displayed astounding powers of recovery. Shaftesbury thought on 8 February that Handel

> is better than he has been for some years, and finds he can compose Chorus's as well as other music to his own . . . satisfaction. His memory is strengthened of late to an astonishing degree. . . . [Dean, *New Grove*, p.69]

These late flowerings were apparently dictated, owing to Handel's blindness, to J.C. Smith Jr. The big revival for 1757 was *The Triumph of Time and Truth* with Beard, Frasi and some new singers (11 March, Covent Garden), for which five new airs were added to this, Morell's translation and adaptation of the old Roman *Il trionfo del Tempo e della Verità*. But apart from that revival, Handel wrote a new duet and chorus, 'Sion now her head shall raise' for *Esther*, revived at Covent Garden on 25 February. Later in the year he was dictating new additions to *Belshazzar* for the 1758 season. His cure in the late summer of that year at Tunbridge Wells with his librettist Morell seems to have given him a new, if limited, lease of life, for by 1759 he was only just able to attend this his final oratorio season; but he was facing the end with his usual courage and equanimity:

DIARY NOTE, OR LETTER, WRITTEN BY SELINA, COUNTESS OF HUNTINGTON (Spring 1759?)

I have had a most pleasing interview with Handel – an interview which I shall not soon forget. He is now old, and at the close of his long career; yet he is not dismayed at the prospect before him. Blessed be God for the comforts and consolations which the Gospel affords in every situation, and in every time of our need! Mr Madan [Chaplain of Lock Hospital] has been with him often, and he seems much attached to him. [Deutsch, p.813]

The Covent Garden (not Foundling Hospital) season ended on 6 April with *Messiah*, 'Being the last time of performing IT this Season', and the next day, we read:

FROM THE *Whitehall Evening-Post; or London Intelligencer*, 7 April 1759

Last Night ended the celebrated Mr Handel's Oratorios for this Season, and the great Encouragement they have received is a sufficient Proof of their superior Merit. He began with Solomon, which was exhibited twice; Susanna once; Sampson three Times; Judas Maccabaeus twice; and the Messiah three Times.

And this Day Mr Handel proposed setting out for Bath, to try the Benefit of the Waters, having been for some Time past in a bad State of Health.

This report was countermanded a few days later:

FROM THE *Whitehall Evening-Post*, 12 April 1759

Mr Handel, who was in Hopes to have set out for Bath last Saturday [the 7th], has continued so ill, that he could not undertake the Journey.

Two days later, on Saturday, 14 April 1759, Handel died. He was seventy-four. The following letter gives us details of Handel's last days:

JAMES SMYTH TO BERNARD GRANVILLE

London, April 17th, 1759

Dear Sir,

According to your request to me when you left London, that I would let you know when our good friend departed this life, *on Saturday last at 8 o'clock in the morn died the great and good Mr Handel*. He was sensible to the last moment; made a codicil to his will on Tuesday, ordered to be buried privately in Westminster Abbey, and a monument not to exceed £600 for him. I had the pleasure to reconcile him to his old friends; he saw them and forgave them, and let all their legacies stand! In the codicil he left many legacies to his friends, and among the rest he left me £500, and has left to you the two pictures *you formerly gave him*. He took leave of all his friends on Friday morning, and desired to see nobody but the Doctor and Apothecary and myself. At 7 o'clock in the evening he took leave of me, and told me we 'should meet again'; as soon as I was gone he told his servant '*not* to let me come to him any more, for that he had *now done with the world*'. He died as he lived – a good *Christian*, with a true sense of his duty to God and man, and in perfect charity with all the world. If there is anything that I can be of further service to you please to let me know. I was to have set out for the Bath to-morrow, but must attend the funeral, and shall then go next week.

I am, dear Sir,

Your most obedient humble servant,

James Smyth.

He has left the Messiah to the Foundling Hospital, and one thousand pounds to the decayed musicians and their children, and the residue of his fortune to his niece and relations in Germany. He has died worth £20,000, and left legacies with his charities to nearly £6000. He has got by his Oratorios this year £1952 12*s*. 8*d*. [Deutsch, pp. 818f.]

NOTE

James Smyth = the perfumer who was to accompany Handel to Bath.
Codicil = it was signed on 11 April (Wednesday); among the estranged friends was, foremost, John Christopher Smith the Elder.
Rembrandts = Bernard Granville had given Handel only the smaller (see above, p.272).
Doctor = Dr Warren (mentioned by Burney).
Apothecary = John Cowland (see above, p.274).
Servant = Duburk (see above, p.271).
Handel's credit = £17,300 at the Bank of England. (These notes are taken from Deutsch, p.819).

Handel had wished to be buried in Westminster Abbey, in itself an extraordinary proof that he considered himself (rightly) to have become a national hero; and no one thought otherwise:

FROM THE *Whitehall Evening Post*, 14 April 1759

This Morning, a little before Eight o'Clock, died (between 70 and 80 Years of Age) the deservedly celebrated George Frederick Handell, Esq; When he went home from the Messiah Yesterday Se'nnight [6th April], he took to his Bed, and has never rose from it since; and it was with great Difficulty he attended his Oratorios at all, having been in a very bad State of Health for some Time before they began.

FROM THE *Public Advertiser*, 20 April 1759

This Evening the Remains of Mr Handel will be buried in Westminster Abbey. The Gentlemen of his Majesty's Chapels Royal, as well as the Choirs of St Paul's and St Peter's, will attend the Solemnity, and sing Dr Croft's Funeral Anthem.

FROM THE *London Evening-Post*, 24 April 1759

On Friday Night [the 20th] the Remains of the late Mr Handel were deposited at the Foot of the Duke of Argyle's Monument in Westminster-Abbey; the Bishop, Prebendaries, and the whole

Choir attended, to pay the last Honours due to his Memory; and it is computed there were not fewer than 3000 Persons present on this Occasion.

Those who have followed the astounding course of Handel's life will have noticed his dogged courage, his refusal to bow to, though severely buffeted by, adversity. This tenacity is more than mere stubbornness: it is also an implicit belief in his own worth. Naturally he adopted a pragmatic approach to his compositions in the face of such endless failures, but it is touching to see how long it took before he would finally abandon opera, the darling of his heart. With our hindsight, we may wonder why he did not continue in the grand line of *Israel in Egypt* and *Messiah*; but both those epic works failed miserably in London, and it is clear that, if Handel were to survive, he thought he must try other kinds of oratorios – and non-oratorios: for *Semele* and *Hercules*, and perhaps even *Susanna* (certainly *Alceste*) have nothing to do with oratorio except that they now, wrongly, share the title if not the content. Alas, the British public did not really take to those pseudo-operas. But much though we might like to displace some of the endless popularity of *Messiah* in favour of these other, cruelly neglected works, it does not appear that we are going to succeed, at least in the foreseeable future; the tercentenary in 1985 gave us almost his whole *œuvre*, but it remains to be seen how many of the revivals will be of a permanent nature. Centenary performances are obviously of an ephemeral nature.

It would be nice to think that his beautiful operas, which contain some of the great arias of all time – Handel's particular favourites, as Hawkins quotes the composer, were 'Ombra cara' from *Radamisto* and 'Cara sposa' from *Rinaldo* – will return to the repertoire; but there are prejudices to overcome. On the one hand, Winton Dean writes in 1982 (*New Grove*, p.106), 'This comprehensiveness of mood and dramatic approach gives his operas a depth seldom attained in the history of the art', while Gregory Sandow, writes a year later,

> Handel's operas are an acquired taste. On the one hand, nothing happens; according to the conventions of Handel's time, characters parade their passions in aria after aria, interacting with each other only in recitative. And on the other hand, the things that do happen

> are silly. The sad truth is that Baroque operas appeal nowadays to the most refined listeners, but have plots so silly that the blood and thunder of *Il Trovatore* looks, by comparison, as mature and restrained as a Chekhov play. [*Ovation Magazine* September 1983, p.42]

Apart from *Messiah*, certain groups of Handel's works are now showing signs of permanent popularity, and they include the instrumental music (not just the Concerti Grossi and the *Water Musick* and *Fireworks Musick*, but also the exquisite trio sonatas, which Hans Keller judges to be in part as fine as Bach's), the solo harpsichord music (uneven though it is) and – the latest addition to what appears to be the regular repertoire – the church music. In this latter group are the Roman Vespers and other Italian pieces, the Chandos anthems, the Coronation music (which, when I was young, was hardly ever played at all, except at Coronations) and the Royal Chapel Anthems, all of which are now performed with great regularity.

Nevertheless, I do not believe it is possible to consider Handel without placing *Messiah* in a position of special eminence, as I have done in this survey. It would be saying too much to view all Handel's earlier music as leading up to *Messiah* and all subsequent works as leading away (or rather down) from it; this was the Victorian view, but it will not withstand any kind of scrutiny; and now that we know the earlier works such as the Roman Vespers, we realize that, in some respects, Handel never surpassed them for perfection of form and concise power of expression (even though he had neither trumpets nor kettledrums in those pieces of Roman church music). Yet *Messiah* still continues to occupy its place of pre-eminence in the Handelian canon: for all their beauties, *Solomon* or *Jephtha* or *Athalia* or *Judas Maccabaeus* simply do not attain the perfection of *Messiah* nor, for that matter, the grandeur of *Israel in Egypt*.

Naturally Handel invites comparison with J.S. Bach; but when this was done hitherto, it was always at the expense of Handel, and this was particularly the case the more one moved geographically east of London: Handel is still largely a lost cause in Italy or Austria or Hungary. Not even Handel's greatest admirers have ever pretended that their hero reached the sublime heights of the Bach *Passions* or the depths of his organ music. But Handel has his sublime heights, too; only they are usually born of, or related to, opera (without opera, no *Messiah*, for example), round which *rotated* his whole life. Handel was a very *public* man, used to coping with the necessities of box-offices, the whims of famous opera singers, and the fickleness of the public – dealings with which Bach hardly had any experience at all. For Bach it was the flicker of church tapers; for Handel the smell of grease-paint and that curiously dead air that enfolds one as the great curtain of the opera stage rises. It is said that Handel, towards the end of his life, was a devout man. Burney (1785, pp. 33f.) relates that although Handel was 'so rough in his language, and in his habit of swearing, a vice then much more in fashion than at present, he was truly pious, during the last years of his life, and constantly attended public prayers, twice a day, winter and summer, both in London and Tunbridge.' And Hawkins (v, pp.408f.) tells us, Handel 'was a man of blameless morals, and throughout his life manifested a deep sense of religion. In conversation he would frequently declare the pleasure he felt in setting the Scriptures to music: and how much the contemplating of the many sublime passages in the Psalms had contributed to his edification . . .'

There is no reason to doubt the veracity of these quotations, but in seeking to find *Messiah* less important, some critics have tended to find these protestations of piety an exaggeration: they prefer the idea of Handel, 'the old Pagan'. Those who have wished to see Handel as a tower of Protestant faith have also felt their idol to be under the shadow of Bach, who was in many respects a genuine mystic, a seeker of Truth, slightly other-worldly, untainted by the gleam of gold from the box-office. There seems no necessity to make Handel something different than he was, an experienced man of the world, hard-headed and astute in business matters, but with tremendous depths to his rather opaque outward personality; a man of infinite goodness, tenderness and compassion, whose violent temper was matched by a profound sense of irony (perhaps accentuated by the country of his adoption).

As for his private life, George III's annotated copy of Mainwaring says that Handel 'scorned the advice of any but the Woman he loved, but his Amours were rather of short duration, always within the pale of his own profession.' Although a very public man, Handel nonetheless led a very private life within his walls in Brook Street and, like most public figures, he evidently regarded his privacy highly for there are many questions that remain unanswered. As to his personality, readers of this biography will be acquainted with his ready wit, his sense of humour, and his abundance of charisma; the numerous anecdotes add colour to our portrait of the great composer, as well as being a reminder of how Handel was regarded by his contemporaries. Charles Burney adds his touch of colour to the picture by recalling the man's qualities of fire and dignity, reflected in Handel's features:

> He was impetuous, rough, and peremptory in his manners and conversation, but totally devoid of ill-nature or malevolence; indeed, there was an original humour and pleasantry in his most lively sallies of anger or impatience, which, with his broken English, were extremely risible. His natural propensity to wit and humour, and happy method of relating common occurrences, in an uncommon way, enabled him to throw persons and things into very ridiculous attitudes . . . Handel's general look was somewhat heavy and sour, but when he *did* smile, it was his sire the sun, bursting out of a black cloud. There was a sudden flash of intelligence, wit, and good humour, beaming in his countenance, which I hardly ever saw in any other.

Of all the portraits, perhaps that painted by Thomas Hudson in 1756 reflects this aspect of Handel the most tellingly: it is a face so full of power as to be nearly frightening, with a stubborn mouth and fine (though heavy) features.

Many opinions have been offered about Handel, during his life and after his death; but about one aspect of his multi-faceted personality no one was ever in doubt – his universality. That is the single quality which has made his music endure and his popularity rise steadily after a certain neglect and misunderstanding which, fortunately, began to disappear after the Second World War. It is this universality which, in microcosm, is reflected in the fact that he composed fluently in German, Latin, Spanish, French, Italian and English, and which continues to strike us breathtakingly in every one of his great works.

Select Bibliography

GENERAL

Note: An excellent and critical bibliography, the newest and the most complete, may be found in the 'Handel' article in *The New Grove Dictionary of Music and Musicians*, pp. 167–79, also available separately; the present select bibliography therefore contains only the key works; it also omits the scholarly articles used, and cited, in this book at their first appearances.

Burney, Charles: *A General History Of Music*, 4 vols. London, 1776–89 (edited by Frank Mercer, London 1935, reprinted New York, 1957). Contains a detailed account of Handel's London seasons and valuable observations on the singers, some from first-hand experience; B. worked with Handel in the 1750s.

Burney, Charles: *An Account of the Musical Performances in Westminster-Abbey, and the Pantheon, May 26th, 27th, 29th; and June the 3rd, and 5th, 1784. In Commemoration of Handel*, London, 1785. Contains many details of Handel's life furnished by his contemporaries, including B's description of Handel as he passed through Chester *en route* to Dublin.

Chrysander, Friedrich: *G.F. Händel*, (unfinished) 3 vols. Leipzig, 1858-67 (reprinted 1979). Still essential for its research, especially for the years in Germany, containing letters, etc., that are now lost.

Coopersmith, J.M.: 'A List of Portraits, Sculptures, etc., of George Friedrich Handel', *Music & Letters* xi (1932), pp. 156ff. Essential for reconstructing the authentic portraits of Handel.

Coxe, William: *Anecdotes of George Frederick Handel and John*

Christopher Smith, London, 1799 (reprinted 1980). Contains important information gathered from Smith, Jr.

Dean, Winton: *Handel's Dramatic Oratorios and Masques*, London, 1959. A great, humane book by the finest Handel scholar of our day and a model of how a vast and complicated subject can be treated lucidly.

Dean, Winton: *Handel and the Opera Seria*, Berkeley & Los Angeles, 1969. The only reliable and up-to-date book on Handel's operas.

Dean, Winton: *The New Grove 'Handel'* (work-list: Anthony Hicks), revised when off-printed, London, 1982. Probably the finest single article about a composer in *The New Grove*; the work-list is also a model of its kind.

Deutsch, O. E.: *Handel: a Documentary Biography*, London, 1955 (reprinted New York, 1974). The essential source for all the then-known contemporary references to Handel: although (incredibly) out of print, it has no replacement.

Hawkins, Sir John: *A General History of the Science and Practice of Music*, 5 vols. London, 1776.

Lang, P.H.: *George Frideric Handel*, New York, 1966 (reprinted 1977). Prejudiced, choleric and undisciplined, this is nevertheless a highly important book.

Larsen, J. P.: *Handel's Messiah*, Copenhagen 1957 (revised second edition, 1972). A very important book, both for its penetrating analysis of Handel's music – also other than *Messiah* – as well as its epochal analysis of the Smith scriptorium.

Mainwaring, John: *Memoirs of the Life of the late George Frederic Handel*, London, 1760 (reprinted 1964, 1967). Although (as said in the Preface) inaccurate as to chronology, this book nevertheless remains our principal source of information about the early and formative years of the composer, with much of the information furnished by Handel's pupil, J. C. Smith, Jr.

Mattheson, Johann: *Georg Friedrich Händels Lebensbeschreibung*, Hamburg, 1761 (reprinted 1976). A translation of Mainwaring but containing many additions and corrections by this old friend and companion of Handel's in his Hamburg days. Incorporates information previously published by Mattheson in his *Grundlage einer Ehren-Pforte* (Hamburg, 1740, reprinted 1969).

Myers, R. M.: *Handel's Messiah: a Touchstone of Taste*, New York,

1948. Contains many valuable observations on the peculiar position of *Messiah*, both as a work of art and as a religious phenomenon and cult figure in Anglo-Saxon countries.

Robinson, P.: *Handel and his Orbit*, London, 1908. Contains penetrating observations on Handel's 'borrowings' and in particular an ingenious (though possibly erroneous) solution to the so-called Urio *Te Deum* and Erba *Magnificat*, namely that they are works composed by Handel in the north Italian towns of Urio and Erba rather than being works of Padre F.A. Urio and Dionigi Erba.

Shaw, Watkins: *A Textual and Historical Companion of Handel's Messiah*, London, 1965. The essential book dealing with the versions of, and sources for, *Messiah*.

Smith, William C.: *Concerning Handel: His Life and Works*, London, 1948. Full of new discoveries and containing valuable information on some Handel portraits.

Smith, William C.: *Handel: A Descriptive Catalogue of the Early Editions*. London 1960 (revised second edition, Oxford 1970). The essential standard work.

Streatfeild, R.A.: *Handel*. London, 1909 (revised second edition, 1910, reprinted 1964). A work so finely written and containing so many profound truths that it still remains essential reading for all Handelians.

Taylor, Sedley: *The Indebtedness of Handel to Works by Other Composers: A Presentation of Evidence*, Cambridge, 1906 (reprinted 1979). A brilliant analysis of selected 'borrowings' of Handel, still indispensable.

Tobin, John: *Handel's Messiah. A Critical Account of the Manuscript Sources and Printed Editions*, London, 1969. Valuable not only for its examination of the sources but even more for questions of performance (double dotting, ornamentation, with useful suggestions for the latter). Hence the book is of general importance to conductors.

OTHER SOURCES

Händel-Jahrbuch (edited by Rudolf Steglich and others), Leipzig 1928–33 (reprinted), 1955 et seq., contains essential biographical, musical and bibliographical information, e.g. the bibliography of

Handel published by Kurt Taut in the 1933 issue.

The standard edition of Handel's music is: *Georg Friedrich Händel's Werke. Ausgabe der Deutschen Händelgesellschaft. Herausgegeben von F. Chrysander*, Leipzig, 1858–1902. Although not complete and textually antiquated in some cases, it is of course essential; of the reprints, one might single out the edition, reduced in size, reproduced photo-mechanically, by E.F. Kalmus, New York, (n.d.). This edition is generally abbreviated 'HG'. The new critical collected edition, still in a very unfinished state, is the *Hallische Händel–Ausgabe im Auftrage der Georg Friedrich Händel–Gesellschaft*, edited by M. Schneider, R. Steglich & c. Kassel, 1955 et seq. Abbreviated 'HHA'. Many of the volumes are unscholarly and the whole project is now apparently being reorganized by American and British scholars with (or possibly without) the cooperation of the Handel Society in Halle, DDR. Many important works by Handel are still unpublished at the time of writing (1984).

BIBLIOGRAPHICAL ABBREVIATIONS

Burney 1785: *An Account of the Musical Performances in Westminster Abbey and the Pantheon, May 26th, 27th, 29th*; and *June the 3rd, and 5th, 1784, in Commemoration of Handel*, London, 1785.

Dean New Grove: Winton Dean: *Handel, New Grove* (revised), London 1982.

Dean: Winton Dean: *Handel's Dramatic Oratorios and Masques*, London 1959.

Deutsch: Otto Erich Deutsch: *Handel, A Documentary Biography*, London 1954.

Hicks: Anthony Hicks: 'Handel's Early Musical Development', *Proceedings of the Royal Musical Association*, ciii (1976–7), pp. 80–9.

Kirkendale: Ursula Kirkendale: 'The Ruspoli Documents of Handel', *Journal of the American Musicological Society*, xx (1967), pp. 222–73 & 517f.

Larsen: Jens Peter Larsen: *Handel's Messiah: Origins, Compositions, Sources*, Copenhagen 1957.

Mainwaring: [John Mainwaring:] *Memoirs of the Life of the late G. F. Handel. To which is added a Catalogue of his Works and*

Observations upon them. London 1760 (reprinted, with a foreword by J. Merrill Knapp, Da Capo Press, New York 1980).

Mattheson: Johann Mattheson: *Grundlage einer Ehren-Pforte*, Hamburg 1740 (translated in Deutsch, pp. 501–5).

Shaftesbury: *The Earl of Shaftesbury's Memoirs of Handel* [Autumn 1760]. Transcribed in Deutsch, pp. 844–8.

Smith: William C. Smith: *Concerning Handel, His Life and Works*. London 1948.

Streatfeild: Richard Alexander Streatfeild: *Handel*, London 1909.

Valesio: F. Valesio: *Diario di Roma*, vols. iii, iv, ed. G. Scano & G. Oragli, Milano 1978.

Weinstock: Herbert Weinstock: *Handel*, New York 1946.

Acknowledgements

The authorities of the British Library, in which are housed the great Handel collection from the King's Library, kindly allowed me to study and to trace the watermarks of the Handel autographs and authentic copies which must form the bulk of any study of Handel. My old friend, the Music Room's Keeper, Mr O. W. Neighbour, was as usual of the greatest assistance. I must also record the kind help of the Fitzwilliam Library in Cambridge, the Santini-Bibliothek in Münster (Westphalia), the Gesellschaft der Musikfreunde in Vienna (and the courteous attention of its Archivist, Dr Otto Biba), the Library of the Royal College of Music in London, the Vatican Library (and especially its Ottoboni Archives and the Ruspoli Archives) in Rome – where both I and my wife worked under very pleasant and civilized circumstances – and the Museo Correr in Venice, where in our research in 1983 we were shown every possible kindness. Among my colleagues and friends, I must thank Dr Warren and Dr Ursula Kirkendale, Dr Sven Hansell, Dr David Wyn Jones, Mr Robert Court, Mr Ian Cheverton, Mr Gerald Coke, Professor Ellwood Deer, Professor Karl Geiringer and (as always) my kind friend, Mr Albi Rosenthal of London and Oxford, who lent me his first edition of Mainwaring's Handel biography. My faithful editor, Charles Ford, with whom I have collaborated for some fifteen years, prepared this book for the press and was of great kindness in many other respects as well. At Weidenfeld and Nicolson, Barbara Mellor, the picture editor, Robert Turnbull, and the author formed (in Nelsonian language) a *tria juncta in uno.* My wife, Else Radant-Landon, was of great help in the initial research, especially for the long Italian chapter.

Appendix of Musical Examples

I
The Beginning of Rinaldo's Aria 'Or la tromba' from *Rinaldo*

II
Thematic Index to the *Water Music*

- i Horn Suite in F
- ii Trumpet Suite in D
- iii Flute Suite in G

III
Extract from Final Figure (Alleluja) of 'Nisi Dominus'

IV
Extract from *Zadok the Priest*

I

Allegro
Tr.
I
II
III
IV
Timp.
Ob. I
Vl. I
Ob. II
Vl. II
Vla.
RINALDO
Bassi

Or la trom-ba in suon/le - stan- te mi ri - chia-ma a tri - on - far
Soli
mi ri - chia-ma_a tri - on - far
mi ri - chia-ma_a tri - on - far

II

Horn Suite in F
1. Overture
Largo
tr
Allegro
2. Adagio e staccato
Adagio e staccato
[Viol I]
[Oboe]
p
3. Allegro – Andante
Allegro
[Horns]
[Str]
tr
Andante
[Oboe]
tr
Allegro da capo
4. Presto
Presto
tr
tr
5. Aire
tr
6. Minuet for the French Horn
[Viol. I,II]
7. Bourrée
Presto
3 times
8. Hornpipe
3 times
9.
[Oboe]
10 F.
11 F. Alla Hornpipe
tr

Trumpet Suite in D
Allegro
[Trumpets]
10 D. Allegro
[Viol.]
11 D.
12. Trumpet Minuet
3 times
Lentement
13. Lentement
14. Aire
3 times
iii Flute Suite in G
15.
Presto
16. Presto
17. Menuet
18.
[Discant recorders 8va↑]
19. Country Dance
[Discant recorders 8va↑]

III

Ob. I
Vl. I
Ob. II
Vl. II
Vla. I
Vla. II
S
A
T I
T II
B
Org. e
Bassi
Oboe Solo
Tutti Viol
unis.
et in se-cu-la se-cu- lo-rum. A -
A - men. a
A - men. a -
A - men. a
A - men. a

men. a - men. a men. a - men. a
men. a - men. a men. a men. a
men. a - men. a men. a men. a
men. a men. a men. a men. a

IV

90
I
Tr. II
III
Timp.
I
Ob.
II
I
Vl. II
III
Vla.
S.
e-ver, a-men, a-men, al-le - lu - ia, al - le-lu - ia, a - men, a
A.I
A.II
T.
B.I
B.II
Org. e Bassi
6 7 6

93
men.
men.
men.
men.
men.
men.
Al - le - lu - ia,
Al - le - lu - ia,
Al - le - lu - ia,
Al - le - lu - ia,
Al - le - lu - ia,
Al - le - lu - ia,
6 6 6 6

Index